W9-BNI-111

DEATH ON OCEAN BOULEVARD

"The Rebecca Zahau case is one of the great crime mysteries of modern times. It took an author of Caitlin Rother's caliber to bring it into sharp focus. A riveting read."
—**Gregg Olsen**, #1 *New York Times* bestselling author

"Using her innermost understanding of suicide, Caitlin Rother connects you with the heart-wrenching details of the Coronado mansion case. Prepare to be deeply immersed in this beautifully written, impeccably researched book right up to the gripping epilogue. The new facts never before exposed about this case will shock you!"
—**Alan R. Warren**, author and host of *House of Mystery* podcast

"Caitlin Rother skillfully chronicles one of the most fascinating and controversial cases of the past decade. Big money, sex, and a questionable death make for an addictive read."
—**Kathryn Casey**, bestselling author of *In Plain Sight*

"Rother's meticulous journalism shines through in this authoritative account . . . along with some significant surprises. If you think you know this case, think again. And read this book."
—**Katherine Ramsland**, forensic psychology professor and author of *The Psychology of Death Investigations*

"Rother is a rare talent, and *Death on Ocean Boulevard* an instant classic of the genre."
—**Kevin Deutsch**, author and host of *A Dark Turn* podcast

"A suspicious headline-making death proves to be only the beginning as Rother unlocks the door of this real-life mansion of horrors to reveal a shocking true story of money, power, duplicity, and scandal."
—**Michael Fleeman**, *New York Times* bestselling author

I'LL TAKE CARE OF YOU

"Rother has written another 'ripped from the headlines' page-turner. Journalistic and thorough, this title is sure to be popular."
—*Library Journal*

DEATH ON OCEAN BOULEVARD

Inside the Coronado Mansion Case

CAITLIN ROTHER

CITADEL PRESS
Kensington Publishing Corp.
www.kensingtonbooks.com

CITADEL PRESS BOOKS are published by

Kensington Publishing Corp.
119 West 40th Street
New York, NY 10018

All Kensington titles, imprints, and distributed lines are available at special quantity discounts for bulk purchases for sales promotions, premiums, fund-raising, educational, or institutional use.

Special book excerpts or customized printings can also be created to fit specific needs. For details, write or phone the office of the Kensington sales manager: Kensington Publishing Corp., 119 West 40th Street, New York, NY 10018, attn: Sales Department; phone 1-800-221-2647.

CITADEL PRESS and the Citadel logo are Reg. U.S. Pat. & TM Off.

ISBN-13: 978-0-8065-4089-4
ISBN-10: 0-8065-4089-3

First Citadel trade paperback printing: May 2021

10 9 8 7 6 5 4 3 2

Printed in the United States of America

Electronic edition:

ISBN-13: 978-0-8065-4090-0 (e-book)
ISBN-10: 0-8065-4090-7 (e-book)

To Rebecca and Max,
my thoughts are with you.
May you both rest in peace.

DEATH ON OCEAN BOULEVARD

Preface

When I first heard about the Rebecca Zahau case, I was intrigued, just like everyone else. But due to the parallels in my own life, the more I learned, the more haunted I became.

On April 22, 1999, three days after I told him that our marriage was over, my husband, Rich Rose, was found dead in a motel room in San Quintín, Mexico. His driver's license and bank card were on display nearby, apparently for identification purposes.

Rich, who was the former chief investment officer for the San Diego County pension fund, died by hanging. However, unlike the Zahau family, I wasn't surprised when I got the news. I was actually expecting it, because he'd threatened to commit suicide several times before.

I will always remember our last phone conversation, when he called me after crossing the border into Mexico. Even after ending our chaotic relationship, I was still worried about him.

"Do you feel like hurting yourself?" I asked.

"Not right now," he said ominously.

A few days later, he was dead.

As tragedy struck at the Spreckels Mansion in July 2011, I had no idea that this case would become so all-encompassing, that every time I would try to walk away it would pull me back in.

Faced with the possibility that a killer was on the loose, I was scared for my personal safety, not to mention the legal liability of writing about a case without so much as an arrest. So, for years I sat on investigative reports, death scene and autopsy photos, and other materials that trusted sources had passed to me early on. Only when the case hit the courts did I feel it was safe to dig deeper.

Yet, even as I voiced my journalistic objectivity and neutrality, parties from all sides tried to draw me in, persuade me, and involve me in the fight for the "truth" in a way I hadn't experienced with previous book projects.

The search for answers was at times frustrating and difficult, but I persisted. Thankfully, I'm quite a determined investigative researcher, so the roadblocks placed in my way only fueled my compulsion—obsession even—to solve this mystery.

Chapter 1

A man sounding flustered and out of breath made a 911 call to the Coronado Police Department at 6:48 on a Wednesday morning.

"I got a girl, hung herself in the guest house," the caller said, but he didn't know the address. "It's on Ocean Boulevard, across from the hotel—the same place that you came and got the kid yesterday."

The caller was Adam Shacknai, whose brother, Jonah, a multi-millionaire pharmaceutical tycoon, owned the historic beach-front home, just down the street from the Hotel del Coronado.

Adam, a forty-seven-year-old tugboat captain who hauled barges up and down the Mississippi River, either forgot or didn't know that Jonah's summer house was a local landmark known as the Spreckels Mansion. He also sounded so confused that he got the timing wrong about the day paramedics had attended to his nephew after a tragic fall from an interior balcony.

The police dispatcher promptly passed Adam over to the fire dispatcher, who needed an address to send paramedics.

"What's wrong?" she asked.

"She hung herself, man, I just woke up," Adam said, panting, in a five-minute 911 call peppered with grunting, cussing, and a mysterious eight-second muted pause.

After Coronado police officers pulled up to the cream-colored mansion a few minutes later, they entered through the front door, which was wide open, and scurried through the house to the rear courtyard.

There—not in the guest house, as Adam had stated—they found the body of a woman in her early thirties, lying on the grass next to a brick walkway between the main house and the guest house.

But this was no ordinary death scene. The woman's slender, athletic body was not only completely naked, but her wrists were bound behind her with red boating rope, which was also tied around her neck and ankles. A blue T-shirt, used as a gag, was wrapped around her neck on top of the rope, and her knees were bent to the side in an almost ninety-degree angle. Above her, a long piece of the same red rope hung down from the iron railing of the second-story balcony.

Although Adam reported her death as an obvious suicide, it appeared far more suspicious and elaborate than that to the sheriff's homicide detectives who were called out to the scene minutes later.

How, they wondered, could a woman tie up and gag herself, then jump over a balcony, with not just her hands tied behind her, but her ankles bound together as well? What woman would do this while naked, and, more important, why? And why didn't Adam ever mention on the call that he knew the woman, his brother's girlfriend, Rebecca Zahau?

Chapter 2

Two days earlier, on Monday morning, July 11, 2011, Jonah joined Rebecca in the kitchen of the Spreckels Mansion, where she was making pancakes for his six-year-old son, Max, and her thirteen-year-old sister, Ariel. After Jonah worked out at the gym, they were all going to the beach, then to the zoo.

Ariel had just flown in the night before from Missouri, where she lived with their mother and their oldest sister. Because Ariel didn't get to see Rebecca much, the monthlong trip to California was a treat for Ariel's upcoming birthday.

Rebecca was a nurturing soul, who spoke proudly of her two youngest siblings as if they were her own children. She was also very close to Max, who loved her just as much as she loved him.

Max was a cheerful, sweet kid, a natural athlete whose first spoken word was "ball." Already on the soccer field at a precocious twenty-two months, he grew into a sure-footed striker and joined an accomplished club team with boys two years older than he was.

He liked to play games in the house too, but he'd been told he could only kick the ball in the front entranceway, where he and his older brother often played "hole soccer" between two doorways.

Even though Max had also been warned not to ride his Razor scooter in the hallways, he showed off to Ariel by doing so the evening she arrived. Nonetheless, he still couldn't go very fast on the pile carpet, because it was too thick for him to get up much speed, so he never got close to the wooden banister that ran along the second-floor hallway and zigzagged down the stairs to the first floor.

Max's teenage brother and sister liked to slide down that banister, high-fiving the chandelier's glass crystals on the way down. But Jonah had never seen Max imitate his half siblings, who had flown off to stay with their mother in South Carolina that morning.

Max loved his scooter, a recent gift from his mother and aunt. Jonah, however, never liked the scooter and didn't think it was terribly safe. In fact, when he saw Max thinking about riding it down the stairs one day, he took it away from him. This was only temporary, though, because Max got it back as soon as he returned to his mother Dina's summer house in Coronado, which was right around the corner.

Dina had a slew of complaints about Rebecca, and blamed her for Max's fussiness about food lately. But good nutrition had always been a topic of disagreement between her and Jonah. And now that Jonah was with a fitness fanatic and health-conscious eater, just like him, the sugar and junk food intake by Max and the teenagers from Jonah's first marriage were regulated during their time at the mansion.

Still, as Max picked at his breakfast that morning, Rebecca told him he had to eat one more silver-dollar pancake and clean his messy room, or he couldn't go to the beach.

After Jonah left for the gym, Ariel and Max finished their meal, then headed upstairs to their rooms on the second and third floors, respectively. Ariel wanted to take a shower, the first since she'd flown in the night before.

* * *

About twenty minutes later, Ariel was getting dressed for the beach when she heard Rebecca screaming downstairs.

"Ariel!"

As Ariel emerged from the guest bedroom, she looked down from the landing to see a state of chaos in the foyer below: Max was lying in an alcove near the bottom of the stairs, surrounded by a mess of scattered glass shards from the broken chandelier that lay nearby.

Rebecca was cradling Max's head in her lap as Ocean, her fourteen-month-old Weimaraner, paced around, barking. Known to bark when strangers were in the house, he was also big and strong enough to push over an adult.

"Call 911!" Rebecca yelled.

But in all the commotion, Rebecca couldn't remember where she'd left her cell phone. Ariel ran upstairs to the master bedroom to look for it, then scrambled downstairs again, locating it in the kitchen.

While Ariel fumbled with the unfamiliar phone, Rebecca blew some breaths into Max's mouth.

"Max!" she kept screaming, hoping the boy would come to.

Ariel connected with the 911 dispatcher at 10:10 A.M., and may have put the conversation on speakerphone, because Rebecca could hear the dispatcher's questions and tried to help Ariel communicate what was going on.

But given the high level of urgency and emotion, it was difficult for Ariel to talk and listen to both women at once. Not only that, but the Zahau family were Burmese political refugees who fled first to Nepal, then to Germany, so English was not Ariel's first language.

"My sister is trying to—" Ariel started, pausing, for the right word.

"Resuscitate him," Rebecca called out.

"—resuscitate him," Ariel said.

"Resuscitate who?" the dispatcher asked. "Where are you calling from?"

"1043 Ocean Boulevard," Rebecca called out. "He fell down the stairs! Just tell them to come!"

After the 911 dispatcher transferred Ariel's call to the fire department, a series of miscommunications began.

"Ma'am, tell the operator what's going on."

"Hello, my sister is trying to resuscitate a boy," Ariel said.

"I'm sorry?" the new dispatcher asked.

"She can't breathe."

"She can't breathe? What's your address?"

Flustered, Ariel asked Rebecca again for the address, then gave the operator the wrong house number.

"How old is she?"

"Six."

"Okay, what happened to her?"

"She fell down the stairs."

The dispatcher mistakenly thought that Rebecca, who was calling out high-pitched tones of distress, was Ariel's mother, and that the injured child was Ariel's sister.

"He's a young boy," Rebecca called out.

"Okay, how old are you?" the dispatcher asked Ariel.

"Thirteen."

"And that's your mom in the background?"

"No," Ariel said.

"Is she there?"

"No."

"I don't want to talk to her, I'm just asking if she's there."

"Yes."

"Is your sister awake?"

"Yes," Ariel said.

"Is she breathing right now?"

"Yes."

"She's just having trouble with her breathing?"

"Yes."

"Okay, is she alert? Is she responding to you guys?"

"No," she said.

Apparently, Ariel realized that the dispatcher was asking about Max, but this only confused the dispatcher further.

"Does she have difficulty talking?"

"No."

"Is she able to talk at all?"

"No."

"Is she changing color?"

"I don't know."

"Is she clammy, like cold and sweaty?"

"He passed out," Rebecca called out.

"She passed out?" the dispatcher said. "Okay, so she's not waking up right now?"

"He's not breathing," Rebecca called out.

Time was wasting, but the dispatcher was finally able to determine what to do next.

"Okay, I need your mom to lay her flat on her back."

The rest of the call consisted of long pauses, crying, and rustling sounds as the dispatcher tried to elicit responses from Ariel, who had stopped answering questions as the dog barked in the background.

"Ocean!" Rebecca yelled. "Ocean!"

With all the background noise on the recorded call, it's unclear what exactly was going on and who was talking to whom. Was someone else there with them?

As Coronado police officer Van Erhard pulled up to the mansion at 10:12 A.M., he could hear a woman screaming inside.

The front door opened as he approached, and a teenage girl stepped outside. Erhard could see a little boy lying in the foyer.

Once he alerted the paramedics that he'd located the victim, Erhard went inside, where he saw Rebecca kneeling next to the boy. He was lying on his back beneath the staircase, with his feet facing the wall, his head pointing toward the front door, and a Razor scooter across his right shin. The base of a broken chandelier was on the floor near his left shoulder, directly under where it had been hanging, and a soccer ball was resting nearby. Rebecca was sobbing, calling out Max's name as the boy lay still, his face ashen.

As several other officers pulled up to the house, the paramedics were not far behind. One officer began chest compressions, trying to get Max's heart beating again until the paramedics could take over.

Once they arrived, they moved him away from all the broken glass to continue compressions, and injected him with epinephrine.

Rebecca told the officers that she had given Max mouth-to-mouth, but she couldn't recall if she'd found him on his back or had flipped him over per the dispatcher's instructions. Erhard wrote in his report, however, that "at no time did I observe Rebecca perform CPR."

After the paramedics arrived, Rebecca called Jonah to alert him to what was going on, but she purposely didn't say anything, so he could listen to her talking to the first responders. He jumped off the exercise machine at Hollywood Fitness and sprinted home.

Jonah saw a fire truck, police cars, and an ambulance parked out front, with officers milling about, but they stopped him from entering.

"You can't come in here," they said.

"This is my house," Jonah said. "What's going on?"

"There's been an accident. Your son."

From his vantage point outside, Jonah could see paramedics working on Max near the front door. He watched his son being loaded into the ambulance as paramedics continued to do compressions and helped him breathe with an air bag.

When he went inside to grab his wallet, he noticed a blood-stained patch on the rug, about five by seven inches wide, where Max had been lying. Tearing back outside, he got into a patrol car to follow the ambulance to Sharp Coronado Hospital, the nearest trauma center.

Psychologist Karen Hancock was riding with Officer Robert Kline that morning, when they responded to the 911 call.

As soon as the ambulance drove off, Hancock followed Kline into the mansion, noting that the broken chandelier's electrical cord had been "severed."

Hancock found Rebecca on the couch with her sister in the downstairs living room. Tearful, trembling, and clinging to Ariel, Rebecca looked visibly shaken. Ariel seemed upset too, although she wasn't crying.

Looking back later, Hancock didn't think Rebecca seemed depressed or suicidal. She was simply—and understandably—distressed after what had happened to Max while in her care.

Rebecca told Hancock that she'd been in the first-floor bathroom under the stairwell when she heard a thunderous crash, about twenty minutes after Max had gone upstairs to his room. She ran out to find the boy on the floor next to the stairs.

Clearly worried, Rebecca asked Kline if he could take her and Ariel to the hospital. En route, Rebecca got a call from her younger sister, Snowem, to whom she was the closest, even though Snowem still lived in Germany.

"Snow, I can't talk to you right now, we had, Maxie had, a horrible accident," she said. "We have to go to the doctor's now and we are driving."

"Okay, good, I'll call you later," Snowem said. "I'll be praying for you."

Jonah called too, telling Rebecca not to come to the emergency room so as to avoid a messy scene with his ex-wife Dina, with whom she had clashed over multiple issues, including Max.

"I suggested she go back to the house," Jonah recalled. "We were desperately trying to get ahold of Dina. It would have been an incident, it would have been unpleasant, and the last thing we needed to do was take the attention away from Max."

But Rebecca was already on her way there, and they didn't turn back. However, she respected Jonah's wishes by staying in the patrol car with Ariel while the officer went inside to check on the boy's condition.

In the meantime, Rebecca called her oldest sister, Mary Zahau-Loehner, a nurse practitioner in Missouri. "Something terrible happened today," Rebecca said. "Max fell, I think. I'm not sure what happened, and Max is unconscious."

Between calls, Hancock tried to keep Rebecca occupied with conversation. Seeing that Rebecca was still shaking and anxious, the psychologist asked if she'd eaten anything that morning. Rebecca said yes, pancakes.

After Rebecca expressed concern several times about how Max was doing and whether he'd been transported to Rady Children's Hospital yet, Hancock went inside to find out.

When she returned, Rebecca and Ariel exited the car and another officer invited them into the ER waiting area. As Jonah ran in and out of a hospital room, he didn't come and talk to them, so they left.

On the way back to the car, Rebecca pulled Hancock aside for some advice about Ariel. "Do you think I should send her back to Missouri?"

That would be up to Rebecca, Hancock said, but she suggested waiting twenty-four hours to decide, when Max's prognosis would be clearer.

"Dina is going to kill me," Rebecca said as she and Ariel climbed into the backseat.

Back at the mansion, Officer Kline and Karen Hancock tried to calm Rebecca by asking her about the landmark property, which was listed as one of the city's "historic resources." Jonah had bought the mansion for $12.75 million four years earlier, when he and Dina were still married. Just as he and Dina had, Jonah and Rebecca spent summers in Coronado, and the rest of the year in Paradise Valley, Arizona.

As Rebecca led them down the driveway into the rear courtyard, she described the minor renovations she and Jonah had done so far, and their more major remodeling plans for the future.

"We do a little each year," she said.

Heading back inside, they sat at the kitchen table and drank water, but didn't talk much about that morning's events. Instead, Hancock tried to lighten the mood by inquiring about Rebecca's family. Rebecca boasted about the excellent grades that Ariel and their little brother had earned, and told Ariel she was sorry her trip had been interrupted by all of this.

As they wandered back to the foyer, Rebecca asked if she could clean up the glass shards that littered a twelve-by-fifteen-foot area. After Kline moved the broken chandelier over to a sidewall, Rebecca and Ariel began to pick up the glass and put it into a bag.

But as Ariel was carrying the bag out to the trash, a sharp point poked through and pierced her leg—the second time that day a minor had been injured while under Rebecca's care.

Rebecca called her sister Mary again. "We were cleaning up the chandelier, and Ariel cut her leg," she said. "Do you think she needs stitches?"

Saying she couldn't tell without seeing how bad the cut was, Mary asked Rebecca to send photos. After seeing them, Mary said Ariel would need at least two stitches.

"Should I take her to the emergency room or urgent care?" Rebecca asked.

Mary told her to look online for an urgent-care facility nearby, because they would keep her waiting too long at the ER.

Rebecca ended up taking Ariel to Coronado Bay Urgent Care, which was actually off the island and farther south in Imperial Beach, where they arrived around 1:00 P.M.

While Rebecca and Ariel were sitting in the waiting room, the doctor's assistant heard Rebecca talking on her cell phone to a man with a stern voice, to whom she apologized several times.

"I'm sorry, I didn't know," Rebecca said. Her phone records don't show the number of the incoming call, only that it was "private."

As the doctor stitched up Ariel's cut, Rebecca seemed stressed, staring off into space. At one point, she felt faint and had to sit down, but he figured her light-headedness was from watching the needle going through her sister's skin rather than the morning's events, about which Rebecca had confided in him. She said she'd heard Max verbalize several unintelligible words before he lost consciousness. She'd told Officer Erhard, however, that the last thing she'd heard Max say was her dog's name, Ocean.

When a detective contacted the doctor several days after Rebecca's death, the doctor was surprised to learn about the circumstances, because he didn't sense any state of mind to harm herself.

* * *

Max still didn't have a pulse when he arrived at the ER. It took two doses of epinephrine to get his heart going again, by which point he'd been down for twenty-five to thirty minutes. But because Rebecca told Jonah that she'd given Max CPR before paramedics arrived, he believed his son had a chance of surviving.

Staff at Rady Children's Hospital, who had been immediately alerted to Max's condition, drove over the bridge from San Diego and took over his treatment at Sharp. As soon as they restarted his heart, he was taken for a head CT scan.

Meanwhile, Jonah repeatedly tried to reach Dina at her house on G Avenue in Coronado, where she stayed during the summer and took care of Max under their fifty-fifty custody arrangement. But she wasn't answering her cell phone.

She and Jonah had agreed by text at eight o'clock that morning that she wouldn't get Max at noon, as planned, but rather at 5:00 P.M., because she wasn't feeling well and hadn't slept. So she put in earplugs, took something to help her sleep, and turned off her phone.

Shortly after the CT scan showed a fracture on the top of Max's skull, he was transferred by ambulance to Rady, which offered more cutting-edge treatment for pediatric traumas and head injuries.

As Jonah rode over with them, he texted his best friend of sixteen years, who was also Max's godfather. Dr. Howard Luber, a dermatologist in the Phoenix-Scottsdale area, immediately booked a flight for San Diego, arriving at 8:30 P.M.

By the time Dina realized that Jonah had been calling and texting her, it was midafternoon, and Max was already at Rady. When she and Jonah finally talked, his voice had a "sense of gravitas," Dina said, but he wouldn't say much more than it was "something serious."

"You need to get here right now," he said. "A detective will come get you. They'll be there any minute."

Jonah had asked detectives to bring Dina to Rady that afternoon, around three o'clock, because he didn't think it was a good time for her to be driving. He also cautioned hospital staff that once she arrived, she would likely have a difficult time coping with the situation.

But Dina didn't understand what was going on, and was frustrated at having to wait for a detective when there were officers already parked outside her house. Unaware that officers had been banging on her door earlier at Jonah's request, she wondered why she couldn't drive herself to the hospital.

"I was chomping at the bit," Dina recalled.

Jonah said Dina got to Rady around four-thirty or five o'clock, although she thought she arrived earlier than that. They were getting along better these days than during their volatile divorce, but it was not unusual to get contradictory statements from the former spouses.

Either way, Dina was shocked and unprepared when she saw Max hooked up to a ventilator, with tubes coming out of his nose and mouth, bruises across his forehead, up the center of his back, and around his right eye.

Jonah, who was still wearing his workout clothes, told her that Max had fallen over the banister and apparently had grabbed at the chandelier, which came down with him. He said Ocean had saved Max by barking to alert Rebecca, who rushed out of the bathroom to give him CPR, because he had no pulse. Max had recently been diagnosed with a systolic heart murmur, but hadn't yet followed up with a pediatric cardiologist.

"We are so lucky we live in Coronado," he said, explaining that the paramedics had arrived within a couple of minutes and continued resuscitation efforts.

But Max was still struggling. The doctors had drilled a hole in the top of his head to insert an intracranial-pressure valve, with the hope of reducing the brain swelling.

"I didn't realize how serious the injury was," Dina said later. "It was hard to see him like that, but I absolutely thought that he'd get through it."

Chapter 3

Jonah responded to Rebecca's calls and texts about Max's condition throughout the day, but, as he acknowledged later, maybe not as often as he should have.

"I gave her what reassurance that I could under the circumstances, which was to thank her for doing her best for taking care of Max," he said, but he still didn't want her coming to the intensive care unit at Rady because of Dina.

During one conversation, Rebecca told him she was going to board Ocean in a kennel while she was busy ferrying Jonah's extended family and friends between the airport, the ICU, and their lodgings. She hadn't done that in Coronado before, but when it got hot in Paradise Valley, she'd put Ocean into a day camp so he could run around more comfortably with other dogs.

After returning from urgent care with Ariel, she called Camp Diggity Dogs at four o'clock and asked if someone could come pick up her dog because she was pressed for time.

"Rebecca was kind of crying," kennel worker Ted Greenberg told police later. She said her "daughter . . . had been in an accident and she needed to get to the hospital," and "there was no other way of getting the dog to us."

Greenberg was strapped for time himself, because he'd been

in a first-aid class all day and a coworker had gone home early. He also explained to Rebecca that the kennel required dogs to be properly vaccinated before being exposed to other dogs.

After a number of calls, including one to Rebecca's vet in Arizona, Greenberg said he couldn't take Ocean that day because he was missing a shot, but he could take him to Rebecca's vet in Coronado the next day and keep him isolated until the medicine kicked in.

Later that evening, Jonah asked if Rebecca would pick up Nina Romano, Dina's fraternal-twin sister, at the airport around 9:00 P.M.

Nina, who had flown down with her teenage son from Northern California, had no idea how severe the boy's injuries were either. But based on the report that Rebecca had started CPR before paramedics arrived, Nina also had the impression that Max was going to pull through.

As Rebecca got out of her SUV to join Nina on the sidewalk, Nina thought Rebecca was going to open the trunk to stow the luggage. But instead, she gave Nina a bear hug.

"I'm so glad you're here," Rebecca said, and started to cry.

Holding Nina tight, Rebecca put her face into Nina's neck, and would not let go. She held on for so long, and with such emotional intensity, that Nina felt uncomfortable.

Something's weird about this, she thought.

Nina didn't know Rebecca very well. They'd only seen each other a couple of times—once at a school function for Max, where Rebecca and Dina had a confrontation, and once at his birthday beach-bonfire party in June in front of the Del, which was also attended by Dina, Jonah's parents, and his two teenagers.

"I'm glad I'm here too," Nina said. "Thanks for picking me up."

On the ride to Rady, Nina told Rebecca that she'd heard "bits and pieces," but she didn't understand what had happened to her nephew.

"I heard that Maxie was walking up the stairs and he had a cardiac arrest. That doesn't make any sense," she said. "He's six years old. He's a healthy boy, he plays soccer."

"I know," Rebecca said.

"Where did he fall from?"

"He fell from the bedroom," she said.

"How do you know that? I thought you didn't see him."

But Rebecca never answered her question. "Are you good with directions?" she asked, handing her cell phone to Nina.

Nina was caught off guard. She wanted answers, but Rebecca seemed to be lost and needed help finding the hospital, where Nina assumed she'd already been.

"If I was her, and I was picking up a family member of a boy that I was watching, I would give full disclosure of everything I knew, everything I saw, everything I did," Nina recalled.

After she got dropped at Rady, Nina saw Dina, but she wasn't allowed to visit Max because it was after visiting hours. So a friend of Dina's drove her back to the house on G Avenue in Coronado.

Rebecca wasn't much more forthcoming with Jonah's friend Howard, who didn't know her that well either. Howard and his wife, Lisa, had been close to Jonah's first wife, Kim, and because Lisa and Kim had stayed in touch, it was awkward for them to hang out socially with Jonah and Rebecca. But Howard was still Jonah's best friend and talked to him most days.

He and Jonah had had a heart-to-heart talk early on about the twenty-two-year age difference between him and Rebecca, and also the possibility that she was a gold digger. Jonah said he'd found a new level of peace and happiness with Rebecca, because their relationship was unlike any he'd ever had. He just didn't see her as someone out for his money.

"He loved her," Howard told detectives, "and I think for Jonah that's a pretty big statement. Very big. They were very close. They were very compatible. She brought a tranquility to his life that was remarkable, because his life, until he met her, was pretty turbulent, especially with increasingly turbulent divorces . . . I think that she loved him also."

To start, Jonah and Rebecca shared views on exercise and nutrition. A quasi-vegetarian and a pescatarian, Jonah kept no animal meat in the fridge. House pancakes were made with whole wheat and plant protein. He also stayed away from sugar, processed foods, and alcohol, as well as garlic and onions, to which he was allergic. Rebecca was even more self-disciplined than him about sweets—declining to join him for the occasional ice cream or frozen yogurt.

"He's sort of a fanatic with those things and he found a mate who understood exactly what he wanted, which was new to him," Howard said.

That said, some of the people in his life, including his daughter and two ex-wives, didn't approve of the relationship.

"There were people that thought it was odd, or not right, because of the age difference, so he tried to sort of ignore that, which he did successfully. But he knew how people felt," Howard said.

Because Howard also arrived at the hospital after visiting hours, he talked with Jonah in the lobby until Rebecca showed up. After Jonah returned to Max's room, she and Howard chatted for a bit before she took him back to his house in Coronado.

In the car, Rebecca seemed sad and upset as Howard tried to piece together what had happened to Max. She told him much the same story that she'd told Jonah.

"She didn't say a lot. We talked more about how could this happen, 'cause I couldn't understand it."

After dropping him off, Rebecca delivered Nina's luggage to Dina's place, then headed home, where Ariel was waiting for her.

A little while later, Jonah got a ride back to the mansion with another friend, Rady's chief of dermatology. Jonah was waiting for Max's latest test results, so he had only an hour to shower and change. He also wanted to take a look at the stairs to try to figure out what had happened that morning. He asked Rebecca about Max's fall again, but she kept saying she didn't know.

Jonah quickly got dressed, grabbed the sandwich Rebecca had made for him, and caught a ride back to the hospital with his doctor friend. He tried to get a room at the Ronald McDonald House (RMH), which is across the street from Rady and provides overnight lodging for parents whose children are seriously ill or injured. But their beds were full, as were several other hotels nearby.

Jonah texted Rebecca at 1:21 A.M. to let her know he was looking for a hotel "to crash for a few hours." She replied two minutes later that she was thinking of him, and encouraged him to get some sleep.

Luckily, one of the nurses found him a hotel room, but he got lost trying to find it, panicking as the deadline neared for holding the room.

He pulled up at 1:55 A.M., with five minutes to spare. After dozing off for a several hours, he was back at the hospital by 6:00 A.M. on Tuesday.

Around 8:00 A.M., Rebecca called the kennel again to ask if they could come and get Ocean. She answered Ted Greenberg's knock at the front door and led him upstairs.

"C'mon," she said in a soft, whispery voice.

Rebecca didn't seem to be in a cheerful mood, and her voice was so "very, very quiet" that Greenberg felt a "little bit scared" and uncomfortable walking through the big "dark and eerie" mansion, just the two of them.

On the upstairs computer, she filled out the required forms on the kennel's website, though she left the "emergency contact" line blank, saying it was just her and Jonah. He wouldn't be available, she said, because he was at the hospital.

Leading Greenberg back downstairs to a big Tupperware container of dry dog food, she measured out some for him to take.

Why, Greenberg wondered, *with such a big house and a yard, would she put the dog in the kennel while she went to the hospital? For that matter, why is she home and not at the hospital with the child?*

Later, he asked the detectives if she ever went there, noting that Rebecca told him at one point that she wanted to "get rid of" the dog. Perhaps, he suggested, she felt responsible for what had happened to Max, and now thought, *Well, I've already screwed up with the kid, I don't want to be left with the dog too.*

The detectives defended Rebecca, saying it made sense to them that a professional dog-watcher would feel differently about dogs than other people did.

"The last thing you need to be, I don't want to say 'bothered with,' but with people coming in and out of the house for the next several days, it makes sense that the dog is the last thing you want to deal with," one detective said.

About a week earlier, Jonah had flown in a Doberman security dog that they had selected as a puppy the previous year, and had paid a professional in Wisconsin $10,000 to raise and train him.

Caroline Niles, who lived in an apartment over the garage, heard a lot of barking in the courtyard as the trainer introduced the Doberman to Ocean and taught Jonah how to handle the new dog.

Caroline stopped to chat with Jonah on her way out. "I met your dog earlier," she said. "It's cute."

When she returned a couple of hours later, Rebecca stepped outside to talk to her. "Do you really think the dog is cute?" she asked.

Caroline confirmed that despite his breed's reputation, the Doberman didn't look ferocious at all. But this was clearly not what Rebecca wanted to hear.

"We really wanted a guard dog that was scary and intimidating," Rebecca said. "When they got off the plane with the dog, I wanted to cry."

Although Jonah wanted to keep the dog, he did as Rebecca asked and had the trainer take the animal back to Wisconsin.

When Rebecca told Caroline as much a couple of days later, she also added mysteriously, "But now I'm kind of wishing we'd kept it."

Noticing that Rebecca's knee was bandaged, Caroline asked her about it. Rebecca replied that she'd taken Ocean with her on a bike ride, and he'd pulled her down, scraping her knee.

"Don't tell Jonah," she said.

When Caroline recounted these conversations to detectives later, she said she couldn't help but wonder why Rebecca said she wished she'd kept the Doberman.

But by sending back the guard dog and boarding Ocean in the kennel, Rebecca had unwittingly ensured that she would have no protection that night. There would be no dog to bark at intruders, or to watch out for her safety when all hell broke loose at the mansion.

Once Ocean was gone, Rebecca texted Howard to offer him a ride to the hospital. On the way, they stopped to pick up bagels for the nurses—which he thought might help Max get better care—and some bread that Jonah liked.

By then, Dina had gone home to get some rest, so Rebecca stopped by Max's room. She wanted to come in and sit with him, but Jonah was worried that it would be too upsetting for her to see him in such a wrenching state when she was already feeling bad about what happened. He was also concerned that Dina might come back, or that Nina or a friend might stop by, which "would cause a stir."

"I think it's not good for you to be here," he told Rebecca, who stood at the door, crying. She didn't say anything and left.

Howard stayed, however, and helped Jonah get a room at the RMH for the night.

Chapter 4

Adam learned about Max's condition from his father, Gideon Shacknai, who called Monday afternoon, sobbing. Gideon said Max had suffered a horrible accident, fell down some stairs, and "may be dying." Adam had never heard his father sound so upset.

But he wasn't eager to get on an airplane. He enjoyed his time on land between twenty-day shifts on the tugboat. At times, he'd also had "substantial fear of flying," experiencing near panic attacks, so he didn't want to fly to California if he wasn't really needed. Not being a doctor, he didn't know how he could help, and he didn't want to be in the way.

Nonetheless, his girlfriend, Mary Bedwell, who was a nurse practitioner, encouraged him to go and support his family. "This is what people do," she said.

Still on the fence, Adam spoke to Rebecca by phone about whether he should make the trip.

"Follow your heart," she told him.

That night, Adam hit the YMCA steam room to mull it over, during which time his wallet, with all his credit cards, was stolen.

When he decided the next morning to fly out, he paid for an

outrageously priced ticket with a check. Although he offered to get a rental car in San Diego, Rebecca said she would pick him up.

With everything that was going on, Rebecca didn't think it would be much fun for Ariel to stay in Coronado, so she'd booked her a Southwest flight back to Missouri for that afternoon. She managed to coordinate a single trip to drop off Ariel and pick up Adam after his four o'clock flight arrived.

Adam and Jonah lived in the same house the whole time they were growing up in the small community of Suffern, New York, where their father owned his own business and their mother was a teacher and guidance counselor.

Nearly seven years apart, the two brothers had very different personalities and made dramatically different career choices. But they felt it was important to take care of each other, perhaps even more so for Jonah, who was the older and increasingly wealthier brother.

Looking back, Adam recalled how Jonah used to pull him around the neighborhood in boxes for fun when they were kids.

"He's always looked after me," he testified. "He always extended himself to me."

That premise would hold true as this story continued to unfold.

While Jonah excelled in his high school studies, worked on the newspaper, and scooped ice cream after school, Adam earned varsity letters in several sports, including lacrosse.

Jonah went on to attend Colgate University, a small private liberal arts college in central New York, where he majored in political science and classics, while tending bar and working as a short-order cook.

After graduating in 1978, Jonah took classes at Georgetown University Law Center in Washington, D.C., often at night, while working days full-time for U.S. Representative James Scheuer, a Democrat from New York. At twenty-one, Jonah was one of the youngest chiefs of staff on the Hill.

Adam, on the other hand, didn't possess the same kind of ambition, and preferred a much less intense lifestyle.

"They were living in two different worlds, and I don't believe that Adam wanted to live in Jonah's world," Dina said.

Adam entered George Washington University in Washington, D.C., in 1981, but stopped going after a couple of years. After growing up in the Northeast, he wanted a change. So he headed to the South, landed a job as a camp counselor, and ended up in Memphis in 1987, where he studied to be a river guide. As a Jewish man, he said, he hoped he would encounter less anti-Semitism than he had in the Northeast, where "some of the anti-Semites are actually Jewish."

In his mind, he wasn't trying to get out of Jonah's shadow. He just wanted to be his own man. While Jonah wore business attire, Adam was more of a T-shirt and earring kind of guy. But both men were focused on staying physically fit.

Adam's job demanded it. Starting as a tugboat deckhand with Midland Enterprises in 1990, he worked his way up to leadman, then to pilot in 1997. At some point, the coast guard licensed him as an "able-bodied seaman."

Still working for Midland, he returned to college in 1998 to complete his studies in American literature at the University of Memphis, graduating in 2000. Over the years, he wrote satirical essays, and jotted down ideas for plays, hoping to get published someday.

Despite his odd schedule, he enjoyed his life on the tugboat, pulling barges, three or four stories tall and two football fields long. During his time off, he worked out at the gym daily, played tennis, and enjoyed watching live music. He also spent time with Mary, his longtime companion, who was seventeen and a half years his senior.

Adam met Mary at a fund-raiser in 1992, when she was a registered nurse and he was still a deckhand in his twenties. Because she had come to the event alone, his friends urged him to dance with her.

The next night, they went to dinner at a Thai-Vietnamese restaurant. Although they never expected a romance to bloom because of their age and religious differences, they've been in a committed, monogamous relationship ever since.

"He did seem to have a genuine affection for this woman," Dina said.

When his mother and father were suffering from cancer in 1999 and 2016, respectively, Adam was the one who took unpaid time off work to care for them in their last days.

In all the years I have known Adam, he has never accepted one penny from Jonah or anyone else, Mary wrote in an email. *Even when their mother left them a modest inheritance, [It] was Adam who insisted they give it to their dad. Also, in all this time he has never harmed anyone physically or otherwise.*

In July 2011, Adam was about to turn forty-eight. He'd had girlfriends in high school and college, but even after all those years with Mary, he still lived alone. Asked why Adam would describe himself to police as "single," after dating Mary for twenty years or so, Jonah said he meant "unmarried."

"I've never really lived with anyone other than my family," Adam said.

Adam liked Rebecca, and they got along fine. She was certainly different from Jonah's two previous wives. But she was like Dina in one way; she "got" Adam.

They had met several times before, including a trip to New York with Jonah to celebrate his father's seventy-fifth birthday.

"[From] what I saw, she was okay," Adam recalled later. "We had a great time in New York . . . My dad's a fun guy."

One night, they all went to see jazz singer Barbara Carroll in a subdued hotel nightclub. "I had to go under the table because I was laughing so hard," Adam recalled, adding that Jonah had a "very comic presence, because he's like a straight man."

But as Rebecca drove Adam to the children's hospital in San Diego that Tuesday evening in 2011, the mood was quite somber.

By the time Howard was ready to leave for the airport, Dina and Nina were back at the hospital, and it was a good time for Jonah to take Howard to his flight. When they saw Rebecca and Adam pull up, they decided to go in one car, and have dinner afterward.

But even with four of them in the car, Howard said, "Everybody was quiet. There wasn't much conversation."

It was a short hop from the airport to the Fish Market, a popular bayside restaurant with long picture windows and a deck overlooking the dark blue-green water of San Diego's harbor.

"We're trying to piece together the sequence of events," Jonah said to Rebecca, asking again for any other details she could remember. "It's really important."

"I don't know," she said. "I just found him there. I don't know what happened."

They ordered their usual sushi and seaweed salad, but Rebecca ate little or nothing.

"I have no appetite," she said. "I'll get something to eat at home."

After dinner, Rebecca drove them back to Rady. As they went up to Jonah's room at the RMH, she asked for a private moment with him, leaving Adam in the lobby. Adam was impressed with how close she and Jonah seemed, and how well they were getting along at such a stressful time.

Inside the room, Rebecca embraced Jonah and started crying softly. She didn't let go of him for five or six minutes.

To Jonah, who was eager to get back to Max's bedside, it

seemed like an unusually long hug. But at the time he'd been so focused on Max that he hadn't thought much about how hard Rebecca might be taking what had happened to the boy.

"I didn't pay enough attention to that," he said later.

As Jonah recently described those moments together in the hotel room, he stopped and got choked up with tears, noting that in retrospect the hug reflected "her extraordinary despair." At the time, he had no idea that those moments would be their last.

As Rebecca drove Adam back to Coronado for the night, he too broached the topic of Max's accident.

"So he fell down the stairs or whatever?"

"Yeah," she said, noting that Max "was black-and-blue when she found him," and that she had tried to do CPR, which Jonah had already told him. The doctors were checking for any preexisting heart condition that might explain more, she said, but things "could have been different" if the Doberman had still been there.

As they pulled into the driveway, shortly before eight o'clock, Adam figured they would go inside to visit for a bit. He didn't see himself as a "touchy-feely person," but he'd flown out to "be a good family member" and offer support where he could.

To him, that meant giving Rebecca a chance to talk more about what happened, but he didn't want to get in her face about it. At the time, Rebecca reminded him of himself when his mother was dying of cancer.

"[Rebecca] was probably the most vulnerable out of everybody, and it shows," he told detectives later. "She probably shouldn't have been by herself."

He knew that she and Jonah didn't drink alcohol, and neither did he. But before she went in, she said: "If I ever drank, I think I would drink tonight."

Yet, she seemed intent on being alone, so they said good night in the driveway.

"I wanted to give her space," he told detectives. "She said, 'I'm going in.' I said, 'Okay, that's perfectly okay,' the opposite sex . . . diplomacy, or being appropriate, all that stuff."

He carried his two carry-on bags down the path to the guest house, where he'd stayed on previous visits. The three-level building was quite spacious. The first floor had a living room, galley kitchen, and two bedrooms, each of which had its own bathroom.

As he later told investigators, he settled in, drank a Diet 7UP, and showered "to wash the airplane off me." With no TV in the guest house, he took an Ambien, called his "lady friend" back in Memphis, and was happy to be in bed by nine o'clock.

Jonah walked out of the hospital around 12:30 A.M. on Wednesday, and called Rebecca from his room at 12:48 A.M. As he later told police, he cried during the sixty-two-second voice mail he left for her as he related the blunt prognosis from Max's doctor a few hours earlier: Under the best scenario, the boy would never walk or talk again.

When she didn't answer, he thought maybe she was in the shower. He was a little concerned that she didn't call him right back, but after waiting a few minutes, he figured she was probably sleeping, so he went to bed. He later wished that he'd left a message simply asking her to call him back, with no explanation.

He woke up about four hours later with a bad feeling. Fearing that Max might have taken a turn for the worse, he called the ICU nurse at 5:13 A.M.

"Is there any change in his condition?" he asked.

Reassured that Max was no worse, he dozed for a bit longer, until Howard called to ask how he was.

Because parents are asked to leave the ICU during a nursing shift change, Jonah called Dina to see when he should come down. Then he threw on some clothes to get his morning coffee from the cafeteria around ten to six, before returning to shower and change.

Rebecca still hadn't called back by the time he headed over to the hospital shortly before seven o'clock.

Chapter 5

As Adam told investigators later that day, he got up around three in the morning to use the bathroom, checking his watch a few times during the night. It seemed like the hours were dragging as he waited for it to get light.

He woke up again, around 6:15 A.M., feeling fitful. Knowing he still had some time to kill before joining his brother at the hospital, he pulled out his cell phone and went to a porn site. Hoping to dispel some nervous energy, he pleasured himself, took a shower, and got dressed.

Adam wanted to go into town to get a bagel and coffee, but thought he'd be a good guest and head over to the mansion to invite Rebecca to join him.

As he walked out of the guest house around 6:40 A.M., he noticed something in the courtyard out of the corner of his eye. When he turned to look, he thought he saw a mannequin hanging from the mansion's second-story balcony, a joke the kids had rigged up.

Those damn kids.

But as he got closer, he saw it was much more horrifying than that.

Rebecca's slender five-foot-three-and-a-half-inch frame was

hanging naked from the balcony railing by a red rope, about two feet above the ground, with her ankles bound together and her wrists tied behind her back. As if that weren't enough, some kind of blue scarf was tied around her neck and stuffed into her mouth.

Over time, Adam would tell several versions of what he did next, but, essentially, he decided to cut her down. So he ran through the unlocked kitchen door, grabbed a serrated knife from a butcher block in a drawer, and called 911 at 6:48 A.M.

After what had happened with Max under her watch, Adam said he immediately assumed that Rebecca had committed suicide. But the law enforcement officers who showed up that morning saw it quite differently. To them—and to the general public, who learned about the mysterious death as it hit the news that day—Rebecca looked like a victim of foul play.

The 911 dispatcher asked Adam for an address so she could send help, but he couldn't produce it.

"I'll call you back," he said.

"Sir, is she still alive?" the dispatcher interjected before Adam could hang up.

"I don't know."

Adam later said he didn't know for sure, because Rebecca's Asian skin was a different color than his, and he "couldn't tell if she was blue or stuff."

Although he didn't explain what he was doing, the dispatcher could hear a lot of grunting and cussing, scraping and knocking, in the background. To get high enough to cut Rebecca's body down, Adam later explained that he had to drag over a wooden table to stand on. On the recording, the old teak table could be heard scraping across the walkway as a broken leg fell off and bounced onto the bricks.

"Sir, are you there?" the dispatcher asked, but got no answer.

Holding the knife, Adam climbed up on the table, held Rebecca's body against him with one arm as he cut the rope with his other hand, then climbed down and laid her on the lawn.

"Are you alive?" Adam asked. Then, speaking into the phone, he said, "Hello? Hello?"

"Yes, sir," the dispatcher replied.

"Did you get the address?" he asked, panting.

"No, sir, I need the address."

"I'm going to do CPR right now," he said, sounding exasperated. "You came here yesterday to pick up a little boy."

The dispatcher said she didn't know where he was, because she wasn't working the previous day, and she couldn't find any record of a call on Ocean Boulevard. That's because it had been *two* days earlier.

When she repeated that she couldn't send paramedics without an address, Adam ran around to the front of the house to look for it, still holding his phone. After giving her the address, he continued to breathe heavily as he entered the house through the unlocked front door, and headed back out to the rear courtyard.

"Is she still alive?" she asked.

"I don't think so."

Nonetheless, the dispatcher transferred him to her counterpart at the fire department to guide him through resuscitation efforts.

"Okay, what's wrong?" the fire dispatcher asked.

"She hung herself, man, I just woke up."

"When was the last time you saw her?"

"Last night."

"Okay, is she beyond help?"

"I been trying, giving some, I'm doing, I'm compressing her chest right now—"

"Did you cut her down?"

"Yes, I did."

The dispatcher directed him to do thirty compressions, then breathe twice into the victim's mouth.

"Count out loud if you want to," she said.

Even though Adam had been answering her questions aloud, he spontaneously began his count at "twenty-eight, twenty-nine, thirty," as if he'd been counting all along.

Adam never mentioned that he knew the "girl" as his brother's girlfriend. He later claimed that he didn't even know her last name. And despite his initial statement that she'd "hung herself in the guest house," where he'd spent the night, Adam told investigators that Rebecca was never there, nor had he been in the main house.

Coronado police Officer Robert Kline was the first to arrive at 6:52 A.M., pulling up to the same mansion he'd responded to two days earlier with psychologist Karen Hancock.

Seeing the front door wide open once again, Kline went inside and called out to identify himself as law enforcement.

"Out here!" a man's voice yelled from the backyard.

Making his way through the house, Kline headed into the grassy courtyard, where he saw Adam on his knees, leaning over a naked woman who was lying in a contorted, awkward position, wrists and ankles bound, with her knees bent.

Adam said he'd been trying to give her CPR, but it was clear from her body's position that it would be difficult to do effective chest compressions. That said, Kline told Adam to move aside so he could assess her condition, then started doing compressions himself.

Moments later, his supervisor, Sergeant Mitch McKay, arrived, right behind the paramedics. McKay had also been there for the previous 911 call.

As McKay pulled out his defibrillator to try to start Rebecca's heart, one of the paramedics kneeled down and touched her face. Feeling that her jaw was cool and seeing that rigor mortis had already set in there, he officially pronounced the time of death.

Authorities later said they couldn't offer an estimated time of Rebecca's death, because it wasn't clearly defined by any one factor.

Officer Kline led Adam to the northwest side of the house, trying to calm him down. Adam was clearly nervous, pacing back and forth, saying he needed to call his brother.

Adam called, then texted Jonah, starting at 6:53 A.M. When Jonah didn't answer, Adam texted him again a few minutes later: Call me, it's urgent.

At the time, Jonah was in Max's hospital room, twenty miles away. Not wanting to answer the phone in there with Dina, he stepped into the hallway to call his brother at 7:02 A.M.

"Are you sitting down?" Adam asked.

Jonah could tell from his brother's voice that he needed to find someplace that was even more private to have this conversation, so he did.

"Rebecca took her own life," Adam said.

Jonah was so shocked that he had to hang up and call Adam back. Only when pressed did Adam tell his brother anything more. But he still gave no graphic details, most of which Jonah said he learned later from police.

"I'd rather not tell you right now, man," Adam said.

Adam's first call to Jonah lasted two minutes and seventeen seconds, but they spoke repeatedly that morning, sometimes for as long as thirteen minutes.

He told police how much pain Jonah was already suffering because of Max's condition, so he didn't think his brother could handle the grisly truth about the scene in the courtyard that morning. He was right. Even days later, Jonah still didn't want to hear the details.

Adam knew he needed to call their father, but wasn't sure how to break the news. He dialed the number, but hung up before Gideon could answer, deciding it was better to call his stepmother, Marcelle, and ask for her help.

Adam said he wondered if Rebecca had done this to herself so that he, the only other person on the property that night, would find her in the morning.

"I hope it wasn't a message to me or some s—t, because it was the first thing I saw when I came out," he told detectives.

Once the police's mobile command vehicle had parked in front of the house, Officer Kline took Adam inside for some coffee and bagels.

"This must be traumatic," Coronado police Lieutenant Lou Scanlon told Adam. "Officer Kline will stay with you."

Adam didn't respond immediately. "This is f—ing crazy," he finally said. "I don't think my bedside manner is that bad."

Adam mentioned several times, without prompting, that he couldn't believe Rebecca could take her own life by hanging herself, noting that he'd had to remove a blue "gag" before breathing into her mouth.

While he was waiting, Adam called Jonah again. He also called his girlfriend Mary at work.

"Are you sitting down?" he asked. "The plot thickens. Rebecca has taken her own life."

Surprised, Mary was speechless for a minute. Her first thoughts went to a troubled Asian female coworker, whom she'd feared was feeling suicidal. Wondering if this was a cultural thing, she mentioned that to him.

"She hung herself," he replied.

Mary, who had wrongly assumed Rebecca had overdosed, was surprised again.

"Guess who had to cut her down?" he asked.

Don't the police have someone to do that for you? Mary wondered. *Adam must have been the most able-bodied one there, so that's why they had him do it.*

Chapter 6

Officer Kline took Adam from the command post to the Coronado police station for questioning by sheriff's detectives Henry "Hank" Lebitski and Dave Hillen. Adam told them he didn't need an attorney, because he didn't think he had done anything wrong.

"Go ahead and do whatever you want to do," he said.

The detectives asked him to run through the last couple of days' events, and inquired specifically about Jonah's relationship with Rebecca, her relationship with Dina, and even Adam's relationship with his brother.

"We've got each other's back," he said of Jonah. "That's why I came out."

"Do you have any injuries on you right now?"

"Not that I know of, you want to check me?" Adam replied coolly.

"We might."

"I understand you got to do your thing," but it "kind of makes you think twice about Samaritism," Adam said, mispronouncing the religious term *Samaritanism*. "My brother said most people wouldn't have even cut her down."

"What do you think happened?"

"I assume she killed herself," he said. "Maybe some of this is cultural. I just don't know. I never thought all that s—t through, all the tying. We've all had our down moments."

After establishing a general timeline, the detectives had a forensic tech check and photograph Adam's body for injuries and signs of a struggle, scrape under his fingernails, and take a DNA swab.

Then, at Adam's request, the detectives dropped him at the National Car Rental office near the airport.

Adam called his girlfriend several times that day, giving her additional details about the bindings on Rebecca's body, and "that gag in her mouth."

When Mary heard the "gag" detail for the first time. the whole scenario changed into something possibly more nefarious.

"Adam, a suicide?" she asked skeptically.

"You think?" he asked incredulously. "Who? Why?"

"We tossed around the usual possibilities," Mary recalled later. "It was very obvious to me this was the first time he considered the possibility that she'd been murdered."

Asked to undergo a polygraph exam later in the day, Adam said he needed to talk to his brother before consenting. After Mary and Jonah both advised him to proceed without an attorney, he agreed to meet with detectives again that evening at sheriff's headquarters in Kearny Mesa.

Shortly into the two-hour exam, which started at 6:40 P.M., he received two calls from the same number on his cell phone, which he didn't answer. Checking his voice mail, he told detectives that it was an attorney.

"I knew what they were going to say," Adam said later, referring to the lawyer. "I said, 'F— it, kiss my ass.'"

The calls were from Paul Pfingst, who had served as San Diego County's district attorney (DA) for eight years and had since become one of the best-known criminal defense lawyers in town. But Adam, being from Memphis, had no idea who Pfingst was.

At the time, Pfingst told the media that he'd been hired to represent "someone connected with this case," but he wouldn't say who or by whom, only that it wasn't Jonah.

"I'm not Jonah's lawyer," he said. "I've never spoken to him."

Pfingst recently acknowledged that he'd gotten a call from someone representing Jonah that morning, saying that his brother needed an attorney, so Pfingst went to the mansion to find Adam.

"I thought he might be there, so I wanted to meet with him," Pfingst said.

In a move that prompted conspiracy theories, Pfingst was allowed to cross the yellow crime-scene tape, and was photographed talking to detectives, one of whom had an arm around Pfingst.

Told that Adam was being interviewed elsewhere, Pfingst called 911, describing the incident as a "homicide."

"I'd like to have the police please stop talking to my client and I'd like to find out where he is," he said.

When he found out that Adam was at sheriff's headquarters that evening, taking a polygraph, he called the station directly and asked to speak to the watch commander.

"I was directed ultimately to where he was being interviewed, told he was in an interview, and couldn't be disturbed," he recalled recently.

He also tried calling Adam on his cell phone, but got no answer.

Detective Hillen told Adam that an attorney would tell him not to take the polygraph, but Adam said he "had nothing to hide," and wanted to continue.

By the time Pfingst finally connected with Adam, he was already finished with the exam and said he didn't need a lawyer.

During the exam, Adam couldn't remember whether he had dialed 911 before getting the knife and pulling over the wooden table in the courtyard, or vice versa, that morning.

Detective Angela Tsuida's report had Adam pulling the table over first. When he decided Rebecca's body was too high for him to cut her down, he went to the kitchen to get a knife, climbed up on the table, and cut her down.

The polygraph examiner's report, however, quoted Adam saying he got the knife from the kitchen first, pulled the table over, called 911, pulled the "gag" out of her mouth, then started CPR.

At trial seven years later, he offered a third scenario: He called 911, tried to figure out how to get her down, pulled the table over, then got the knife to cut the rope, which seems to match the sounds on the tape.

"I was pleased with how it went," he testified.

In an interview on *Dateline*, Adam said he thought Rebecca was already dead, but he called 911 in case she wasn't.

"It never even occurred to me that someone would look at this like a crime scene," he said. "That was the furthest thing from my mind."

During Adam's polygraph test, examiner Paul Redden asked Adam multiple variations of several questions: Before you met Rebecca, do you remember ever hurting anyone when you were drunk or angry? Did you, yourself, do anything to Rebecca that resulted in her death? Before you met Rebecca, do you remember lying to anyone in your family? Did you physically do anything to Rebecca that caused her death? Before you met Rebecca, do you remember doing anything sexual that you are ashamed of? Regarding the death of Rebecca, do you know for sure if anyone did anything to her that resulted in her death? Regarding the death of Rebecca, were you in that guest room that she was found hanging from at any time during the night?

Although no question demanded it, Adam volunteered the very personal details that he had masturbated to porn on his iPhone about half an hour before finding Rebecca's body, then showered and got dressed.

That unsolicited admission later caused the Zahaus' first attorney, Anne Bremner, and others to speculate that he offered it up because he believed his DNA would likely turn up in the house or on Rebecca's body, and he wanted to supply an alternative reason why.

"You could have done a whole lot worse on the test," Redden told Adam after the exam. "You could have done a whole lot better there too."

"Sheesh," Adam said under his breath.

"Based on what I've got there, we're in the inconclusive range—" Redden said.

Adam sighed loudly. "God," he muttered.

"—which really doesn't bother me that much," Redden finished.

While the exam was under way, Detective Tsuida called to ask if Adam would leave his shoes and have his fingerprints taken. He agreed.

Redden determined that the overall polygraph results were "inconclusive," but he believed that Adam was being truthful. He later said that although he recommended another test be administered, he wasn't asked to do so.

Asked later why no additional exam was conducted, Sheriff Bill Gore said there was no point to administering more tests that would likely repeat the same inconclusive results.

But Louis Rovner, one of several outside polygraph experts who have reviewed Adam's test, came to a different conclusion: Adam's answers clearly showed deception.

"I think he failed his polygraph. No doubt about it," Rovner said, adding that an additional test should have been administered regardless.

Chapter 7

Although Coronado is actually on a peninsula, this sunny resort town of multimillion-dollar homes, with neatly groomed
yards, many of which are gated, is affectionately known as Coronado Island.

Circled by the San Diego Bay and the Pacific Ocean, the
small community is surrounded by beautiful sandy beaches,
marinas, yacht clubs, and private docks, offering gorgeous
views in every direction. Traveling to mainland San Diego is as
simple as hopping on the Coronado Bridge or crossing a strip of
land known as the Silver Strand.

With three working bases dating back to at least World War
II, Coronado is home to thousands of active and retired military
officers, which lends it a strong patriotic presence. American
flags flap in the sea breeze and palm trees stand guard like tall
soldiers.

But back in 1885, Coronado was just a big piece of undevel-
oped land, purchased and subdivided by two retired businessmen from the Midwest. They sold off the lots, but held on to a
hotel development project that became the famous Hotel del
Coronado, funded in part by a $500,000 investment by John D.
Spreckels, heir to the sugar manufacturing fortune and the eldest child in California's wealthiest family. In time, Spreckels

came to own the Del, most of the land on Coronado, and much of downtown San Diego as well.

When the Del opened in 1888, it was one of the town's first landmarks, and has been a tourist draw ever since, in part because the iconic movie *Some Like It Hot* was shot there.

John Spreckels first built a palatial estate on five acres overlooking the bay, now known as the Glorietta Bay Inn, where he lived and moored his 226-foot yacht. He then commissioned architect Harrison Albright to design a smaller Italian Renaissance home on the beach side of the island in 1908, now known as the Spreckels Mansion.

When Jonah Shacknai first came to town in the 1980s, he gave a speech to a national small-business group, and stayed at the Del. Years later, he returned as a successful business owner, the CEO and founder of Medicis Pharmaceutical Corp., headquartered in Phoenix. By this time, Coronado had become a popular vacation destination for families who wanted to escape the searing summer temperatures in Arizona, and he was eager to join them.

In 2000, while going through a divorce from his first wife, Kim, he bought a three-level beach house on G Avenue for $2.2 million. Seven years later, he was married to his second wife, Dina, and their son, Max, was two, when he bought the nearby Spreckels Mansion as a summer home. They lived in Coronado from Memorial Day to Labor Day, but he hoped to relocate his family to the more spacious property permanently someday.

"Nothing bad could ever happen here," Dina said at the time.

From their sweeping front lawn, the Shacknais could see the red cone-shaped towers of the Del to the south, just around the bend of Ocean Boulevard. Across the street, they looked out to a row of massive craggy rocks along the sidewalk, down a slope to iceplant-covered dunes, a flat stretch of beige sand, and an azure strip of ocean that was close enough to hear the lulling sound of waves breaking on the shore.

Blessed with the county's lowest crime rate, Coronado had no history of home invasions, and in 2011 had seen only one murder in the last twelve years, the murder-suicide of a couple. Knowing that bicycle theft was the most common crime, many of the island's 24,000 residents, including the Shacknais, didn't even lock their doors.

Because a thirteen-year-old girl had been present during the 911 call to the same address two days earlier, Coronado Sergeant McKay told his officers, Van Erhard and Marc Langlais, to do a quick "protective" sweep of the main house.

An unlikely setting for such a bizarre series of events, the 12,750-square-foot property also had three other residential structures on it—the guest house, caretaker's cottage, and a garage apartment—offering *many* places for a killer to hide, in addition to the mansion's basement, attic, and three levels of living space.

The first floor had a foyer, living room, sunroom, kitchen, and dining room. The second level had two bedrooms, one of which was used as both a guest room and a painting studio for Rebecca. She and Jonah slept in the master bedroom on the top level, where his three kids each had a bedroom.

Finding no one on the first floor, Officer Langlais headed upstairs. In the hallway outside the guest bedroom, the carpet was spattered with four drops of blood next to a green-and-white-striped towel, which was also marked with dried blood.

As Langlais entered the bedroom, he passed a cryptic message painted in two lines of black capital letters, with no punctuation, on the white door:

SHE SAVED HIM

CAN YOU SAVE HER

Inside the small room, he had to step over a red rope, which was anchored to the leg of an antique-replica bed and trailed out two French doors to the balcony. He also navigated around two paintbrushes, a tube of black paint, a chef's knife, a steak knife, a cell phone, a white plastic bag, and an overturned white wicker chair.

As Langlais testified later, he found the right-side French door latched closed, so he walked through the open left-side door, and stepped one foot out onto the small balcony, which was covered with a layer of dirt and dust.

Looking down, he could see the rope hanging above Rebecca's naked body on the grass below. However, Detective Angela Tsuida wrote in her report that when she went to the room later that day, she found both French doors to the balcony "closed, but not locked." It's unclear whether Langlais misremembered or if someone else closed the door, but investigators aren't supposed to touch or step on evidence at a crime scene.

Based on its obviously suspicious nature, McKay told Langlais and Erhard to secure the entire property with yellow crime-scene tape across the front lawn.

It didn't take long for Coronado's police chief, knowing his department's limitations and lack of experience investigating murders, to ask the San Diego County Sheriff's Department (SDSD) to head up the investigation. After getting the call at 8:20 A.M., sheriff's officials promptly dispatched a homicide team to the mansion.

Chapter 8

As word quickly spread to the media, at least one news helicopter was flying over the mansion by 9:00 A.M., capturing video of the naked woman whose body was left outside in the sun all day long, exposed to the elements.

Although the county Medical Examiner's Office was notified at 8:09 A.M. of Rebecca's death, Deputy Chief Medical Examiner (ME) Jonathan Lucas and investigator Dana Gary didn't arrive to examine and collect the body until 7:14 P.M. In the meantime, kids and adults in neighboring homes stood on balconies and rooftops, unable to stop themselves from gawking at the spectacle below.

Designated as the lead detective on the case, Angela Tsuida arrived at 9:20 A.M. and joined nearly a dozen officers for a briefing in the driveway about twenty minutes later.

Soon the property was swarming with more than two dozen forensic techs and investigators, including four special agents with the state Department of Justice (DOJ), who were embedded in the sheriff's homicide unit.

Among their first tasks: canvass the neighborhood to establish whether anyone had seen or heard anything, photograph forensic evidence while they waited for search warrants to be

approved, and identify people of interest in the case. This included those closest to Rebecca and anyone who might have
had a motive, opportunity, and access to harm her. Additionally,
it meant those who had insight into her state of mind over the
past couple of days since Max's fall over the interior railing.

Investigators started by walking through the mansion, mark-
ing relevant pieces of evidence with numbered plaques and photographing them, but they didn't secure the guest house until
10:20 A.M., three and a half hours after Adam called 911.

At 12:30 P.M., the SDSD issued its first brief news release,
based on admittedly "fragmentary" information: Its homicide
detail was investigating the death of an unidentified woman at a
scene that "showed suspicious circumstances."

Reporters did live shots in front of the mansion, and after
learning that Jonah was at Rady with Max, news outlets sent reporters there as well.

"They had to cordon off the [ICU] floor, because there were
TV cameras and reporters, and they were waiting in the parking
lot," Jonah said. "I literally had to go through a back door of the
hospital, and go around the perimeter, just to get to the Ronald
McDonald House and avoid the onslaught of reporters."

The first search warrant came through in the midafternoon,
which allowed investigators to begin collecting evidence and
processing the main house for fingerprints and DNA at 4:26 P.M.
They didn't start in the guest house until two hours later, at six-
thirty.

The first forty-eight hours after a death are the most important for homicide investigators. Told that this case was a top priority, they worked all night and into the next morning.

Assigned to talk to neighbors, sheriff's detective Troy DuGal
and DOJ Special Agent Sonia Ramos went door-to-door on

Ocean Boulevard and Star Park Circle. But no one except Marsha Allison, who was in her seventies and lived with her husband, Jeff, two doors down, had anything significant to report.

Over the next couple of days, several pairs of detectives spoke to Marsha, but the investigative reports sometimes differ from interview tapes and from her memory of what she told them she'd heard the night Rebecca died.

In her first interview, she said she was sitting near an open window bordering Ocean Boulevard and watching one of her favorite TV shows about rebuilding houses, which started at 11:30 P.M.

At first, she heard some kids talking outside. Then, a few minutes later, she said, she heard a woman screaming, "Help! Help!"

When the witness wanted to add to her statement, two detectives returned that evening. This time, she told them the woman sounded like she was in her late twenties or early thirties, and called out, "Ah, ah, help, help!"

But Marsha wasn't exactly sure where the sound came from. "As clear as it was, I don't think she was in the back, I think she was in the front. It was clear, not muffled. It wasn't far off," she told detectives. "It could've come from the back, but I don't think so."

Nonetheless, Detective Troy DuGal wrote in his report that Marsha was "confident" that the voice she heard came from the sidewalk area in front of her house on Ocean Boulevard. Marsha added to her story during her deposition in 2017. She said she initially heard some kids bouncing a ball near her driveway for about ten minutes, but the kids had gone silent by the time she heard a high-pitched woman's voice calling out.

"She just screamed real loud, 'Help me! Help me!'" she said. "It was coming from high up, because you could tell."

Marsha said she turned down her TV to listen more closely,

but went back to her show after she was sure things had quieted down ten minutes later.

Asked why she didn't call the police, she replied, "Because I'm a chicken. You stand up and look out the window, they might shoot you. She quit yelling and so I thought she was all right."

Marsha said she'd seen the ambulance come two days earlier but didn't know the little neighbor boy had been hurt until her husband told her. She also didn't know Rebecca more than to wave to in passing.

"She had a little boy with her and they were throwing a ball," she said.

Asked if she recalled telling the police that the person screaming was out front on the sidewalk, she said, "No."

Some of the detectives had upset her with the way they treated her, she explained, particularly a blond female detective, whom she described as "snotty." The detective told Marsha there was no way she could have heard a scream from the Spreckels courtyard balcony while sitting in that front room.

Marsha acknowledged that she saw a group of people on the sidewalk when she looked out to see what the boys were doing, about five minutes after hearing the scream, but they were gone.

After their third interview with Marsha, sheriff's detectives dismissed her as a relevant witness, determining that what she'd heard were kids playing or people talking on the sidewalk in front of her house.

Chapter 9

According to Dina, she was sitting at Max's bedside when Jonah came into the hospital room around seven o'clock on Wednesday morning and tossed a bagel in a bag to her. Then he sat down and stared silently at his son's limp body.

"I've got to go," he said abruptly.

Dina didn't understand what could be more important than their son at this crucial time, but Jonah left without explaining.

When he returned a few minutes later, he looked even more upset.

"What's going on?" Dina asked.

"Rebecca killed herself."

Dina was stunned. "Oh, my God. I'm so sorry. Why would she do that?"

"I've got to go," he said.

When Jonah came back a little later and sat down, Dina asked him again.

"What happened?"

This time, he looked at her and made a stabbing motion to his stomach, as if to indicate hara-kiri.

"Asian honor," she quoted him as saying.

Jonah subsequently testified that he never made that comment. He later acknowledged that some details may have gotten conflated once he learned that one investigator's report quoted Dina as saying that Adam told her "Rebecca committed an honor killing using a knife."

Jonah then recalled telling Dina something about Rebecca doing this out of "honor," and conceded that he may have made the hara-kiri gesture to indicate suicide, but he never said a knife was involved.

"The whole thing was so bizarre to begin with, I don't clearly remember," he said recently.

When Dina called to tell her sister the news, Nina immediately thought of Rebecca's bear hug at the airport.

Oh, my gosh, she probably knew something, and her guilt, she couldn't take it. What on earth did she do that she couldn't live with?

But once she heard that Rebecca was found naked, bound, and gagged, she had the same reaction as everyone else.

How bizarre. How do you even do that?

She didn't know Rebecca well, but from what she did know of her: "If she was going to do something, it was going to be all out," Nina said. "There was no turning back."

The Zahau family claims they never received any official notification from the authorities about Rebecca's suspicious death, which is the county ME's responsibility. The autopsy report states that notification was given at noon on July 13 by "law informant" to Doug Loehner, her sister Mary's husband, who was erroneously described as the decedent's "brother."

The person who actually called to deliver the information was Jonah, who asked Doug, then a police officer in St. Joseph, Missouri, to break the news to Mary and the rest of Rebecca's family.

As soon as Doug got the call, he drove to the clinic where his wife worked in Kansas City to tell her in person.

"Rebecca's gone," he said.

"What do you mean?" she said. "I just talked to her last night!"

After hearing what little Doug knew, Mary wanted to know more, so they called Jonah back from Doug's truck, still reeling from the shock.

When Jonah said he didn't know anything else, Mary asked who did. Jonah suggested they talk to Adam, and gave them his cell number. Mary called Adam right away and said they had this odd conversation:

"I'm Becky's sister," she told Adam, crying. "Tell me this is not true."

But Adam didn't say a word.

"What happened, Adam? Because I need to know everything," she said. "I need to know what happened to my sister."

"I don't know if I'm supposed to be talking to you," he said.

"It's okay."

"It's not a good idea," he told her. "I don't want to push somebody else off the edge."

Mary handed the phone to her husband, who took over the questioning. Adam said a bit more to Doug, but still didn't go into much detail.

"He just said it was suicide," Doug recalled. "He never said anything about her being tied up."

Adam's manner put Mary off, and his comment about not wanting "to push somebody else off the edge" has nagged at her ever since.

Adam also made odd comments to detectives that day, which were noted in the investigative reports, such as his unsolicited "bedside manner" comment to Lieutenant Scanlon. Given his concerns about not wanting to upset Jonah and his father with graphic details, it's possible that he didn't want to further upset Mary, but he ended up doing that anyway.

His girlfriend, Mary, said Adam can be reserved and appropriate, but he often makes "flippant," "inappropriate," and "ir-reverent" comments when he is trying to lighten the mood in a difficult situation.

"It was his lame attempt at levity," she said to explain his comments to police and Rebecca's sister that day. "I mean, look at what he'd just gone through. He was out of his mind and was using flippancy to overcompensate. All I know is that it sounds just like him."

Adam told detectives that he'd tried to be there to talk to Rebecca, but she hadn't seemed *that* upset. Confirming Mary Zahau-Loehner's sentiments, Adam said Rebecca certainly wasn't a "basket case that just can't cope." In fact, he said, she "comported herself in an admirable, appropriate way," and never said she felt responsible for Max's fall.

He indicated, however, that perhaps he hadn't judged the situation correctly, or had failed to say what was necessary to comfort her before she went into the mansion alone, when, he believes, she was in so much pain that she took her own life.

When the detectives asked him how Jonah reacted that morning when he heard the news about Rebecca, Adam said his brother was "very distraught. Wanted to know how she did it, and s—t like that, I didn't f—ing tell him. I said, 'I ain't going to tell you.' I'll tell him someday. I want to talk to a mental-health professional before I even . . . Apparently, people are more on the edge than what I think."

After Jonah spoke to Mary Zahau-Loehner on the phone that morning, they also exchanged texts as they tried to understand why Rebecca might have committed suicide.

Did you or someone blame her for what happened to Max that she feels there was no way out? Mary texted shortly after she got the news.

No. He seems to had [*sic*] cardiac arrest, then fall. Of course not, Jonah texted back.

Mary texted that she wished someone had been at the mansion "to hold" Rebecca. Why did she think she had to do this? Mary said she could have come to Coronado, or Rebecca could have come back to Missouri. Why???

I'm not sure what happened, Jonah replied. I cannot believe she would do this. I cannot.

Mary said she couldn't either. She should never have been alone.

The two of them continued to console each other by text for weeks.

Chapter 10

As detectives pieced together a timeline for the past few days and explored the complicated configuration and dynamics of the Shacknais' and Zahaus' extended families, they started by nailing down who was where and when.

Although they were investigating Rebecca's suspicious death the same way they would a homicide, they were still trying to establish whether it was a murder or a suicide. Also, whether Max's fall was causally related to Rebecca's hanging, and if so, how.

Building an investigative tree with Rebecca at the center, detectives branched out to include those who were physically and emotionally closest to her, as well as Max's family members who might have blamed Rebecca for the boy's injuries. Were other people upset with her, or with Jonah, for some reason yet to be identified?

Searching for answers, Detectives Mark Palmer and Todd Norton went straight to the hospital to interview Jonah as their colleagues were talking to Adam. Their initial questions focused on Rebecca's emotional state, whether she'd communicated any suicidal ideations or indications that she might harm herself.

"Not at all," Jonah said. "I absolutely am astonished." When

Adam had texted him that morning, "I was so shocked I couldn't even speak to him."

Looking back, though, he wondered if Rebecca had other reasons for boarding Ocean in a kennel. "It kind of makes sense," with her driving back and forth between the airport and hospital. "I sort of got it, but it seems a little weird."

Based on her emotional reactions leading up to that morning's events, "I can't help but think she felt responsible in some [way]." Noting her Asian background, he said, "They just look at things a little bit differently in terms of responsibility. I think of how I would feel, if even just a friend asked me to watch their kids, and they went running or something, and when they came back, the kid was dead or near dead. I mean, who could live with that?"

As a kid, Jonah recalled, he'd been watching a friend's dog, which ran away and got hit by a car. "I just couldn't face the people. I just ran and ran and ran . . . in the middle of New York City, for, like, fifty blocks."

Asked about his relationship with Dina, he described it as "not close, but functional," and Dina's relationship with Rebecca as "at the edge of civil."

Dina's access to the mansion? "Everybody has access to my house," Jonah replied. "There's a dog door that, you know, a football player could probably get through. We're not very—"

"Security conscious?"

"Well—"

"Not very security smart."

Questioned about the circumstances of Max's fall, which were still murky, Jonah said the doctors were exploring whether an unusual medical condition might have caused Max's heart to stop spontaneously.

"He may have had something called Long QT syndrome," he said, a heart rhythm abnormality that can cause sudden cardiac arrest and make a healthy guy drop dead while playing basketball. "That's probably the best guess as to what's going on here, because if he doesn't have any other trauma injury, there's just no other explanation for this."

Although he'd never caught Max sliding down the banister, he said he'd seen his older son, Kevin, doing it.

"You said Max was a big climber."

"Yeah, he was a climber," Jonah said, but he would climb a wall or a small tree, not a palm tree or a chandelier. "You'd say he takes reasonable risks."

Asked to recount his whereabouts the previous night, Jonah told them about the voice mail he'd left for Rebecca after leaving the hospital, saying that when she didn't call back, he assumed she'd gone to bed.

But he said it was worrisome that two of the people closest to him had been involved in such serious and bizarre incidents at his house within two days of each other.

The investigators said they couldn't answer certain questions about the investigation, but they knew right away that this was no straightforward death scene.

"Things are suspicious," one detective said.

"Are they?" Jonah asked. He sounded surprised, yet he also voiced concern that he might have been the real target, and that he and his other kids might be in danger.

"I mean, do I need protection?" he asked.

"I don't think so."

"It's too early to—" Jonah said.

"If we have any inkling that you do, we will let you know."

"Okay, 'cause I have the means to arrange it. I work for a company that would consider it a priority. My question is, what happened?"

"That's what we're trying to figure out."

On the one hand, Jonah said, he could understand Rebecca doing this to herself if she felt responsible for Max's injuries, but he also thought that "she would have wanted to take care of me. She would not have wanted to add to my problems, unless it was just unbearable."

Jonah said he didn't ask Adam for details about where he'd found Rebecca, so the detectives vaguely outlined that it was below a second-story exterior balcony in the courtyard near the guest house.

"This hadn't even occurred to me, but if you genuinely believe this is suspicious, she had an ex-husband, who had exceedingly insistent contact with her, who texts her almost every day," Jonah said, describing the "strange" pleading texts from Neil Nalepa that Rebecca had shown him.

He said Neil didn't seem to be stalking her, but he asked her to lunch, told her he missed her, and said, "I'll do anything I can to make this work." The texts also included "almost fanatical religious statements," because Neil believed that Rebecca was living in sin with Jonah.

"Do you know why Neil and her broke up?"

"She claimed that he was unfaithful," Jonah said, "that he was with someone else."

Jonah said he wanted to be sensitive to her family, who had specifically asked him not to allow the authorities to do an autopsy, because they wanted to bring her home intact and try to "save her."

She still might have chance, pls, Mary had texted Jonah, with an apparent religious reference, that morning.

Nonetheless, the autopsy was conducted the next day.

Chapter 11

I started following this case from day one, knowing it could make quite a compelling book someday. As the media jumped on every new detail, this sensational story spread faster than a California wildfire. Due to the suspicious nature of the death scene, coupled with Jonah Shacknai's wealth and international reputation in the pharmaceutical industry, the story quickly went global.

Most observers believed Rebecca had been murdered, so it wasn't surprising that the media attention generated many calls to the sheriff's department with tips, theories, dreams, and possible suspects, including one woman's ex-husband, whom she offered up as Rebecca's killer. People who said they knew Rebecca, as well as alleged psychics, criminal law students, and retired detectives, all claimed to have important information to contribute.

Many also believed that the incidents involving Max and Rebecca were not just related, but sequentially causal. Although the public wanted facts, detectives kept specifics to themselves—such as wording of the message on the door. However, this only prompted armchair detectives to speculate, based on scant or inaccurate details printed in the media or in comment sections below news articles. Amid escalating disillusionment with government and mistrust of police agencies, numerous alternative conspiracy theories grew out of skepticism of "official" sources, a trend that continues today.

For years to come, these theories flooded the internet on blogs and online forums that discuss big crime cases, such as Websleuths, Reddit, and Tapatalk. The rare, if not unique, circumstances surrounding Rebecca Zahau's naked hanging made it one of the most hotly debated, controversial real-life mysteries since the JonBenét Ramsey and O.J. Simpson cases.

On the morning of Wednesday, July 13, 2011, Jim Haager heard sirens and helicopters near his summer rental home in Coronado. Hopping on his bike, he rode a few blocks toward the source, where he saw the yellow tape wrapped around the Spreckels Mansion. He approached the command center and offered to tell investigators what he'd witnessed there the night before.

Haager, a fifty-three-year-old visitor from Austin, Texas, had been coming to Coronado with his family for the past thirteen years. Out for a bike ride Tuesday night, his wife and two young boys stopped to look at a possum while he rode up ahead to the mansion, where some movement caught his eye. As he stopped and stood on the sidewalk under the streetlamp, he saw a woman standing at the front door, "fidgeting" with the doorknob and looking around, as if it wasn't her house.

The mansion was completely dark as the woman turned, walked slowly down the steps, and headed toward him on the front path. Hesitating, she looked around again, changed direction, and pivoted toward the driveway.

He said she was a bit stocky, heavier in the hips, between five feet five and five feet nine inches tall, forty to fifty years old, with dark shoulder-length hair pulled into a ponytail. She was wearing a black-and-white short-sleeved shirt with black pants, and was carrying a black shoulder bag.

As she made her way up the driveway toward the rear court-yard, Haager's family caught up to him and they continued their ride. Stopping at Starbucks a couple of blocks away, his wife bought some tea at 10:25 P.M., so he figured he saw the woman between 10:00 and 10:20 P.M.

After Haager learned on the news that the homeowner's ex-wife Dina Shacknai lived in a house nearby, he found a photo of her online. Pretty sure that she was the woman he'd seen at the house, he rode back to the command center to report his findings.

Some months later, he saw Dina's sister, Nina Romano, on TV saying it was she who had been at the mansion, and that she was holding a pink wristlet purse, not a black shoulder bag. Nina's hair was significantly lighter than Dina's.

However, when Haager contacted the authorities to confirm that it wasn't Nina he'd seen, but the dark-haired Dina, he was told the case was closed and to "do what you have to do." He subsequently contacted Anne Bremner, and conveyed the story to her investigator. So did Haager's wife, who said she, too, saw a woman with dark hair, and it was not Rebecca Zahau.

When Nina learned of Jim Haager's report, she said she could understand how someone could mistake her for Dina, because they had similar body types. Dina was thinner and had darker hair, but they had the same broad shoulders. In the dark, with no lights on at the house, and with Nina wearing dark clothing, she could see how it might be difficult to tell them apart.

"But it is one hundred percent a mistake," she said. "She was at my nephew's bedside."

Hospital records show a nurse's notation that Dina and Jonah were in Max's room, talking to Dr. Francisco Recalde at 10:38 P.M., shortly after Haager said he saw a woman fitting Dina's description at the mansion.

Security video from Rady shows Dina walking in and out of

the hospital's front entrance throughout the night, and Jonah leaving at 12:30 A.M. on his way to the RMH.

The next two nurse notations at 1:13 and 2:06 A.M. don't mention if either parent was at Max's bedside overnight, but only one of them was allowed to stay in the room after visiting hours.

"[Dina] was there when I left that evening and she was there when I came back the next morning," Jonah said recently. "I have no idea what transpired in between."

Chapter 12

As investigators worked through the night on Wednesday and into Thursday morning, they focused their efforts on areas where they found the most relevant evidence. All the items collected from the guest bedroom, where the hanging was initiated, seemed to have come from within the house or the garage.

They found dried blood on the carpet outside the guest room and on a towel nearby. They also found a drop of blood in the master bathroom shower, one level up. However, because they determined there was no trail of blood between those areas, or any sign of a struggle, they didn't spend much time in the master bedroom or bathroom. Nor did they test the blood or hair they found there.

Criminalist Michael Macceca, who looked for shoe prints throughout the house, found a wet, muddy trail on the kitchen floor, leading from the back door to the knife drawer. He also found multiple shoe prints in the basement, but the sole had a different pattern.

The kitchen drawer contained a knife block with eleven slots, six of which were empty, with one knife lying across the top. Two of the missing knives were in the guest room—a chef's knife, with an eight-inch blade, and a steak knife, with a four-and-a-half-inch blade. A third knife, with a serrated blade, which Adam used to cut Rebecca down, was outside in the courtyard. Each one had a black handle, with three round silver rivets.

On the balcony from which Rebecca had been hanging, Macceca found several impressions in the layer of dust that covered the floor and iron railing. Drawing a diagram, he noted two somewhat V-shaped impressions, one to the left of the doorway and one just inside the railing, as well as one single larger impression farther to the left of the doorway. Of the two disturbances in the dirt on the railing, one was about eleven inches wide, and the other was a half-inch area about four inches to the right, where the rope was hanging over.

Based on the indentation in the carpet where the bed leg that anchored the rope normally sat, Macceca measured that the metal frame had moved seven and a half inches, apparently pulled by the force of Rebecca's body dropping over the railing.

Nina, who knew her visit to the mansion the night before could be important for the police's timeline, informed detectives at the hospital on Wednesday.

Back at Dina's house on G Avenue that night, Dina was having a tough time with the latest news about Max's declining condition when two DOJ agents showed up around nine-thirty to question her.

As they broached the topic of Rebecca's death, Dina became "very emotional" and "visibly distraught," Special Agent Victor Resendez wrote in his report. He said she alternately texted, answered her cell phone, and sobbed "uncontrollably" as he tried to interview her. She also refused to allow him to record their conversation. When asked if she "had any information on what happened to Rebecca Zahau," Resendez wrote, Dina said Adam told her it was "an honor killing," a comment she later attributed to Jonah.

Because it was "a very difficult time for Dina," Resendez noted that he couldn't get much out of her other than she'd asked Jonah several times what had caused Max to fall and he'd replied that Max had fallen from the balcony. As Dina continued to receive calls, she became "increasingly emotional," stated that "she could no longer speak to us, and terminated the interview."

Moving on, Resendez and another agent interviewed Dina's sister, Nina, for about fifty minutes, during which time she agreed to do a polygraph exam another day. It was late by then, and Nina didn't want to leave her autistic son at the house, so forensic techs came to her at 11:00 P.M., collecting a DNA swab, her fingerprints and palm prints, and half a dozen strands of hair. They also scraped under her fingernails, photographed her body and hands, and took the clothes she said she'd worn to the mansion the night before, which included a brand-new pair of yoga pants.

"I don't know what's going on, so anything I can do to help you guys figure out what's going on," Nina said, "I will."

To her knowledge, no one ever took prints or photographed Dina's body.

"The reason why is because she wasn't at the mansion," she told KFMB-TV later. "The only reason they did it to me is because I told them I went by there."

On July 17, Dina's life coach, Ken Druck, called sheriff's detectives to say that his client had information she wanted to convey. A man claiming to be Dina's attorney subsequently said he wouldn't let Dina talk to them, but she ended up meeting with detectives at her home in Paradise Valley, Arizona, as scheduled. However, she still wouldn't talk much about what happened to Rebecca, wanting to focus on her son instead.

As Detective Tsuida took one last walk through the mansion to collect any items that might have been overlooked, she came across a book on a shelf in the guest room, *Buckland's Complete Book of Witchcraft*. She took it as evidence, because it featured hand-drawn pictures of "subjects bound in different positions."

The book was about Wicca, a "good witch" type of religion, art, and magic, in which some participants perform rituals naked or wearing robes. Tying bindings and removing clothing weren't done as punishment, but for ceremonial reasons. As a section on death and resurrection states: *She laid down her garments and her jewels and was bound, as are all who enter the Realms of Death the Mighty One.*

The book includes a few pages showing naked people, including an instructional diagram of a woman being blindfolded and bound—curiously, with a nine-foot length of red rope—during an initiation ceremony. But other than having her wrists tied behind her, the bindings and markings on the woman's body aren't similar to Rebecca's.

At 10:18 A.M. on July 14, Dr. Jonathan Lucas, the deputy chief medical examiner, conducted an autopsy on Rebecca's body, with five law enforcement officers observing. The resulting nineteen-page report noted a number of findings with which outside experts and observers significantly differed later on.

For instance, Lucas noted that Rebecca had several evenly spaced areas of sticky, tan-gray tape residue on both legs, and smears of black paint on her right nipple and left breast. Paint smears were also found on the right side of her lower back, her upper arm, clavicle, ring fingernail, index finger, and the base of her thumb. In addition, she had four subgaleal hemorrhages on her scalp.

The pathologist noted that she had petechiae, or tiny broken blood vessels, on her face and in her eyes and mouth, which are found in cases of both hanging and strangulation. Her upper eyelids had been cosmetically tattooed with blue eyeliner and her eyebrow area was also tattooed with color.

Rebecca's body fell a greater distance than in most hangings, which are only one or two feet. But, despite the nine-foot "long drop" from the balcony, her spinal cord and cervical vertebrae were intact; her cricoid and thyroid cartilages and hyoid bone were only fractured.

These fractures later became a primary point of contention in the suicide-murder debate, just as they were in the 2019 death of Jeffrey Epstein, who was found dead with ligature marks on his neck and three fractures of his hyoid bone. Authorities determined his death was a suicide, but some outside experts said the injuries were more consistent with murder.

Abrasions and contusions were found all over Rebecca's body—on her back, abdomen, upper buttocks, arms, and legs. Lucas's report said they "appeared consistent with impact with large plants under the balcony," but experts said her arms, face, and front of her body should also have been scratched under that scenario. In addition, she had dirt on the soles of her feet and on her left hip and thigh.

Although she had dried blood on both of her upper inner thighs, genital area, and on two fingers of her right hand, she had no visible bleeding injury. She did have a laceration on one finger, but it didn't look fresh. The report didn't state this, but to the naked eye, the laceration looked like a rope burn. It seemed deep even for that, so it also could have been a two-day-old cut from picking up the glass shards, but she wasn't treated for that when she took Ariel for stitches.

Blood was noted inside Rebecca's vagina and around her cervix, but "no visible trauma" or signs of sexual assault, such as semen. Toes on both feet also had dried blood on them, but it was never tested to determine if it was menstrual blood.

Livor mortis, or lividity, which consists of visible purple areas where the blood has settled due to gravity after the heart stops beating, was "posterior, red and fixed . . . appropriate for the decedent's position," the report said.

Experts have strongly differed with this finding as well, noting that this pattern of lividity—markedly horizontal along the rear portion of her buttocks, her entire right calf, in the lower lateral portion of her left calf, and across her back—indicated that she'd been lying on her back for some time, with her legs bent to the side, as the authorities found her. If she'd been hanging by the neck for several hours as Adam claimed, they said, the blood should have been pulled down by gravity, pooling in her feet and lower extremities.

During the autopsy, Lucas removed the bindings around Rebecca's wrists, and placed them around cardboard tubes to preserve the knots. This section of rope had apparently been cut from what was originally one long water ski rope cut into three sections.

The rope around her right wrist was tied with a slipknot, but it was loose enough for that hand to be slipped out of the binding loops "with mild pressure." The rope on her left hand, however, needed to be loosened to free it. The end of the rope, which Lucas said was used to tighten the noose, was still clutched in her left hand, and had some black paint on it at the wrist.

The bindings around her ankles were tied with a similar slipknot. At the end of the rope was a yellow plastic tube serving as a "water sport tow rope handle" with this warning: *intended only for towing up to a maximum of two people or 340 pounds on an inflatable tube.*

Curiously, Lucas noted, there was not one, but two "ligature furrows," or red purplish bruised areas, leaving a "dried red abrasion," on both sides of her neck.

The long-sleeved blue T-shirt was wrapped three times around her neck, on top of both the rope and her long black hair, with the ends of both sleeves tied in a double knot near the cuffs.

Observers argued that Rebecca's hair being underneath both the rope and the shirt countered a woman's natural impulse to pull her hair free. The autopsy report made no mention whether any secretions on the T-shirt were examined, what size it was, or to whom it belonged.

Rebecca wore three silicone bands on her wrists, a black "Bionic Band" and a yellow "Livestrong" on the left, and a "Power Balance" on the right, which are marketed to improve an athlete's "strength, balance and energy."

Lucas's report noted that Rebecca had no history of depression, and no scars on her wrists indicating previous suicide attempts.

On July 18, Captain Tim Curran, who headed the sheriff's Central Investigations Division, requested that the ME's office keep the autopsy report and toxicology test under seal so as not to "seriously hamper the successful resolution of the homicide investigation."

When toxicology results came back a couple of weeks later, they showed no alcohol or drugs in Rebecca's system. But the report—and its conclusions about the cause and manner of death—wasn't released until September.

Chapter 13

The day after Rebecca's death, sheriff's detective Todd Norton and DOJ Special Agent Sonia Ramos asked Jonah's best friend, dermatologist Howard Luber, for his perspective on the case.

Howard told them how special and different Jonah's relationship with Rebecca had been compared to his two previous marriages, which were doomed by their volatility and incompatibility.

Asked about Jonah's relationship with his brother, Adam, and whether there was any jealousy between them, Howard said no.

"You're a smart guy, you've been around the block a few times," Norton told Howard, saying they were open to hearing any medical theories that could help shed light on the two incidents now that Max's bleak prognosis was more definitive. "What do you think happened?"

"It's unimaginable to me that these are independent events," Howard said. "It's possible, but how can that be?"

"But related how?" Norton asked. "That's the question."

When Howard first heard that the events leading to Max's fall were a "pure accident," that scenario made no sense. "He's brain dead . . . but not enough physical damage to warrant that. Then either he fell and his heart stopped, which would be really unusual, or his heart had stopped before he fell. So he's hanging over the banister with a heart attack and falls, or something happened to him on the second story where his heart stops, and he's unconscious, and he somehow has to get to the next floor with a bunch of glass on top of him . . . So somebody suffocates him, but has to sit there for some minutes."

Norton pointed out that during training officers are cautioned that carotid holds on an adult's neck can cause irreversible brain damage in only a minute, and even faster on a six-year-old child.

"We've got things in play here," Norton said. "He wasn't alone in the house, and all we know is what people have told us. We know there was a dog there, we know that her sister was there, we know that Rebecca was there. It's a big dog. I have big dogs and I've seen the weirdest things happen. We know that Max liked to play soccer inside. What happened with that? I mean, we've got way too many questions than we have answers."

Howard laid out his thoughts. "If somebody did something to Max, then they come back two days later and they do what they did to Rebecca? That makes no sense to me. Unless the person on the first go-round is looking for Rebecca, ran into Max, he started making noise, and they had to sort of get him out of the way. And then the dog with the fall, they scoot, then come back, because they really want Rebecca."

"But what would the motive be?"

"Hatred."

"Toward who?"

"Toward Rebecca or Jonah."

Howard said he'd even discussed this scenario with Jonah. "Who dislikes you enough to do this?" he asked, but Jonah couldn't think of anyone.

"Who would dislike Rebecca?" Howard asked, with the same

answer. However, as he told detectives, "Many people knew that Jonah and Rebecca spent summers at the Coronado mansion."

When Jonah first told Howard that Rebecca had committed suicide, Howard figured she'd felt responsible for Max's injuries. After seeing Max, all banged up in the hospital, she might have thought that even if Jonah didn't blame her, others might, and she "didn't want to endure that."

Still, he had a hard time understanding why she would do it in such an extreme fashion, and asked the detectives if they'd ever seen anything like it before.

Norton said he'd seen people hang themselves by accident, attempting autoerotic asphyxiation, but he had to admit he'd never seen anyone do it purposely, or as elaborately as this.

Howard said he hadn't heard Dina, Nina, or anyone else place blame on Rebecca for Max's condition, although he did over-hear this exchange:

"We really want to find out what happened here," Jonah told Dina.

"Duh, how does he just topple over onto the floor and the chandelier lands on him?" Dina replied.

Chapter 14

With so much going on at Medicis, Jonah didn't have much time to wallow in grief. The company's stocks, which had been strong and rising in the first half of the year, took a tumble the day after Rebecca's death, sending him and his staff into damage-control mode.

"It's just a little panic selling," one analyst in New York told Newsmax.com on July 14. "There's no question that Jonah is very much the face of the company and very much a part of the overall vision and strategy."

Detectives Angela Tsuida and Todd Norton did a second interview with Jonah, on Friday, July 15.

Since his conversation with detectives two days earlier, Jonah's perspective had changed a bit. In hindsight, Rebecca's boarding Ocean at the kennel, for example, made sense after all.

He also offered further explanation on some topics. Rebecca decided to send Ariel back to Mary in Missouri, he said, because they'd planned a fun summer of taking Max and Ariel to Disneyland, and sending Ariel to camp, but everything changed when Max fell. She talked it over with Mary, and they both felt Ariel should go home.

"I should have just had Ariel stay," Mary later told Jonah, stopping midsentence when she realized that it could have been worse. "Well, what might have happened to Ariel?"

The detectives said they assumed that Jonah had heard that Rebecca was found bound, which led to a discussion about any ropes, ties, or zip ties kept around the house. Jonah said he still hadn't heard or read any more details, because his brother told him he couldn't handle it, so he'd purposely avoided looking at photographs and most of the news accounts.

"I mean, was she, was she assaulted? I mean, these are things, like, I am curious intellectually, but I don't think I really want to know. Right now, anyway," he said.

As for the rope, Jonah said, "The only thing that I would have had would have been some boating line."

"Um-hm," Tsuida said.

"To tie up a boat."

"Okay, and where would that have been?"

In the garage, there were some metal shelves, where they kept an inflatable inner tube for the kids, he said.

"I was thinking, like, big boats," she said.

Jonah said he had two of them: a forty-seven-foot Eastbay powerboat, and a nineteen-foot Sea Ray "cruise the harbor" boat, both of which were kept at the Glorietta Bay Marina.

Pressed for more details, Jonah said he preferred using white rope, but he recalled that they used some kind of thin nylon rope to hitch the inflatable boat to the dock. Other than that, he said he didn't really know what was in the garage.

"I'm not a fix-it guy," he said. "I don't know how to use tools."

"Do you recall seeing any red rope anywhere in the house?" Tsuida asked.

Jonah said he had a recollection of some red or orange boating line that came with the inner tube, which he'd bought five years earlier. But the only time they'd used one of the bigger boats was July 4, when he and Rebecca watched fireworks.

When Tsuida inquired whether Rebecca typically slept in the nude, Jonah said she usually wore pajamas—sweats or medical scrub pants that tie at the top—or one of his T-shirts to bed.

"That's usually how she'd start out," Jonah said. "And then if it was warm, or we had sex or something else, she might easily wind up nude."

Tsuida asked who had been over to the house recently because they'd found a bottle of Dr Pepper on the top of a hamper in a mansion hallway. However, she never mentioned the women's panties that they'd found in the trash in the guest house bathroom, but didn't test, or the women's clothing they found on the floor, the glass of clear liquid on the nightstand, or the makeup wipes on the dresser.

Jonah said his fourteen-year-old son, Kevin, had a friend sleep over for four or five nights before he and his fifteen-year-old sister, Cindy, left for South Carolina to stay with their mother, Kim. Cindy also had a party with friends in the guest house, and alcohol was involved, which angered Jonah enough to go buy a breathalyzer at Fry's to do random testing on her. He said a couple of plumbing crews had been to the house in the past few weeks to clear the sewer line and fix a toilet that had overflowed in the downstairs bathroom.

Tsuida said they were still in the initial investigation stage, trying to figure out what had happened, amid "a lot of speculation out there" and "a lot of different theories being thrown out." But if this was foul play, she asked, who would have a motive to kill Rebecca?

Then Tsuida answered her own question. The detectives hadn't been able to talk with Dina yet, because she'd said she wasn't up to it, "but, I mean, when we're looking at if this is foul play, who has the motive? Dina."

Jonah conceded that Dina had had a "high degree of interest in Rebecca for a long time," but in terms of what happened with Max, Dina had been "really adamant that I press Rebecca, because her theory was that Ariel was somehow involved in what happened to Max, not intentionally, but that they were playing. She must have asked me fifty times on Monday night and on Tuesday, 'Ask Rebecca what happened. I've got to know what happened. Can I speak to the little girl myself?'"

"Is she the kind of person that has the ability to do something like this?" Tsuida asked.

"She herself would not have been strong enough to subdue Rebecca," Jonah said. "Rebecca was pretty strong. I mean, she used some martial arts. I don't think she was a super expert."

"Um-hm."

"So the more interesting question—'cause I have to say, I've contemplated, but I wouldn't like to think it's true—is would Dina have hired someone to do this or gotten someone to do it? It's unlikely, but not impossible. I wouldn't like to think it's true. It was, I mean, I guess I should just spill it out, right?"

"Right."

"Because I really am not looking to hang Dina, she's just suffered unimaginable loss. She was almost giddy. She had one reaction when she sort of heard about this, then she became almost giddy that Rebecca was dead. She didn't say it, but her whole demeanor was inappropriate—"

"Um-hm."

"—given that we had a kid dying. And, you know, for someone like, you know, even she didn't like Rebecca, it's like, 'Okay, I have my beef with her, but this is tragic that she's dead.'"

Noting that Dina had "always hoped that we might get back together," Jonah later conceded that her odd reaction might have had other origins. "Maybe it was just the shock of the news," he said. "It may have just been nervous laughter."

But at the time, he couldn't say it was impossible that Dina was involved in Rebecca's death, and yet he also couldn't see how she could have done it by herself. "Physically, would it be impossible? Yeah, there's no way. Rebecca would pulverize her."

"Unless she caught her off guard, just hypothetically," Tsuida said.

"But how would she have dragged [Rebecca]?" he asked, noting that Rebecca was "not weak" and would have fought back.

"Would Rebecca do this to herself?" Tsuida asked, almost nonchalantly, in the middle of her less important questions.

Jonah said he'd been mulling that question constantly and had been vacillating. If she felt responsible or thought their relationship would be forever changed because *he* thought she was responsible, then maybe. But he was leaning the other way.

First, she loved him, and if she were going to harm herself, she wouldn't do it on the property. She would have calculated that, and thought, *What am I doing to Jonah here?* He just didn't see it.

"I'm pretty convinced not," he said. "It's hard to accept because it would have been so inconsiderate, and she was anything but inconsiderate. She was excessively considerate. But I don't know what goes through someone's mind when they're taking their own life. So I'm not pretending to be a shrink."

Playing devil's advocate, Tsuida asked Jonah to consider why Rebecca might have felt that he *did* blame her: He told her not to come to the hospital to see Max, he didn't talk to her much Monday night when he came home to shower and change, and he repeatedly asked her what had happened to Max. Perhaps Rebecca interpreted his reaction as: *He doesn't believe me, why does he keep asking me the same questions over and over again?* And finally, the voice mail he left her, relaying Dr. Bradley Peterson's prognosis that the boy wouldn't walk or talk again.

But Jonah said he couldn't see that either. "I shared that with her, but not in a blameful way," he said, insisting that he didn't feel any blame toward her.

"Um-hm."

"It was more like I was so upset. And I was a little surprised that she didn't call me back. I mean, it was atypical of her not to do that. So, the only way would be if she not just felt responsible, but there's more to the Max story than we know. That's the only way you could convince me that she did this herself."

This same thing could have happened to anyone, he said. "I've left Max for twenty minutes with Cindy, my fifteen-year-old daughter. Of course, a kid can have an accident . . . She was resuscitating him. I went out of my way to tell several people that she saved his life, and I told her how much I appreciated that."

But even if she *had* wanted to kill herself, he said, she wouldn't have done it while Max was still in the hospital, or "in such a sensational way that would be just so bizarre" and "only would have hurt me." It was more likely that she would have disappeared, gotten into the car and driven somewhere like Missouri. "I mean, she was my support system."

When he called Doug to notify Mary, he said he used the words "she's taken her own life," because that was what Adam had told him. "I felt I had to notify them. And her first reaction was 'That's impossible. This would never happen.'"

If the detectives could present him with "conclusive forensic evidence that she did this to herself," then he'd believe it, but it would have to be something definitive like a toxicology screen. Otherwise, Jonah said, "It's so counterintuitive at so many different levels. It's so inconsistent with her behavior patterns."

That's when Tsuida pulled out a new angle. "I'm not saying this is the case with her, but, you know, the situation, when we've seen it, it's more like a *screw you*, because she's pissed off, and here she's devoted her life to you," she said.

But Jonah dismissed that theory too. "No way," he said. "You would in one hundred years never sell me on that story." If she felt responsible and driven to this, it would stem from a "strong sense of shame," not anger, and she would be more apt to cut herself in a car than this.

However, now that Dr. Peterson suggested that Max could have been smothered, Jonah said, he realized that *he* could have been the real target.

"Is that a possibility? I think it is," Jonah said. "So, my concern here is, is there somebody running around that, you know, is this about me in some way? Is someone trying to take things away from me that are important? It's true that Max, he's the world, and Rebecca too. She was fantastic. So, if someone really tried to hurt me, man, they did it."

After discussing this scenario with Howard and trusted colleagues at Medicis, Jonah said they'd come up with three possible suspects, all of whom had attended corporate events at his house, and one of whom had run into Jonah and Rebecca while jogging in their neighborhood in Paradise Valley. One man had been unable to find a job after leaving the company a year earlier. Another employee had been fired after he and another employee were accused of sexually assaulting a woman at an out-of-state event. One of them went to another company, then texted Jonah out of the blue on July 14, sending "thoughts and prayers."

"We fire people all the time," Jonah said. "You get the right combination of someone's feeling that they've been treated unjustly, and I'm the leader of the company and stuff happens."

He also noted that he wasn't even supposed to be in Coronado that week; he was supposed to be in Phoenix from Monday night to Wednesday night.

"A lot of people knew that," he said, because his calendar was visible to most Medicis employees.

Finally, Jonah had a request to make. His company's general counsel, "through people that he knows in San Diego, have approached both the sheriff and the DA to get you guys to make some sort of statement that I'm not a suspect, because our stock has been depressed out of—I mean, it seems unbelievable to me, I have to say—out of some concern that somehow I'm involved in this. So, if you don't think I'm involved—and if you do, you're out of your minds—it would be helpful to our company and to our shareholders' economic interests if there could be some declaratory statement at some point to sort of say that."

"Right," Tsuida said. "I can tell you this. I have not seen the press coverage myself. But I know that my captain did make a statement yesterday." Even if she believed he wasn't a suspect, she said, "in these kinds of investigations, you just can't [say that publicly]." Besides, she added, she was under the impression that the news conference the day before "kind of squashed that" possibility.

"Not entirely," Jonah replied, because he'd looked online for news about his company's stock performance and found a story on CNBC, which "basically speculated what would happen if I was mixed up in this." That kind of coverage could cause problems for Medicis, and it wouldn't be "helpful for our shareholders" to get the wrong impression. "If something could happen to me, they wouldn't allow me to be the chief executive of the company."

Tsuida said she would talk to her superiors "and see if we can help you out with that."

"I probably would not have mentioned this if our stock had not swooned," he said. "It didn't even occur to me that someone could imagine that I was a suspect," but "you know there's five percent out there" who might. "I lost my son, I've lost Rebecca, and my life is a circus now, so if you can do something to help, I've got two other kids, I'd appreciate it." He said his company and his shareholders would too.

"Some things are out of my control, but I will see what I can do for you," Tsuida said.

"I'm going to help you and cooperate no matter what," Jonah said. "And maybe you can't just make this decision, but if you can be an advocate, it would be helpful."

"I would do my best. I just don't like making promises. But I will do that."

Jonah said he had nowhere to go. He couldn't go back to the mansion, so he would have to sell it. He didn't even know how he was going to face getting his belongings out of there.

"Even Max alone would have been enough. And now this?" he said. "Maybe nothing happened with Max. I don't know, but it's just this coincidence of events is just extraordinary. You wouldn't necessarily say these two things are absolutely connected, but you'd think in one house, how did these two things happen within two days of each other?"

"We are looking into everything," Tsuida said, "Max and Rebecca separate, we're looking at them together, we're looking at it from every angle. You know, is it homicide? Is it suicide? Is it accident? What is it?"

"It could conceivably be all those things. It could also be someone trying to get to me," Jonah said, noting he was already taking moderate precautions, and was planning to get the Doberman back. But if investigators had any inkling that "there's somebody running around, and if this is about me, I have to take extraordinary precautions."

"I'm sure you're going to go in all directions," he said, "but, you know, the two people who know her so well are just not buying this suicide. It doesn't mean it didn't happen, but it's a lot easier for me to believe that Dina hired a hit man, and even if I don't think that's what happened, 'cause who would be so stupid as this? I really don't think a con man, I think there's like a one percent chance that happened. But it's a lot easier for me to believe that than Rebecca committed suicide like this, now."

If it wasn't her ex-husband or "some creep from the health club," he wondered, "was it just random? Did someone just see her? Maybe it wasn't intensely personal, I don't know. But she didn't go around pissing off a lot of people. She was extremely pleasant, so it would have to be someone that's off, obviously."

Tsuida tried to reassure Jonah that he didn't need to solve this on his own. "Concentrate on your family, and let us be burdened with trying to figure this out," she said.

"But I can't stop thinking about it," Jonah said.

Securities and Exchange Commission (SEC) records show that Medicis made the first of four $9.8 million annual payments to buy life insurance for eight top executives—including Jonah—in the quarter that started in July 2011. For some observers, this purchase bolstered the "hit man" theory, which was further supported by the remarks Jonah made to Tsuida about his personal safety and the need for further precautions.

However, Jonah said recently that this insurance purchase wasn't done in reaction to the events at the mansion. Rather, it was part of a benefits package that had been in the works for months, an incentive to retain executives during an attempted corporate takeover.

"There was a feeling that it was important to signal to the executives and employees, stay the course, the company is safe, your job is safe," he said.

Chapter 15

As detectives continued to build a portrait of Rebecca and her state of mind, they also tracked her recent activities and interactions with a short list of witnesses, as well as their whereabouts at the time of Rebecca's death. Those people included Jonah, Adam, Dina, and her sister, Nina, Rebecca's sisters and her reportedly abusive ex-husband.

In addition to serving search warrants to obtain phone records and video security footage to cross-check witness statements, investigators examined Rebecca's internet browser histories, texts, and other data stored on her cell phone.

Detectives also collected domestic violence reports that Jonah and Dina previously had filed against each other in Paradise Valley. Drama ensued after the media got ahold of the documents several days after Max was declared brain dead and removed from life support.

As the former couple prepared to bury their son, they issued a joint statement: *These police reports are not reflective of the totality or the precise details of the events during a difficult time in our marriage that we worked through together,* it read in part, then later on: *The release of the records as we grieve Max's recent loss pains us greatly, and we request that the privacy of our family be respected. The unfortunate attention to these records is a distraction from the most important concern of honoring our beautiful son, who lives on in both of our hearts.*

Detectives learned that six months earlier, Rebecca had quit her job—as an ophthalmic technician who aided doctors in Lasik and cataract surgery at a clinic in Phoenix—to take care of Jonah and Max. In the hours after Max's fall, she did just that, constantly ferrying family members and friends to and from the airport and hospital.

Although she was still precluded from visiting Max, she kept her sister Mary updated on his condition and his father's well-being, noting that Jonah was "bawling" and more upset than she'd ever seen him.

It's just bad, Rebecca texted.

Early Monday evening, Jonah texted Rebecca that he planned to keep a vigil at Max's bedside for the next few days, trading off with Dina, who would take the overnight shift.

This is awful, he texted.

Oh babe. I know. I have no words, Rebecca replied, saying he and Maxie were in her thoughts. He will be okay.

As Rebecca repeatedly checked in with Jonah, asking how "our little Maxi" was, there was no visible tension or anger in their text exchanges, in which they called each other "babe," "baby," and "sweetie." As Jonah asked for—or Rebecca offered to bring him—vitamin supplements, clothing, and food, Rebecca's tone didn't seem overly anxious, nor did she apologize or say anything about feeling guilty or responsible for Max's injuries. She just kept repeating that she loved Jonah and his son.

As Rebecca was driving to the airport on Tuesday, her sister Snowem called again, worried that Rebecca had also been injured in the bad accident she'd mentioned the day before. Rebecca said she would have to call her back the next day.

After dinner at the Fish Market that night, Rebecca was back at the mansion talking to Mary, who had thirty minutes to kill while waiting for Ariel's plane to land. Asked why she hadn't come home with Ariel, Rebecca said she was needed in Coronado to help Jonah, who was "picky about his food," so she had to make it for him and get his clothes ready.

But she said she would come visit in September or October. "I want the summer to be over first, and [be] back in Arizona before I come out," Rebecca said.

"Her outlook was positive," Mary recalled. "She was talking about an engagement with Jonah. She was telling me, like, 'We've been talking about it, and I think he'll call you soon about my ring.'"

Rebecca also outlined her plans for the next day: "I've got to go, take a shower and get ready for bed, because I have to get up at five in the morning. I'll keep you posted tomorrow."

Between eight-thirty and nine o'clock, Rebecca texted Mary and Ariel to ensure they had connected at the airport. She also told Mary that it was good to see Jonah smile for the first time since Max's fall.

Breaks my heart to c him so sad, she texted.

When Mary asked if that meant Max was better, Rebecca replied that he still wasn't okay, but the doctors had reduced the "amount of coma," and he seemed "more alive."

She said that although she loved Max as if he were her own son, she knew he wasn't. It was all such an unbelievable "nightmare," but she was trying "to be strong for Jonah."

In her last outgoing texts—to Ariel at 8:39 P.M. and to Mary at 8:53 P.M.—she told her sisters that she loved them.

Rebecca called Mary one last time around 10:00 P.M., asking if she should call their parents to explain how Ariel had cut her leg, and why she'd sent Ariel back early. Mary was already on the phone with their mother, Pari, who was on hold.

"Do you want to talk to them?" Mary asked.

"No, tell them I'll call them in the morning," Rebecca said. "I'm just going to go to bed."

In hindsight, Mary regretted telling Rebecca not to call their parents, so they could have heard her voice one last time.

Earlier that same day, Dina had gotten a ride from the hospital to Coronado with a friend, arriving around ten-thirty in the morning. After showering, she tried to get some rest, but she was too distraught and emotionally spent. Max was her life.

The nurses had told her that Max would probably spend a week in the ICU, about two weeks in a step-down unit, then go through a lengthy period of rehab. Based on that, Dina thought he would miss soccer season, and his entrance to first grade would likely be delayed, but she thought he was going to recover.

According to a detailed interview Nina did with KFMB-TV, during which she recounted her and Dina's activities that day, they drove Dina's car back to the hospital around 3:30 P.M., leaving Nina's son in Coronado with two of Dina's friends.

At the hospital, Nina bought a teddy bear and a book to read to Max from the gift shop. When she finally saw Max's bruised face and body for the first time, she couldn't understand how he could have suffered such serious injuries from falling down the stairs. But even then, they still didn't know how severe those injuries were.

"The doctors didn't know if the cardiac arrest came first, or if the fall caused cardiac arrest," she said. "That was very unclear."

Nina stayed at the hospital when Jonah left with Howard around 4:00 P.M., and another hour after Jonah returned at eight o'clock. By nine, she was ready to go back to the house to get some rest, so Jonah loaned her his car. He and Dina were sharing Dina's, which was parked at the hospital.

On the ride back to Coronado, Nina tried to visualize how and where Max had fallen at the mansion, but she couldn't do it without looking at the actual stairs and where on the floor Rebecca had found him.

I just don't get it, she thought. *I'm going to go ask Rebecca, "Can you please show me where you found him? Show me how you found him."*

She arrived at the house on G Avenue around 9:25 P.M., chatted with her son and Dina's friends in the kitchen, then texted Rebecca at 9:41, asking if she was awake.

I was hoping to stop by, she texted.

She knew Rebecca had her number in her phone because they'd texted about the airport pickup the day before, so she thought it was strange when she got no response. It seemed too early for Rebecca to be in bed.

At 9:55 P.M., Nina decided to walk over to the mansion, which was five minutes away, and talk to Rebecca in person.

Dressed in Reeboks, black yoga pants, and a lightweight dark gray athletic jacket over her tank top, Nina chatted with her cousin by phone as she walked. The pink Coach wristlet purse she wore on her arm was only big enough to fit a tube of lip gloss, a driver's license, and her phone.

As she walked up the front pathway and climbed the several stairs to the front door, she looked for any signs that Rebecca was home. The porch light wasn't on, and as she peered through the frosty-glass pane in the door, the only light inside was the one illuminating the stairwell to the second-floor hallway.

She knocked, waited, then rang the bell—twice. Still, no answer. So, she walked around to the driveway, where Rebecca's SUV was parked. Heading to the back gate, she saw the overhead light was on in the second-floor guest bedroom, but the rest of the house was completely dark, as was the guest house.

It was common in Coronado for people to leave their cars at

home and stroll around the village, so she wondered if Rebecca
had gone out to dinner, or had taken a walk down the street to
the Del.

Or she doesn't want to talk to me.

With that, she turned around, walked back to Dina's, talked
briefly to her son and Dina's friends, and called it a night.

Hospital surveillance video confirmed Jonah's account that
he left the hospital at 12:28 A.M. that night, and his cell phone
records documented his call to Rebecca at 12:48 A.M.

Similarly, Rebecca's phone records showed that the last outgoing call from her cell was to her voice mail at 12:50 A.M.
However, investigators were unable to retrieve the message, and
they were also unable to get a copy of it from the service
provider. All they could tell was that someone had listened to
the message, then deleted it. That meant that no one—not the
authorities, nor Rebecca's family—was ever able to prove what
Jonah's message actually said.

Investigators also didn't try to lift prints from Rebecca's
phone to prove that she was the one who listened to the message
and deleted it. Because there were no other saved voice mails on
her phone, however, they determined that Rebecca typically
deleted messages out of habit. Nonetheless, this missing piece
has raised serious questions for Rebecca's family and other
skeptics.

Why, if Jonah's message contained what he claimed, would
Rebecca delete it if she was planning to kill herself? Conversely,
if she was murdered, it could just as easily have been her killer
who deleted her last incoming voice mail.

Soon after Ariel learned that her sister was dead, she sent a
text to Rebecca's phone, expressing sadness, love, and disbelief, closing with this telling phrase: Come back nothing is your
fault.

*   *   *

Although detectives initially deemed Adam a "person of interest" in the investigation, they were satisfied early on that he was telling the truth and ruled him out as a suspect.

After doing his polygraph, he couldn't go back to the mansion to get his luggage, because investigators were still collecting prints and DNA evidence, so he went to a hotel. Still without a credit card or his shoes, he stayed in town a few days "to help the family and be with Max," then flew back to Memphis.

As he and his girlfriend talked more about what happened, he told her that he was more worried about how his dad was taking the news of Max's injuries, and that, similarly, Rebecca had seemed more concerned about Jonah's well-being than the boy's.

"I think Max is going to be all right," he quoted Rebecca as saying. "It's Jonah I'm worried about."

Mary Zahau-Loehner and her husband, Doug, flew out to San Diego and met with Detectives Mark Palmer and Hank Lebitski on Sunday, July 17. As they talked at the Hyatt Hotel, where the Loehners were staying, the investigators didn't go into any graphic details about the death scene.

Saying they weren't "fixated" on a suicide or murder scenario, they also didn't explain why they were asking particular questions. It only became evident to the Zahau family later that investigators were using this information to analyze forensic evidence they'd found at the scene. Due to the lack of official notification, this brief interview, and the subsequent refusal to release investigative details to Rebecca's family, the Zahaus came to distrust the SDSD.

During the interview, detectives asked seemingly innocent questions, such as whether Rebecca "was poetic" or "into poetry," whether she liked to water-ski, and whether her painting supplies were typically left out in the open in the guest bedroom.

Mary said yes, paint tubes and other items had been visible during her last visit, when she and Rebecca had cleaned up and rearranged the room together. Rebecca told her she'd started painting again.

"What did she paint?" Palmer asked.

"She liked flowers and birds," Mary said, adding that Rebecca also played the guitar and sang too. "She's artsy."

Following up on Jonah's comments about Rebecca's ex-husband, the detectives asked about Rebecca's relationship with Neil Nalepa, and any physical altercations between them. They also asked about Rebecca's recent emotional state, and her relationship with Jonah, his children, and ex-wife Dina.

Asked if Rebecca was a "showy person" who wore expensive jewelry, Mary said she liked to wear pieces that matched her clothes, and she often wore the ring Jonah had given her the year before—an opaque stone like jade or lapis in a gold setting—but not usually a necklace every day. They also asked if Rebecca was "modest and humble," and if she slept naked.

"I know she was found nude, and my sister would never go to bed without clothes on. Ever," Mary said. "She might wear Jonah's T-shirt and underwear, but if she's cold, she'll wear workout pants and baggy T-shirt, and go to bed like that."

Asked if Rebecca drank soda or used drugs, Mary said no. "My sister doesn't even like to take ibuprofen," she said, because Rebecca and Jonah were health nuts. Rebecca was so concerned about eating only natural food that she took forever to order at a restaurant, asking for no garlic, onions, or salt, and only organic lettuce.

"Did Becky seem a little disturbed or distraught or angry that she couldn't be with Max, or that she was kind of being kept away from him?"

No, Mary said, Rebecca told her that she couldn't be at the hospital all the time because Dina was there.

In her last day or two, Mary said, Rebecca had been her usual self. "She always finds something to laugh about," she said. "She always finds a way to cheer everybody up. She doesn't hold a grudge."

Palmer asked if Rebecca had ever expressed any fears about her personal safety or security, or had mentioned any encounters with strangers.

No, Mary said, Rebecca probably wouldn't have even noticed anyone threatening her unless it was blatant. "My sister sees good in everybody," she said. Even if someone asked her for a ride, "she wouldn't think anything about it."

Mary told the detectives at least four times during the ninety-minute interview that Rebecca never would have killed herself.

"I know my sister. She would never do a suicide. Never," Mary said. "She believed in heaven and hell, and she believed that anyone who killed themselves would go to hell."

Rebecca's family members and her friends from Bible college expressed the same sentiments. Why, they asked, would this clean-living athlete, who was brought up in a devout Protestant Christian family, was well educated, and lived with a pharmaceutical magnate, have done this to herself?

It wasn't in her nature, they said. She'd never taken a drink in her life, didn't do drugs, wasn't depressed, and had never talked about committing suicide. She also had no reason to take her own life. She was modest about her body, and never would have "done this to her family"—create such an irreverent spectacle that would naturally draw scandalous attention, thereby embarrassing and humiliating herself, Jonah, and her family. Period.

As Mary told *Dateline*, "We used to tell each other that if somebody ever tried to hurt us, that we would do everything we can to leave something behind so the other one could figure it out."

Nonetheless, sheriff's officials were already discussing the suicide scenario with the media within a few days of Rebecca's death.

"Suicides can appear odd," Sergeant Roy Frank told KFMB-TV. "It's not unusual to have a suicide that appears to be something else."

As Frank told *The Arizona Republic*, "There are five possibilities in her death, and we know it wasn't natural or accidental. We don't want to say 'undetermined' so that leaves homicide or suicide. We want to be very sure which one it was."

Chapter 16

Due to the complex dynamics and drama in Rebecca's life, detectives realized that they needed to go further back into her social history to truly understand her and the issues she faced—not only in her daily challenges with the Shacknais, but from the fallout of her troubled past as well.

Was she the type of unstable, impulsive woman to bind and hang herself naked, staging a suicide that looked like a murder? Or were there people in her past or present life who wanted to do her harm, and had staged her murder to look like a suicide? The responses differed depending on who was interpreting the same set of facts, but the answer was, perhaps, yes to both questions.

Rebecca told people that she was born a Zahau tribal princess in the Falam Township, nestled in the Chin Hills of Burma, now known as Myanmar, where her father and grandfather were tribal leaders.

Her father, Robert Zahau, was away in Thailand when members of the Burmese Parliament were shot in a government coup. Upon his return to Burma, he was sent to prison for nine years because of his political connections to the ousted regime.

Accounts differ on the timing of his marriage and children,

but soon after his release, he returned to his village. He sought political asylum outside the country, then brought his family to join him, but he often left on business trips. So, for some years, his young wife, Pari, had to raise their children largely on her own.

Because Robert was "always in the radar, always kind of a target," as Mary put it, the growing family escaped those dangers by moving near the borders of India and Burma. Mary was born first; Rebecca came next, on March 15, 1979.

When Rebecca was two and Mary was three, the Zahaus migrated as political refugees to Nepal, where they became missionaries with a Christian group, Youth With a Mission. At some point, Robert became an ordained minister, and took the girls back to visit their tribe in case they could never go there again.

Their decade in Nepal was hard. The Zahaus were so poor and hungry that they would put bread crumbs on the table and open the windows to lure pigeons that they could eat. Looking back as an adult, Rebecca said she never wanted to be that penniless again, or wonder where her next meal was coming from.

While they were in elementary school, Rebecca and her two sisters were often invited for sleepovers at the dean's house. This became problematic when the family learned that the dean was touching the girls in a sexual manner.

From what Rebecca's ex-husband, Neil, could glean, the molestation was not a onetime thing, and continued for at least several years, starting when Rebecca was six or eight. The family didn't want to make waves or offend a community leader, so Mary, as the eldest, began going to the dean's house alone.

"Mary would go so they would touch her rather than her sisters," Neil told detectives. "They've all dealt with it in different ways," he said, noting that Rebecca refused to discuss the subject. She "was closed up if you tried to talk about this," forcing him to learn what he could from Mary and Snowem.

Rebecca also never mentioned this topic to Jonah, who

learned about it from detectives during a post-investigation briefing.

"I'd thought she'd had a hard life as a refugee, asylum seeker, someone who had food insecurity," Jonah said. "Had I known that, this would have brought it to an entirely different level of understanding. It certainly suggests that she was far more damaged than I knew at the time."

Neil didn't know how long the touching went on, but said Rebecca didn't leave Nepal until she was sixteen, when the family was granted political asylum in Germany. But Ariel wasn't affected, because they'd left Nepal by the time she was born.

The detectives didn't like having to hear about the molestation from Neil. It was difficult to do their job when the Zahaus weren't volunteering important information or disclosing family secrets, even when it might have helped the investigation. Conversely, the Zahaus were frustrated with the way they and Rebecca's memory had been treated by the sheriff's department.

Later on, Mary downplayed the sisters' experience, testifying that they laughed about it years later, because it hadn't caused them any lasting damage. Not compared to everything else they'd been through, running from country to country, and being so poor.

After leaving Nepal, the Zahaus moved to Erfurt, in eastern Germany, then to Zedin, on the west side. From there, Rebecca left for Austria to attend Calvary Chapel Bible College Europe, which was affiliated with their church in Zedin.

Rebecca was twenty-one when she met Neil there in January 2001, and they started dating six months later. Her younger brothers and Timo Howrath, Snowem's future husband, attended the same college.

Neil, who was four years older, thought Rebecca was one of the most beautiful girls he'd ever met and immediately fell in love with her.

"She was the most sincere, sweet, God-loving girl," he recalled.

Neil had attended Calvary Chapel Bible College in California before going abroad for its European program, where he said they strived to pull "Americans out of their American ways, the thought process, and see what other countries are like."

That November, he traveled to Germany, where Rebecca's family still lived, because he was planning to propose to her and wanted to get her father's blessing.

"I knew she'd say yes," he said.

After she accepted, Neil returned to Long Island, where his mother lived, and filed for a fiancée travel visa so Rebecca could join him there.

Rebecca arrived in New York on April 5, 2002, right before her temporary visa was about to expire, which created some urgency in the relationship. Because she'd left Burma as a political exile, she had citizenship and passport issues that needed to be resolved sooner than later, so they were wed in a simple civil ceremony by a justice of the peace that May. They had a proper church wedding on June 22, which became their formal anniversary date. Rebecca was apparently unable to obtain status as a permanent resident, because she was still worried about not having a proper visa three years later.

She got whatever jobs she could, at a Starbucks, a gym, and then for an eye doctor. With her hardscrabble upbringing, she knew how to take care of herself.

Neil, on the other hand, couldn't hold down a job, which created tension between them. He also became increasingly obsessive, possessive, and paranoid about her and her whereabouts. This put their marriage on an emotional hamster wheel, as Rebecca repeatedly left Neil to get some space and some peace.

The first time they reunited, Neil tried to understand what was going on in her head. "Why did you come back?" he asked.

"I had everything, but I realized I wanted all those things, but I wanted them with you," he quoted her as saying.

But there was more to it than that. Rebecca told her sisters that she'd left Neil because he was abusive, saying he'd choked her and threatened to drive off a bridge with her in the car. Neil acknowledged these stories, but he always denied physically harming his wife in any way. She was his everything.

Chapter 17

The couple repeatedly sought geographical cures throughout their marriage.

In May 2004, they tried to make a fresh start by moving across the country to southern California. Still heavily involved with their church and Bible college, they landed in Temecula, near an extension campus in Murrieta.

Rebecca got a job with a Lasik eye center, while Neil served as a volunteer youth pastor. But as church politics grew more complicated, the stress put their marriage into turmoil once again, and Rebecca suffered a miscarriage.

"Everything was tough," Neil told detectives later. "You have these ideals, some things are the same way. I guess we always thought we could start anew in the next place, and the next place. On top of work, it was very difficult."

One Sunday in October, Rebecca was staffing a vendor booth for the eye center at a 5K fund-raising race in Temecula, geared toward raising awareness about breast cancer.

That same day, Michael Berger, a martial arts instructor, drove down from Glendale to support his mother, a cancer survivor who was running in the race.

It was sunny that morning as Michael strolled through the

booths, waiting for his mom to cross the finish line. He saw Rebecca under one of the canopies, their eyes met, and she smiled at him.

Michael, a former competitive bodybuilder and wrestler, who was six-one and weighed 195 pounds, walked over and started up a conversation with the petite, athletic young woman.

At forty-six, Michael had spent much of his life feeling drawn to Asian culture. He'd first traveled to Japan in 1983, after graduating with a degree in English literature from the University of Utah.

"I fell in love with the culture and the traditions and all of that," he said.

When he met Rebecca, he'd recently left a full-time teaching job at a private prep school to take some classes himself. In between studying physiology and anatomy, he taught martial arts classes twice a week.

Some years later, the pull of the Far East led him back to Japan and China, where he spent eight years earning a master's and a doctorate in Chinese medicine, and becoming a licensed acupuncture practitioner.

At twenty-five, Rebecca was twenty years younger than Michael. But he wasn't drawn to her beauty alone. He also found her "very cheerful, very positive, very kind, and generous."

Because they'd only talked for a few minutes, Michael didn't yet know how much they had in common, only that they were both health-conscious, gentle, and soft-spoken. He was single, and based on how friendly and receptive she was, he thought she was too. She also wasn't wearing a wedding ring.

By the end of their brief encounter, they had exchanged contact information. He emailed her the next night, suggesting they go out for a date. When she emailed him back, Rebecca signed off as "your Shatzi," which is actually spelled *schatzi,* and means "sweetheart" or "darling" in German.

*   *   *

Rebecca and Michael lived about ninety minutes apart, but decided to head south to a Mexican restaurant in San Diego's Old Town. Chatting over dinner, Michael felt a surprisingly strong connection with Rebecca, and apparently, it was mutual.

As they were saying good night inside the restaurant, Rebecca started to cry. After they'd had such a great conversation, Michael was a little surprised by this show of emotion.

"Why are you crying?" he asked.

"I just feel so happy," she said. "I haven't felt like this for a long time."

Michael reached out and gave her a comforting hug. "It's okay," he told her.

But inside, he felt that her expression of passion was more than okay. His feelings for her were strong too, and they'd only just met.

"We had an immediate real love for each other," he recalled.

After that, Rebecca drove to Glendale for future dates. Some weeks later, she began staying at Michael's place for the weekend, leaving for work in Temecula on Monday morning.

Because he'd lived and traveled abroad—including two years in Italy—he had many international friends, whom he made an effort to introduce to Rebecca, especially the ones with whom she could converse in Nepali and German.

She, in turn, introduced him to Tiffany, a coworker and friend from the eye center in Temecula, who came on a number of group outings with Michael's brother and friends.

Michael also took Rebecca to his karate studio for a few training sessions, where he taught her some basic moves. Although she was in very good shape, she never got to the point where she could have defended herself against a male attacker.

"I've seen very, very few women that could overcome a man," Michael said. "They have to be really highly skilled."

They'd gotten together several times, when Rebecca said she wanted to have a "talk" with him.

"I have something to tell you," she said. "I'm separated, and I'm going through a divorce."

Michael was a little shocked and more than a little disappointed. He respected her for telling him, but he wasn't one to mince words about his boundaries. He'd been raised Mormon, but he'd since gravitated toward Buddhism, and, even then, more as a philosophy than a religion. Still, he held traditional values about marriage and monogamous relationships.

"I don't go out with people who are married," he said firmly. "You need to get that resolved right away."

Unable to look him in the eye, Rebecca seemed embarrassed and ashamed. "I will," she said. "I'm working on getting it resolved."

Even though she and her husband, Neil, were still living under the same roof, she said, they slept in different rooms.

"We're separated, we're not even together," she said, insisting that it was merely a matter of waiting for the paperwork to go through. "I don't want to be there. I want to be with you."

But, in truth, neither Rebecca nor Neil had filed any paperwork. This may have been wishful thinking on her part, but it was still a falsehood—one that Michael very much wanted to believe.

Rebecca didn't tell Michael much about her marriage other than it had been arranged by her father, whom she described as a powerful tribal chief. She, as his daughter and a Burmese princess, was in no position to object. That was the way of her culture, she said, which was such an important part of her that she compiled a collection of personal writings about it.

She often signed off her emails with "your tribal princess," "your ruby," and "Your Burmese Princess," the latter of which Michael liked to call her.

Michael got the impression that she was scared of her father. But she also seemed scared of Neil, who, she said, often yelled at her. Tiffany backed up that claim, saying that she'd seen the verbal abuse for herself.

Even so, Rebecca seemed hesitant to talk much about him. "It was like pulling teeth to get any information out of her," Michael said. "She just didn't want anybody to be in conflict."

Although she never said that Neil had hurt her physically, Michael suspected that he had. "She wouldn't tell me that, because she was afraid to. I'm a physical person," he said, and he sensed that she was worried he would harm Neil in retaliation.

She did claim, however, that Neil was using drugs. She didn't elaborate on the type of drugs, or how often he used them.

As her relationship with Michael progressed, Rebecca shared more about her conflicts with Neil, his drug use, and the abuse. Michael encouraged her to leave him.

"You've got to get out of there," he told her. "You don't stay in abusive relationships."

He was pleased when Rebecca finally rented a room in a woman's home in Temecula, where he could see that many of her belongings were stored there the night she invited him to stay over.

But Michael wanted to move forward, and really *be* with his girlfriend.

"Why don't you just come and stay here?" he suggested. "I want you to finalize this divorce."

Although Michael took her to his parents' house in Temecula for Christmas, and also to their home in Utah, he never met her family. Rebecca handed him the phone when Snowem called from Germany, but he never got a chance to speak face-to-face with her or Mary. Rebecca and Snowem fondly characterized Mary as bossy, more like a second mom than an older sister. Rebecca said Mary wasn't happy about her relationship with Michael, and had been pressuring her, as had her parents, to get back with Neil. Rebecca seemed scared of her older sister too.

Meanwhile, Rebecca tried to assuage Michael's concerns about the divorce. They discussed moving in together, but he didn't like the idea of doing that while she was still married.

"I don't want it to be like you're living here full-time with me if you're not divorced," he said. "I'll let you stay here temporarily, until that thing becomes final."

Because money was also an issue for her, he took an active role in trying to solve that problem as well.

"You can get a job up here, I can help you," he said.

To show her how easy it would be, he drove her into downtown Glendale and stopped in front of the first eye clinic they saw.

"Go in and just talk with them," he said.

Rebecca took his advice and won them over.

"She came out and she said that she had a job. They just hired her immediately, and who wouldn't? Everybody loved her."

With that, Rebecca moved into Michael's place in March 2005, and started her new position at the clinic.

Until Michael had his DNA tested years later, he didn't know that his interest in Asian culture was actually genetic, and that his father's ancestors came from Central Asia.

All Michael knew was that he liked Rebecca's traditional Asian qualities and values, such as "accepting a more feminine kind of role." She didn't try to act or look like a man, she enjoyed cooking with him, and she felt it was important to keep their home nice. Although sometimes she could take that to an extreme.

One day, he came home to find her scrubbing the floor on her hands and knees. "What are you doing?" he asked. "You don't have to do that."

"I need to do it, it needs to be cleaned," she replied.

"Oh, my gosh, we have a mop," Michael said, reaching for one. "Here."

In the second week of April, Michael took Rebecca on a road trip to Las Vegas, where a team of his young karate students, ages four to fifteen, competed in an international tournament.

But the few days that the couple spent in Sin City were remarkably sin-free. They spent their days at the tournament and their nights going out for dinner, then walking around the city. Because Rebecca didn't drink and Michael would only have a beer or two, it never occurred to them to see any strippers or hit any bars or nightclubs.

On the morning of April 25, about ten days after the Vegas trip, Rebecca left for work in her Honda Element minivan, wearing her regular scrubs.

The eye center was only a ten-minute drive. A creature of habit, she always left at the same time, to arrive promptly at 8:00 A.M., and to return home by 5:00 P.M.

Michael was home that evening, waiting for her. When she hadn't arrived by six o'clock, he tried calling her cell phone, but got no answer.

He had no idea where she might have gone. She'd only been living with him for a little more than a month, so she had no local friends of her own. She'd said she wanted to try to find a church group, but hadn't gotten around to it yet. Worried, he tried calling her several more times. Still, no answer.

Three or four hours later, he called Tiffany. It was so out of character for Rebecca not to call, he thought something had happened to her. She'd never shown any signs of being impulsive before.

"Have you heard from her?" he asked.

"No," Tiffany said.

"Well, she hasn't come home and she hasn't called, and I can't get through to her," he said.

Michael spent the rest of the night anxiously waiting for her to come in the front door.

Still hoping she would return, he waited until the next night at eleven o'clock, after teaching his class, to go to the police station and report her as missing.

The incident report stated: *She left their residence with no provisions for not returning. . . . None of her friends have heard from her. He* [Michael] *is concerned that her disappearance may be related to her ex-husband and the pressure from the family to remain in the marriage. He is concerned that she may be being held by unknown persons against her will.*

The next morning, Michael called the eye center and was even more worried when they said she'd never shown up for work.

Then, later that morning, she called him—shaky, fearful, and on the verge of tears, from a space that sounded echoey, like a restroom.

"Where are you?" he asked.

"I don't know where I am," she said. "They took me."

"Who has you?"

"I don't know, I don't know."

"Look around," he said. "What do you see?"

"They have something over my eyes," she said, adding that she was only able to make a quick call because her abductors had let her use the bathroom. "I can't talk," she said abruptly, and hung up.

He thought this sounded a bit fishy, but he checked with Tiffany and she said Rebecca had called her with the same story.

Rebecca called him back several times. Michael documented each conversation, and reported them to the Glendale police.

"I want to be with you. I don't want to be here," she told Michael, crying. "I love you."

She seemed to want to let him know that she was okay, but was being held against her will. After he questioned her again, she said that two or three people had abducted her. They had tied her up, put her blindfolded in the back of a cramped vehicle, and were driving her around.

"She didn't know where she was," he recalled.

At one point, a female police officer called to let him know that she'd made contact with Rebecca.

"I talked with Rebecca and she's fine," she said matter-of-factly.

"What do you mean 'she's fine'?"

"I called her on her cell phone and she's fine."

"Of course, she's going to say that. They're threatening her. Someone could be holding a knife to her neck," he said.

Frustrated and angry, Michael called the local Federal Bureau of Investigation office, hoping they would take his concerns more seriously. But because he'd already made a report to local authorities, the FBI said they wouldn't get involved unless requested by police.

And still, Rebecca continued to phone him. In one of her last calls, her voice sounded different. Robotic. As if she were being forced to read someone else's words, like a hostage situation.

"You are not to see me anymore, ever again," she said, continuing in this strange tone until Michael interrupted her.

"What the hell is going on?" he demanded. "Who is making you read this?"

Then he heard her say, "Ow, stop, don't, that hurts. Ow."

"Are you talking to me?" he asked.

"No," she said.

By then, Michael was angry. He could tell she was on speakerphone, because he could hear men's voices in the background as Rebecca rustled around in pain.

As he told them off in harsh terms, they responded in kind.

"I know where you live," one man threatened.

"Fine, I'll meet you out on my front lawn in five minutes."

Rebecca called back a few minutes later and asked him to repeat what she'd said in the previous call to make sure he understood: It was over between them. She had to go back to Neil.

On the morning of April 28, Rebecca showed up outside his house. Michael happened to glance out the window and saw her standing there, looking upset. When he opened the door, she ran to him, and he welcomed her with a warm embrace.

"Get in the house," he said.

She obeyed, following him inside.

"What's going on?" he asked. "What happened?"

"They took me," she said.

"Who had you?"

Clearly distressed, she didn't want to tell him. But little by little, it came out. Neil and two other men were waiting for her in the parking lot at the eye center. Before she could go inside, they came toward her with a baseball bat, smashed the window of her car, grabbed her, and put her into their vehicle.

"We're going to the police department right now," Michael said.

"No, I don't want to," she said.

"You're going. Let's go. Get in the car."

Rebecca said she was hesitant to report the incident because she didn't have a legal visa, and she didn't want to get deported.

"I don't care about that, you're going to the police right now."

As they drove to the station, Rebecca sat silently, looking upset.

When they arrived at 11:15 A.M., Rebecca went to the front desk to speak to the officer on duty. Michael thought they would sit down with detectives, and Rebecca would explain what happened. But instead, he was told to wait while two detectives took Rebecca into a room upstairs—alone.

According to the police report, [Rebecca] *had been entered as a missing person but she was fine. Zahau stated she had been living with her boyfriend,* [Reporting Party] *Berger, for the past 6 months while separated from her husband. On April 26, 2005, she went to work, met with her estranged husband, and decided to reconcile. She stated she had not informed Berger of the reconciliation. Zahau requested her name be removed from the missing person system.*

About half an hour later, Michael said, "They came out all smiles, like everything is fine."

When he tried to have his turn speaking to the detectives, they told him that wouldn't be necessary. "Nope, you can go home, sir."

"Wait a minute, I'd like to go back and talk to you. I've got some things I want to say and I would like to hear."

But they refused, which left Michael frustrated and confused. Why wouldn't they let him explain that, regardless of Rebecca's statement to them, it was clearly made under duress and intimidation by Neil?

Back in the car, Michael asked her what had just happened.

"I told them I was scared because I didn't have a visa, and they laughed and said, 'Do you know how many people in California don't have visas? We don't check that,'" she said.

But that didn't satisfy Michael. "We ought to press charges," he said.

"No, I don't want to make more trouble. I'm afraid."

"Well, are you okay?"

"Yeah, I'm okay," she said.

A couple of days later, Rebecca took off again without warning. Only this time, Michael didn't notify the police. Instead, he called the eye center and asked if they'd seen her. They said she'd called in to report that she had a family emergency in Arizona, but she never called back.

A day or so later, Rebecca emailed to say she was in Oregon, something like, *I'm in Portland. I had to get away and clear my head. I just started driving. I needed to get out of that environment.*

At that point, Michael recalled, "I knew that the wheels were starting to come off."

Whenever Rebecca emailed or called after that, she said she missed him, but she was enjoying her time there. It was so green and beautiful.

On May 2, she wrote that she was meditating, doing a lot of thinking, working through "a bunch of stuff," and that he would be proud of her. *In all the confusion, I know one thing for sure, and that is I love you. Immensely. Please do not worry about me.*

A week later, she said she'd stopped checking emails, scared that he might write something upsetting, or, worse, not at all. *I have died a million deaths, just thinking about you and knowing how much I love you. My beloved, please don't give up*, she wrote.

Another week passed, and she emailed to thank him for his forgiveness. She was indebted to him. *I know it won't be easy for either one of us, but I believe in that what we have left over, our love, it will endure*, she wrote, saying she'd never known a love "so deep and so strong."

She'd come to realize that she'd caused him pain and grief: [But] *in some kind of weird way, I was protecting you. This is not an attempt to come up with a lame excuse, that was all I felt in my numbness.*

They also talked by phone every so often. Michael tried to be understanding about the space she needed, but he wanted her with him and told her, in a tough-loving way, that she needed to "grow up."

"When are you coming back?" he kept asking.

He'd thought the separation was temporary until she told him she'd gotten a job at a health club.

"I just need a little bit of time," she kept saying.

Keeping him on the hook, she told him a guy at the club had asked for her number and had left flowers on her desk. "I took the flowers and put them in the garbage can," she said. "I only want to be with you."

But a few weeks later, instead of coming back to him, Rebecca went to stay with Mary in Missouri.

She stayed in touch by phone, but the excuses continued. She professed her love in handmade cards, sending him paintings and drawings.

I know I will see you again, she wrote. *How long between now and then I don't know.*

In mid-June, Rebecca said she dreamed of him almost every night, and had realized what he must be feeling because of her actions and absence. *Honestly, crazy things have popped into my head, where I think I should just convince you not to love me anymore, or that I should just leave it all be so you could find someone more levelheaded and grounded,* she wrote. *What can I say, babe, everything I do now seems almost in vain.*

She didn't find much satisfaction in her job; she was simply biding time and paying bills until they could be reunited. *The sun and moon pass by without waiting to be noticed,* she wrote.

In late July, she promised she would love him forever. *I will knock down every wall I have built so far and will let you love me,* she wrote. *Together we will venture the deapths [sic] of love and the sea of miracles.*

He got his hopes up that summer when she said she and her sisters were traveling to San Francisco, then would head south to visit him in Glendale.

"I want to come and see you," she said.

He knew she was in San Francisco, because she sent him an

ancient Chinese scroll with a tiger on the front, and a loving inscription. But she never made good on her promise.

Suspecting that Mary had prevented the visit, Michael finally decided to move on. He wrote Rebecca a breakup letter, and read it to her over the phone.

"She was completely sobbing and she was very sad and so was I," he recalled.

Nonetheless, Rebecca told her sisters that she'd been the one to break it off by not returning his calls and emails.

Chapter 18

The truth was that Neil had swept Rebecca away to Portland, where his brother, an agent for the U.S. Drug Enforcement Agency (DEA), had a house. The couple got jobs there, but it wasn't long before things went sideways once again. Only this time, the police got involved.

Neighbors called 911 after hearing them arguing. Reports vary about whether they were in the house or the driveway, and whether it was physical abuse or just yelling, but it was enough for Rebecca to leave him again.

Still, Neil stubbornly didn't want to see the separation for what it was.

"She didn't think it was working out," he said later. "That's what she told me." But as far as he was concerned, "it was actually working. It was, like, a shocking thing."

Rebecca confused matters by crying on the way to the airport, but she tried to let him down gently once she got to Missouri, where she went to help Mary with her new baby boy. "She kind of felt, like, it was set, we should just let it be," Neil said.

But he wasn't ready to give up. Some months later, he decided it was time to return to Pennsylvania, go back to school, "and start new," and that Rebecca should come with him. So he drove to Missouri and picked her up on the way.

That said, they still lived apart. Rebecca landed a live-in nanny job near Bryn Mawr, and they "were trying to date again and stuff, you know, work on things," he said.

When that job ended, she got one at a gym, where Neil was waiting and watching as her new boyfriend, a wealthy computer business owner, dropped her off in the parking lot.

"Who are you choosing here?" he asked. "This guy sees me and dumps you off and takes off, with no idea of what would happen?"

Neil told detectives later that Rebecca didn't respond the way he wanted. "I knew she was seeing a guy, so I basically said, 'That stops or I'm out of here.' It wasn't going to stop, so I left."

In Neil's mind, Rebecca was committing adultery by seeing this guy while she was still married.

"She cheated on me, and I gave it about a month," he told detectives. "I tried everything, just short of going nuts in my head, so I went to Colorado Springs. I just left."

Neil got a job in Colorado Springs and actually started seeing a woman. Things were finally looking up—until Rebecca found out.

"I realize what I did to you. It hurt me when I found out you were seeing someone," she called to say, and this time she was the one who wanted to give it another try.

After a couple of weekend visits in Denver, she told Neil that she wasn't happy with the businessman anymore. She missed spending time at church, and she was ready to leave the East Coast. So she joined Neil in Colorado Springs, where she loved climbing the Manitou Incline hiking trail.

During their two years together in Colorado, Rebecca had Lasik eye surgery, and also got breast implants. "She wanted them, I didn't think [the implants] were necessary," Neil told detectives.

But Rebecca was self-conscious about her chest and the way

she looked. "She used to not be able to wear clothes and lean forward or wear bras. She was flat and just a nipple there," he said. Even so, she didn't go for the full-breasted "look at me" augmentation, because even after the surgery, she was still only an A cup.

Although Rebecca was encouraged that Neil had started nursing school, she grew frustrated again, because he wouldn't finish the program and he still wasn't being financially responsible.

During his deposition, he admitted that he had threatened to crash their car and drive over the side of a bridge, but he described the incident as more of a consequence of not knowing "how else to express the pain."

They tried marriage counseling through the church about half a dozen times, but his threats and inability to keep a job ultimately doomed their relationship to fail. He was constantly asking her for cash, claiming he couldn't go to his parents for it.

"He was financially illiterate," as Doug Loehner put it.

After her death, Neil laughed when detectives asked if he was obsessed with her. "I love Rebecca, yeah. There were times when my obsessive compulsiveness had me call her a lot. Even if she turned the phone off, I'd just call and leave a message or something. But I definitely put her on a pedestal. I thought she was the greatest thing there was."

He'd always worried that she was going to get hurt, because she was so sweet, soft, gentle, and trusting. "I felt like, just suck it up and love her so she could come back and wouldn't be out there," he said.

"She was too naive for our world?" the detective asked.

"Too trusting," Neil replied. "She was a smart girl. I wouldn't say 'naive.'"

Her sister Snowem had a different view. "She was really bold in the sense that she was not afraid of anything or anyone," she told Detective Tsuida, but "she was very naive. She would never think something bad about anyone. She was too good-hearted."

For whatever reason, Rebecca kept coming back to her husband, trying one more time to get it right as they moved from city to city. But they never found that cure.

Neil said he never really understood why she kept leaving him, yet couldn't be truthful about her feelings, but he came to believe that she just didn't want to hurt him.

"Sometimes you hurt somebody, and you can't face what you've done, and it's easier to run," he said.

In December 2007, Neil said, he and Rebecca went to visit his father and stepmother in Scottsdale, Arizona. At the time, coincidentally, Neil's stepmother was working for the Medicis marketing department. She and a coworker were subsequently let go after submitting falsified expense reports.

According to Neil, Rebecca loved warm weather, so they decided to move to Scottsdale and keep working on their relationship. But that wasn't the story Rebecca told her family.

She told her sisters that she moved alone to Arizona in March 2008, got a job, and an apartment in Tempe. Although Neil had agreed that he would stay in Colorado until the lease on their house expired, he showed up unannounced before the lease was up and asked to share the apartment on a platonic basis.

Rebecca told Mary that she was planning to file for divorce, but every time she tried, Neil would beg and plead, "Please give us six months."

Time after time, Mary watched Rebecca give in, lending Neil money and taking him back.

"We're going to try to work it out," she told Mary. "He's going to go to counseling, we're not going to fight anymore, and he's not going to yell at me and threaten me."

Neil told San Diego County sheriff's detectives that he'd wanted to work in Phoenix as a police officer, but his application came to a halt after he admitted some personally incriminating information to the department secretary, who told him those details would cause him to be immediately disqualified.

When detectives asked him to comment on the stories of domestic abuse between him and Rebecca over the years, Neil wouldn't give a direct answer.

"You ever put your hands on each other or hit each other? There are no reports of domestic violence at all?" one detective asked.

Neil stammered, saying, "We had a, a—"

"You're not in any trouble, dude, I'm just curious, just be straight with us."

"No, we had an issue in April 2009, a guy was at our apartment, but she came outside," and prevented Neil from entering. "I think he called police, so I went to work," he said.

During his deposition, however, he said that he knocked on the apartment door, even though Rebecca had already warned him that she wasn't going to answer. When she finally opened up, he saw a man's jacket inside the apartment and started screaming.

"Is someone in there? What, you're sitting here and you just let her come outside, you don't come and address it?" Neil yelled, prompting her male friend to come to the door and threaten him. "He was an ex-cop and he was going to ruin me. I told him I didn't understand how that really works and to go ahead. I believe he called the cops and said I threatened him."

But Neil contended that neither he nor Rebecca had ever gone to jail for domestic violence. Rebecca's ex-cop boyfriend, as well as the businessman in Pennsylvania, suggested she get a restraining order against Neil, but she said she never did, and he was never served.

When detectives asked Mary if Neil had ever been physically violent with Rebecca, she said she'd never seen it personally, but had heard from Rebecca that "he would get really mad and throw things . . . and he would scare her . . . I told her to leave him a long time ago."

In one instance, Rebecca told Mary that Neil had thrown her down on the bed and "acted like he was going to choke her."

"Did he actually choke you?" Mary asked.

"No," Rebecca said, "but he acted like he was going to," putting his hands around her neck, but not exerting any real pressure.

"He was violent several times, where she wasn't actually physically hurt, but it was violent," Mary told detectives.

"She would downplay it," Mary's husband, Doug, interjected.

During his deposition, Neil was asked to explain a text that Mary had sent to him: I also know she left you for a reason.

"Rebecca said I hit her," he replied. "One time, I believe, was in Portland, the other time, I don't know, maybe California. Mary believes that had I not done that, I guess, that things would be different."

Asked if he'd actually hit Rebecca, tried to choke her, or "put [his] hands" on her in Portland or California, Neil said no.

"I might have grabbed Rebecca's arms in California," he said. "I never hit Rebecca. It's my understanding Rebecca told everybody in the family that that's why she left me."

Similarly, the stories differed about whether Neil ever lived in the house Rebecca bought in Arizona. She told her sisters that after kicking Neil out of the apartment, she bought the house, where she lived alone until she moved in with Jonah. However, Neil told detectives that the house was purchased in Rebecca's name, but they "bought it together," and that he lived there with her for a time.

When she and Jonah met in October 2009, she was in the process of moving into the three-bedroom tract home, which was off Route 17 in the Phoenix-Scottsdale area. He visited her there twice.

"She wasn't making a fortune, she wasn't a physician, but I think she was a highly skilled technician who was paid well, and it was a modest home. In those days, it was easy for people to get a mortgage with ten percent down," Jonah said.

There are many such "he said, she said" stories in this case, making it difficult to determine the truth about Rebecca's relationship with Neil and her stories of abuse. Such records may be destroyed after a certain period of time, but in 2019, Phoenix and Portland police had no record of domestic violence incidents involving either one of them, and the SDSD wouldn't say whether detectives ever ran a criminal check on Neil to support his denials.

What is clear is that April 2009 was a stressful time for Rebecca, because she got herself into trouble with the law, and this time it had nothing to do with her estranged husband.

On the afternoon of April 23, thirty-year-old Rebecca was at Macy's on East Camelback Road in Phoenix when she saw some jewelry on display that she liked. But this was no little bauble or pair of hoop earrings, these items were worth $1,090.

Dressed in a black tank top and a black dress, Rebecca was carrying two shopping bags—a brown one from bebe, a women's clothing store, and a pink one from Victoria's Secret, which sells sexy lingerie.

Rebecca casually dropped the jewelry into her bebe bag, then went to the ladies' restroom on the second floor. She entered a stall, closed the door, and removed the security tags, which she placed into the metal bin for soiled tampons. A female security manager, who had witnessed Rebecca in the act, traced her steps to the bathroom stall and found the tags.

From there, Rebecca headed downstairs to the first floor, past the cash registers, and out the door. She hadn't walked more than ten feet when a security guard confronted her and took her back inside, where she was handcuffed and told to wait for Phoenix police.

Police arrested her half an hour later, and read her Miranda rights. Before being booked into the county jail, Rebecca admitted that she knew shoplifting was a crime and said she'd considered paying for the jewelry, but decided not to. Asked if she had any money on her, she said no, only a credit card. The officers checked Rebecca's record and found she had no previous arrests.

Because the items were worth more than $1,000, this was a Class 6 felony, subject to six to eighteen months in jail, up to three years' probation, and fines up to $150,000. But Rebecca agreed to plead guilty to a Class 1 misdemeanor, pay only a $480 fine, and take a diversion course, a "rehab" program designed to address the shoplifting urges, which she completed in August 2009, just two months before meeting Jonah. For all practical purposes, that wiped the charges off her record.

During the period that Neil and Rebecca were reportedly living together in her new house, Neil suspected that she was seeing someone again.

After being hired as an ophthalmic technician at the Horizon Eye Specialists and Lasik Center, Rebecca told him she was doing more "girls' nights out." Although they weren't together romantically at that point, Neil recognized the familiar behavior patterns indicating that she was seeing someone.

He first heard that it was a rich surgeon, but he ultimately learned from his stepmother that it was her CEO, the multimillionaire pharmaceutical magnate Jonah Shacknai.

Knowing that Rebecca had been very poor growing up, Neil realized how important money and financial security were to her. He also knew he couldn't compete with this guy any more than he could with the wealthy businessman in Pennsylvania.

But instead of being up front that she was seeing Jonah, Rebecca told him, "I think you should leave."

Even so, Neil liked to think that it was his idea. He'd started nursing school, but was driving himself crazy with distraction, thinking about Rebecca.

"I couldn't be doing school and wondering where she is," he said. "So I just got my own place."

Neil left behind their Weimaraner, Azul, which Rebecca said she would give to a friend. Neil didn't find out that she'd kept the dog, and renamed him Ocean, until after she was dead.

Neil finally "let her go, but he continued to contact her by text and by phone," Mary said. Rebecca still occasionally gave him $500, here and there, when he needed money.

Rebecca told Mary that she had to give Neil an ultimatum to force him to finalize the divorce: "I'm not going to help you financially anymore if you don't sign my divorce papers," she said she told him.

It appears that Rebecca never told Mary that Neil was the only one who filed for divorce. Rather, she characterized herself as the driving force.

"She could never rely on him to have a job or a steady job," Mary told detectives. Still, "every time she's going to do something, she feels bad for him. That's just my sister."

Chapter 19

In October 2009, Jonah went to get his eyes checked at the clinic where Rebecca worked. She did much of the exam before the ophthalmologist came in and "waved some fairy dust" at the end, as Jonah put it.

While Jonah and Rebecca were alone, they talked and flirted a bit. As he impressed her by recognizing her accent—a "parlor game" of his—he also became intrigued with the engaging, intelligent, and exotic young woman.

"Would you like to have dinner sometime?" he asked.

Their first date was at Pure, a sushi restaurant of Rebecca's choice, on October 19, just ten days after Jonah's divorce was finalized.

He came to pick her up in an unremarkable car, so she had no idea how much money he had or what he'd accomplished in his life. But her coworkers, curious about the patient who was taking out their sweet Rebecca, had either heard of him or did some homework online.

"Do you know who this guy is?" they asked her the next morning.

"No, I don't want to know," she said.

"Oh, yeah, you want to know."

Rebecca also had no way of knowing that Jonah had kids, but he made it clear on their first date that he was not interested in having any more. After two marriages and three children, one of them still quite young, he told her that his business work and home lives were complicated enough, even if it meant they wouldn't have a second date.

"If that's really hard for you, then that probably isn't a good fit for either one of us," he said.

By the second date, Rebecca seemed to have mulled over Jonah's disclosure statement, and decided to proceed. "I never thought that I would consider going out with someone who had kids," she told him.

Knowing that she was from Burma, Jonah remarked that he found Buddhism, the primary religion in her native country, interesting. She responded by animatedly expressing her feelings about religion in general.

"She said all organized religions are populated with people who are hypocrites and do very bad things in the name of religion," he recalled. "I think she was trying to reconcile a deeply religious upbringing and expectation of religiosity from her family with the fact that she was a big doubter. I don't believe she possessed a great deal of faith."

During their nearly two-year relationship, Rebecca didn't go to church more than a couple of times, such as on Easter Sunday. If she had "exhibited characteristics of someone who was deeply religious and Christian," he said, "I don't think we could have been together . . . It just wouldn't have been compatible from the start, and I never saw any evidence of that."

Rebecca found the provider she'd been looking for in Jonah, whom she called her "warrior." He was more powerful, successful, and wealthy than any man she'd ever been with.

"My sister loved him in her own way," Mary said. "She was in awe of him to a certain extent."

By then, Jonah was even more intrigued than before. For him, Rebecca was pleasantly different from his previous partners. They were also more compatible as a couple.

"She was very warm—maybe I'm not the warmest person in the world—but I responded favorably to that," Jonah said. "She was lighthearted. We used to just hang out, time would pass. We worked out together a lot."

He appreciated her education and was impressed by the fact that she had lived all over the world and spoke six languages. She also "had strong views, but a quiet way of expressing them."

Although they came from vastly different backgrounds, their approaches to health and fitness gibed well, as did their personality types—he as the strong, willful patriarch, and she as the nurturing, supportive caregiver.

Born in December 1956, Jonah learned about the power—and responsibility—of the media early on.

As editor of his high school newspaper, the *Mt. Echo*, Jonah was among four staff members who were suspended for three days, and banned from working on the paper, for publishing cartoon caricatures and a story that accused school staff of criminal allegations. Printed without their advisor's approval, which violated school policy, the story accused a custodial manager of "misconduct" for earning "an astronomical $60,000" in overtime pay "for unnecessary work done by coworkers" over the course of a decade.

Already weighing risk-to-reward ratios, Jonah and the assistant editor said they "realized there would be consequences," but ran with the story anyway.

"This doesn't come as a surprise," Jonah told the local newspaper, *The Journal News*, in 1974.

These shenanigans didn't tarnish Jonah's chance for a bright future. After winning a congressional internship, he went on to a private college, law school, and Capitol Hill. While earning his law degree in only three years, Jonah served as counsel to U.S. Representative James Scheuer during his chairmanship of several House committees relating to consumer protection, energy, finance, natural resources, science, technology, and health.

Jonah subsequently became a senior partner of the Washington, D.C., law firm of Royer, Shacknai & Mehle, where he worked as a strategic advisor to pharmaceutical clients.

In 1988, Jonah launched his own company, Medicis Pharmaceutical Corp., serving as its CEO and board chairman. Medicis gained national attention for U.S. marketing and distribution of the revolutionary wrinkle filler Restalyne, and Botox competitors Perlane and Dysport. Other Medicis products included acne meds Solodyn and Ziana, as well as treatments for asthma, eczema, fungal infections, hyperpigmentation, photoaging, psoriasis, and rosacea. The company even made an ultrasound wand that melted fat.

Jonah moved the corporate headquarters from D.C. to New York, where he was living when he met his first wife, Kimberly James, a pharmaceutical saleswoman for a competitor, Johnson & Johnson, at a medical convention in Palm Springs.

As was later chronicled in their ten-volume divorce file, their marriage got off to a rocky start in 1993, prompting him to ask during their honeymoon whether he'd made a mistake by marrying her.

In 1995, he relocated Medicis to Phoenix, where it was more affordable for his employees to live, and he was soon named Arizona Entrepreneur of the Year. Despite, or perhaps *because* of all these life changes and acclaims, Jonah's domestic life took a hit. He and Kim argued a lot, which created tension in the marriage.

When Jonah met Dina in 1997, she, too, was a pharmaceutical saleswoman. Dina came to work for him at Medicis, where, according to his friend Howard, the two became romantically involved while Jonah was still with Kim. Not surprisingly, that added another wedge in the marriage.

Kim filed for divorce in January 1999 at a time when their joint tax return reported an income of about $17 million. A psychologist who evaluated them both during the custody battle noted that Jonah was defensive and had unresolved anger issues, but dearly loved their two children, Cindy and Kevin. The divorce was finalized in 2001.

Jonah married Dina in 2002, and three years later, they had a son, Maxfield Aaron Shacknai. Jonah called him Max and Dina called him Maxie. He got his middle name from Jonah's paternal grandfather.

Things were good for a while. Dina even converted to Judaism. The couple was socially active, volunteering together at the Whispering Hope Ranch Foundation, a philanthropic non-profit for special-needs children, of which Jonah later became chairman. Dina's nephew and a family friend's son were both autistic.

That same friend cofounded a group, now called the Southwest Autism Research & Resource Center, of which Jonah became vice chairman. There, the Shacknais made contacts that helped Dina, who was studying to become a child psychologist, to land a fellowship at the Melmed Center.

Although Dina was a loving person, Jonah's relationship with her was even more volatile than his first marriage. According to Howard, Dina had strong emotions and was also "a party girl," which wasn't a great combination. She stayed up late, and kept

Jonah up as well. But while she could sleep all morning or most of the day, Jonah had a company to run. She didn't take care of the house the way he would have liked, and she seemed to find it difficult to get things done. She also consulted with psychics and shamans.

Just as in his first marriage, Jonah and Dina argued, only this time things got physical and both of them made domestic violence reports to the Paradise Valley Police Department.

In September 2008, Jonah went to the station to report that he and Dina were arguing after she'd mixed prescription drugs with alcohol, when she "came at him and attempted to choke him," a claim similar to one he'd reported in 2007. Dina called police half an hour later to complain that Jonah hadn't stopped his German shepherd security dog, which was the family's dog, from biting her during the argument. She also asked the officer to call her psychiatrist for "background information on her husband's mood and behavior."

Jonah called police a little later to report that when he returned home, Dina was "irate" that he'd notified police, and that he was going to a hotel for the night. Dina's psychiatrist subsequently told police that Dina was "afraid of Jonah and his anger," and felt trapped by his "controlling nature." Dina also submitted photos of numerous dog bites she said she'd suffered during past arguments with Jonah.

The Shacknais' marriage breathed its last breath on Christmas Eve, 2008, when Jonah moved his belongings out of the family home while Dina and Max were away visiting her mother.

Not surprisingly, the battles continued even after one of them filed for divorce. In January 2009, Dina told police that Jonah elbowed her in the breast and swore at her as he drove away from the house. Jonah explained that he was sitting in his car, trying to leave, when Dina reached through the driver's-side window and into the car, slapped him, and tried to turn off the car, yelling, "You cannot leave me!" He said he had to block her with his shoulder to extricate himself before the situation escalated any further.

Despite his personal struggles, Jonah continued to excel in the professional realm, named by a local business publication as one of the most admired CEOs and role models in the Phoenix area. As he continued to build his brand and image over the years, he seemed to hit every note, from education to politics, Wall Street and philanthropy.

Jonah became vice chairman of the Delta Society, now known as Pet Partners, which promotes animal-human bonds. He also received an honorary doctorate from the New York College of Podiatric Medicine, and a national award from the Freedoms Foundation at Valley Forge.

As part of his public service, he served as a scientific advisor to the National Institute of Arthritis and Musculoskeletal and Skin Diseases, and also to the commerce secretary's U.S.-Israel Science and Technology Board, both of which were federal cabinet-appointed positions. He also was named to the Congressional Commission on the Federal Drug Approval Process, to the National Council on Drugs, and to a corporate-community advisory board to the New York Stock Exchange.

Jonah's divorce from Dina was finalized by consent decree on October 9, 2009. When Jonah met Rebecca later that month, he was still haggling with Dina over custody, property, attorneys' fees, and other financial matters.

In August 2010, he sold a third of his Medicis shares, earning $10 million. Over Dina's objections, Jonah had their divorce records sealed, but SEC records showed his annual compensation was $19.6 million in 2011.

Still, as news articles about Rebecca's death investigation

thrust him and his brand into an unwelcome national spotlight, Jonah was not as wealthy as some speculated.

"I became a billionaire overnight because of this," he joked in 2020, referring to inflated reports of his estimated net worth that went as high as $3 billion.

Chapter 20

During the first six months of his relationship with Rebecca, Jonah told Howard that he couldn't believe how happy he was. He'd found someone he saw as "highly educated," whose writing was "exceptional," and who was "infinitely more literate" than his colleagues with doctorates and medical degrees.

"Jonah is a very smart guy and he was intrigued," Howard said. "I just said, 'Be careful,' and he has."

Unfortunately, his two teenage children weren't so happy about the new relationship, his daughter Cindy in particular.

Rebecca moved into Jonah's house in March 2010 while he was on a family trip to visit his parents—before he and Rebecca had properly discussed or agreed that she should do this, and before he'd had a chance to tell his children that she was moving in with them.

After the kids got upset, Rebecca moved her stuff out, only to bring it all back again a month later after things calmed down. She also brought her dog, Ocean, to live with them.

As much as Rebecca loved Max, and he loved her, she had major problems getting along with Cindy, whom Rebecca saw as resentful and disrespectful to her. Once Rebecca came to live with the Shacknais, the whole family dynamic changed.

* * *

As Jonah's relationship with Rebecca progressed, he noticed a couple of strange behaviors in her, one of which was related to food. At the time, he attributed it to her years as a poor refugee, on the run from country to country, without enough to eat.

They were at the airport in Hawaii, heading home from a vacation, when Transportation Security Administration and U.S. Department of Agriculture officials ordered them to throw away a bunch of pineapples and fruit they had stowed in their luggage.

But rather than shrugging it off, she started crying, which Jonah saw as an "amplified" reaction. She had a similar reaction, although to a lesser extent, when even a small amount of food was wasted.

He also thought it was odd that Rebecca always wanted to pose for photos when they went somewhere, which she would then display around the house. The pictures weren't inappropriate or remarkable in any way, he just found it curious.

"I indulged it, and if it made her happy, I didn't see any harm in it, but those were the two behaviors I found the most bizarre," he said.

Rebecca had been conscious about her appearance even before meeting Jonah. In addition to getting breast implants and cosmetic tattoos on her eyebrows and eyelids, she was sensitive about the color of her skin. To prevent scrapes or cuts from getting darker in the sun, she applied athletic tape on her arms and legs.

A few months into the relationship, Rebecca showed up at Jonah's place unexpectedly, shaky and upset. She said Neil Nalepa, her ex, had forced his way into her house, broke the glass frame of an elephant picture she'd painted for Jonah, shoved her around, pinned her against the wall, and screamed at her. She had to run to a nearby coffee shop to seek refuge.

"She just had to see me and get a hug and talk about this,"

Jonah said, noting that she'd told him of other incidents where Neil would "scream at her, push her around, and was abusive." Yet, when Jonah questioned Rebecca whether they needed to get a restraining order against him, she said no.

"I think he's pretty harmless," she told him. "He just hasn't ever gotten over this."

Jonah got a different impression from Rebecca's brother-in-law, Doug, who said he "believed that on one or more occasions, this guy was pretty rough." But neither one had ever met Neil in person.

After Jonah took Rebecca to meet his father and stepmother, she told her sisters that the Shacknais were happy to see Jonah with a woman who made him smile. She also met his brother, Adam, who was quirky and eccentric, but they got along well enough.

Because of the twenty-two-year age difference between Rebecca and Jonah, her sister Mary didn't really approve of the relationship any more than she'd liked the one with Michael Berger.

Still married to Neil, Rebecca was nervous about introducing Jonah to her parents, who didn't know they'd been dating even a year later. The day after Thanksgiving in 2010, the couple flew to St. Joseph, Missouri, where they all met up at Mary and Doug's house.

At Rebecca's urging, Jonah asked her father for permission to date Rebecca, understanding that it was a cultural tradition.

"They were very religious," he said. "I played along," and her father gave them his blessing.

In contrast, Adam never brought his girlfriend, Mary Bedwell, to a single Shacknai family gathering. They, too, had a big age difference, but more important to Adam, his parents were "pretty culturally rooted in our religion," and Mary wasn't Jewish. That said, neither was Rebecca, and neither was Dina, though she converted.

Although Adam introduced Mary to Jonah soon after he started dating her, Jonah didn't see her again for twenty years.

To an outside observer, Mary was a Christian, a mother, well-educated, slender, attractive, funny, and friendly. But in her mind, she was "inappropriate" and "terribly mismatched" with Adam.

"I [could]n't expect him to take [home] a nearly fifty-year-old shiksa from Tennessee, divorced," she said recently. "I guess they wanted something a little bit different. But I was the more hesitant one than him."

Today, they still don't discuss their ages, and when people ask if they're ever going to get married, Mary just laughs.

"Oh, gosh, I can't believe people are still asking that," she said.

Because of the difference in the way they keep house—she has "a place for everything, and everything in its place," while Adam is "constantly 'getting organized,' as he calls it"—they haven't wanted to live together, but they do live *near* each other, in houses that are only a few blocks apart.

"I know we wouldn't have stayed together this long if we'd gotten married," she said. "I've been married and I've never been interested in getting remarried."

Chapter 21

As Rebecca helped Jonah take care of his three children on a half-time custody basis, she didn't think discipline was being meted out enough. She also didn't believe Jonah took her side when she felt criticized or bad-mouthed by his teenagers or ex-wives.

Kim and Dina talked about her behind her back, which Rebecca learned at yoga class, but Cindy made sassy comments right to her face. Rebecca tried to keep the peace, but it strained her relationship with Jonah and stressed her out.

Max loved Rebecca and wanted his two favorite women to get along, so Dina invited her to coffee in September 2010.

Rebecca introduced herself as Rebecca Zahau, never mentioning that her legal last name was still Nalepa. Dressed in an outfit that Dina considered inappropriate for a Sunday morning, Rebecca shared some family photos and talked about competing in triathlons, while Dina ate cookies and tried, unsuccessfully, to discuss books.

When Dina asked how she felt about Jonah's stand against having more children, Rebecca's face turned red. "That is a little bit forward, but maybe he'll change his mind as we move forward," she retorted.

But when Rebecca told Jonah about the meeting later, she sounded more in control of the situation, saying she relayed this message to Dina: "I'm not going anywhere, and I have no quarrel with you. You and Jonah didn't work out, and I came along, long after that, so you have no quarrel with me. We have to find a way to move forward so you're not trying to constantly undermine me."

Dina came away feeling they had little common ground other than Max. But more than that, something felt amiss, which inspired her to do a little digging online with her sister, Nina. However, nothing came up when they tried to Google "Rebecca Zahau."

Investigating further, they learned that Rebecca was not only still married to Neil, but that she'd also been arrested for shoplifting.

"These things were concerning," Dina said. "As a mother, you want to know who's taking care of your child."

Further distressing was news that Rebecca had thrown away a bunch of family photos featuring Dina and Max, which Jonah's housekeeper retrieved from the trash and returned to Dina.

Dina, who had recently earned her doctorate in clinical psychology with the goal of being a child therapist, didn't like the way Rebecca controlled Max's diet, because it had resulted in Max sometimes refusing to eat at all. His mother liked watching him enjoy himself—eating candy and cookies, and performing with his friends on a stage, complete with curtains, that she and Jonah had built out of plywood when they were still together. It was "just a place to horse around and have faux performances that we would sit around and watch," as Jonah described it.

But what really irked Dina was that Jonah brought Rebecca to Max's school events. Dina believed this was insensitive, because she said he'd tried to protect Kim's feelings by keeping Dina away from his kids' school events and hiding his early involvement with her, even after he and Kim had broken up. Jonah disputed that recollection, saying he "never discouraged Dina from going" to events, she just needed to respect that Kim was the kids' mother.

All these tensions erupted one afternoon at the Phoenix Country Day School, where Max was participating in a race that he'd specifically asked Rebecca to attend.

Normally, Max was a happy, gleeful child, with an enormous grin, known to jump up on a big rock at sunset and shout, "It's so good to be alive!" But the rift between his mother and Rebecca was likely weighing on him too—so much so that the star athlete came in second place and, even more uncharacteristically, broke into tears about it.

When Max came over to Jonah and Rebecca for a consolatory hug, Rebecca gave him one, cooing, "Oh, my sweet baby, my sweet angel."

This set off Dina, who was standing nearby. Furious, she lunged between them, and "snatched Max away" from Rebecca, as Jonah put it, taking over what she considered the proper duties of comforting the boy—by his own mother.

"Leave my son alone," she snapped. "He's my son."

Rebecca "was understandably upset" about the incident, Jonah said. Nina also chose this moment to pile on by scolding her about discarding the photos.

"It's not cool to throw them away," Nina told Rebecca. "Just call Dina. Say, 'I don't want them in the house.'"

When Rebecca denied the allegation, Nina wouldn't let her off the hook.

"Rebecca, I'm not going to keep telling you," she said. "I get it. She's an ex-wife, you don't want the photos around."

Rebecca then conceded that she had thrown away some photos, but her explanation didn't fit with what the housekeeper had told Dina.

"Well, there were a few photos," Rebecca said, but "they were from Gideon and Marcelle's wedding, and they were duplicates."

That's when Nina brought up the stories that Dina said Rebecca had been telling Max, that she was an eye doctor and a princess.

"How does one go from being a princess to an eye doctor?" Nina asked snidely.

Rebecca responded with what Nina heard as a purposefully evasive nonanswer.

"I don't know if you know anything about Burma," Rebecca said, adding something Nina didn't understand "about territories and royalty."

Rebecca may have been a nice woman, Nina said, "but she was never what she seemed. She was presenting herself in a way of what Jonah would want."

After the scene at Max's school, Dina was so upset that she asked Jonah to meet for coffee, where she laid out a set of demands. Trying to "mollify" her, he agreed that Rebecca didn't need to come to any more school events—for now—because the end of the school year was approaching anyway.

But he thought some of her other demands, such as preventing Rebecca from taking Max across state lines, were "absurd," because they were already in the custody agreement.

Collectively, these conflicts contributed to Dina's and Nina's suspicions a few months later that Rebecca was more involved in Max's fall than she claimed.

"I think there's more to this," Nina told detectives. "I don't think Max's accident was an accident. I mean, Rebecca had a history. She lied about being married. She lied about shoplifting. She's lied about her past."

Rebecca's sister Mary saw things differently. Although she wasn't aware of the confrontation between Dina and Rebecca, she did know that Dina caused problems by telling Jonah that Rebecca shouldn't come to school events, when she knew very well that Max wanted Rebecca there.

"Dina was very rude and hateful to my sister," Mary told detectives. "I know my sister tried to avoid her."

All of this constant drama took a physical and emotional toll on Rebecca. Mary told detectives that her sister lost more than fifteen pounds during that period, "which is a lot for her. She was usually one hundred fifteen. She dropped down to ninety-five or ninety-eight. She said she wasn't able to sleep."

Jonah differed with that assessment, saying he thought Rebecca had weighed close to one hundred pounds the whole time they'd been together. But he acknowledged that her body composition had changed after she modified her workout routine to do more biking and running, and less bodysculpting with weights.

"I didn't notice any profound body weight changes, but maybe I wasn't observant enough," he said.

What he did notice, however, was that she was "very unhappy with the family dynamic," he said. They both were.

Rebecca's frustrations were documented on her cell phone, where she stored two journal-style entries in the Notes folder, both of which were undated, and didn't appear to have been sent to anyone.

One was a letter to Jonah about a business dinner for thirty people at the mansion in June, which he'd asked her to attend, seated at the same table with him and Cindy. Rebecca initially refused to go, because she was concerned that Cindy would act as hostess, which should be Rebecca's role.

"Let's grow up here. You're just going to have to suck it up," he told her, reminding her that she was the adult and Cindy was the teenager.

After that, Rebecca reluctantly agreed to attend, but the note shows how angry she still was, because of Cindy's "unjustified hatred toward me that she is allowed to freely display both behind closed doors and in public." All Jonah cared about, she wrote, was how her absence would reflect on him and put him in an "awkward situation." Not the resentment he caused by telling her to put her "feelings and hurt on the shelf" for him and his family.

Jonah didn't "ask me or understand how uncomfortable I would be," she wrote, and she was proven right because Cindy "killed me a thousand times during dinner and openly flaunted her disgust at having to sit three chairs down from me."

In contrast, Jonah said he thought the dinner had gone well, with both females acting "socially graceful" toward one another.

Rebecca complained to her sisters that Jonah failed to back her up when Cindy treated her like "a worthless person." Jonah heard Cindy's comments differently, saying he believed Rebecca was overreacting. However, he acknowledged that she correctly assessed that his strongest allegiance was to his children.

Despite what she told Snowem, Rebecca was troubled by the prospect of a childless future with Jonah. *Am I pretending that I will be content without ever having a child?* she wrote.

In the other note, Rebecca spoke poetically about her longing to feel appreciated by a man "with eyes full of love that I would be lost in them like a seaman in the vast ocean." She also described the vast emotional emptiness of her life, and the "enemies" trying to destroy her—his two ex-wives, who "harassed and hated" her.

Although money wasn't a priority for pursuing this relationship, she wrote, [No] *amount of money is worth what I am going through. It is my own fault. I have allowed myself to be completely cut off from my own life. My life does not exist.*

For the first time ever, she couldn't sleep, and she was constantly in tears. She loved Jonah, but she wished he knew how much she'd sacrificed and repressed, so as not to bother him. She was trying hard to be the "best girlfriend" and "caretaker" for the kids she could, because "that is barely what I am."

Despite the "love ring" he'd given her, she didn't know when they would ever get engaged, "let alone get married," but she knew that no one would "take the situation seriously" until they did. Did he expect her to wait patiently until the kids were grown to find the happiness she craved?

Aching for some public affection, she wrote, she realized it was awkward for him, but "god forbid your colleagues think u r holding hands."

Although Rebecca discussed some of these issues with her sisters, she either never revealed how deep her unhappiness really went, or it never registered with them.

She'd told them she loved Jonah and Max, but she was ready to give the relationship a break, and take some time to herself if necessary, as she had done with Neil in the past.

"Becky told me that she did love [Jonah] but that she was disappointed in a lot of ways," Mary told the *San Diego Reader.*

Jonah and Rebecca agreed that if the family dynamic didn't improve that summer, changes would have to be made in their relationship. They even went to a counselor to discuss how best to proceed. At the end of the summer, he said, "we were going to see where we were," and "where things stood."

But for him, he said recently, the situation would have needed to improve dramatically over where it was when the summer started, or they would've had to end the relationship, because he couldn't withstand such a consistent level of conflict. However, he'd still hoped for that outcome.

They had "a strong and good relationship," which "would have been sustainable . . . if we'd been in our own little world," he said, but Dina was being "herself, and there wasn't much I could do about that."

In July, Howard told detectives that Rebecca and Cindy had "recently sort of turned the corner, and they were getting along great, I mean, best friends." Rebecca was getting along well with Kevin too, shooting hoops with him and Max when Jonah was too tired.

Rebecca had conveyed a similar, optimistic outlook to Mary, saying shortly before she died that she and Cindy had "had a good two weeks." In fact, she cut a call short with Mary, saying that Cindy "needs me to help her with something, so I got to go."

Chapter 22

Six months after Rebecca moved in with Jonah, Neil finally broke down and filed for divorce on August 12, 2010, without an attorney.

"I had no choice," he said. "She was never going to do it, so I initiated the divorce."

Neil ultimately relented, he said, because she kept seeing other men while they were still married, which made it "that we're not living right." If they got divorced, "then at the very least what she's doing is between her and God, what I'm doing is between me and him, and if we get together again, it's new."

Still, a year after he filed papers, the divorce was almost dismissed because he dragged his feet in paying $170 in fees. The divorce became final by default in February 2011. Rebecca never responded or filed any paperwork until that April, when she petitioned the court to return to using her maiden name.

In early 2011, Jonah was shocked when Dina told him about Rebecca's shoplifting arrest two years earlier. It didn't fit with the woman he knew.

Nonetheless, he confronted Rebecca about it. He'd already done his own background check on her, but because her records had been purged after she completed the diversion program, nothing had turned up.

Rebecca admitted that she'd been arrested, but she gave him a very different explanation from what is documented in the police report. She said she'd been holding some jewelry at Macy's when she got a distressing call that her brother, Solomon, had been arrested for a serious offense in Germany. She said she was so upset that she immediately ran out of the store, not realizing that she still had the merchandise in her hand.

Jonah took her at her word. "She told a good story about it," he said. "It was convincing. I'm sure I wanted to believe it, because I didn't think of her as dishonest, so I guess I suspended disbelief."

Around the same time, Rebecca told Jonah and Snowem that she was having issues with one of the doctors at the eye clinic, whom she claimed had been propositioning and harassing her about her relationship with Jonah. After her arm got burned with some surgical equipment, she and Jonah decided that she should quit her job and concentrate on taking care of him and Max.

When she said she still needed her own money, Jonah agreed to give her an allowance equaling her clinic salary, with access to his credit cards as well. Also, because she was sending money every month to her parents, who lived near her sister Mary in Missouri, Jonah agreed to cover a $500 monthly payment for that too.

When Snowem flew over from Germany to stay with Rebecca for a month in January 2011, she could tell her sister was stressed. As soon as Snowem got off the plane, she noticed that Rebecca looked "sickly," and about ten pounds under her usual weight.

"What's wrong with you?" Snowem asked.

"Oh, it's just, you know, the kids and lack of sleep."

Over the next few days, Rebecca told her what had been going on. She felt sorry for Jonah because his kids were arguing with him. She'd tried to help resolve the conflict, but it was hard because the situation predated her moving in with them.

"I even saw how they would just argue, loud, and Jonah trying to calm the kids down, but the kids are a little rough, especially the two older ones," Snowem later told detectives.

But not Max, who was "very special," Snowem said. "Becky and him, they really got along with each other. And Becky really loved him . . . He was different than the [older] two. Probably that was the reason why Becky was so close to him."

During a walk with Ocean in the park, Rebecca confided that she was also having conflicts with Jonah's ex-wives. In addition to the nasty, untrue jabs Dina made behind her back at the yoga studio, Rebecca was also concerned that Dina was being irresponsible with Max.

She said Dina kept asking Rebecca to pick him up even when it was Dina's turn to take care of him. Then, one day when Max was staying with Dina for the week, his teacher called and said, "Max didn't show up for school, what's wrong?"

When she and Jonah asked Max about the incident, Rebecca quoted him as saying, "I sat in front of the television the whole day."

Rebecca told Snowem that she and Jonah had discussed taking punitive measures against Dina if she didn't take better care of Max, such as forcing her out of the house and putting her in an apartment instead.

According to Jonah, however, there was never any talk of such penalties. "That's some story," he said recently, though he conceded that Max was late or absent from school a number of times when he stayed with Dina.

Cindy was also having emotional problems, prompting Rebecca to call the girl's mother, with whom relations had improved.

"I still remember Becky calling [Kim]," and that both women were crying, Snowem recalled.

Telling Snowem how surprisingly "evil" Cindy could be, Rebecca showed her a letter she'd written to the teen, discussing what she'd learned in her own family about the importance of showing love and respect to your parents. After the letter, she said their relationship got a bit better, though Cindy continued to act out. Rebecca said she sacrificed many hours of needed sleep by staying up late talking to Jonah about his daughter's issues.

In other matters, Rebecca told Snowem that Jonah had gotten sick after eating a sushi meal in Scottsdale a month earlier, and that he was worried someone had tried to poison him, so they were actively searching for a new security dog. She also said Jonah had promptly called an attorney and asked Rebecca to sign some paperwork.

This information made Rebecca's family wonder if she had signed a will or if the couple had secretly gotten married, because Rebecca had told her family that she and Jonah had been discussing it. As a result, the typically mild-mannered Snowem asked Jonah bluntly one day, "Are you going to marry my sister?"

This caught Jonah by surprise, because the family dynamics were so problematic that an engagement wasn't even on the table.

"I don't know, we'll have to see how things go," he replied, not knowing what else to say.

Asked recently about these stories, Jonah said that he'd never gotten sick after eating sushi, other than from a supermarket, and he'd never been worried that someone was trying to poison him. He said he's allergic to garlic, and perhaps these details got conflated, because he often joked that someone was trying to poison him when a restaurant served him a meal containing garlic.

"When people ask me how bad the allergy is, I say, 'The dose makes the poison, so if there's a lot of it, I'm very poisoned, and if there isn't much, then it's not so bad.'"

Jonah couldn't recall any paperwork they had both signed, other than the immigration application he'd sponsored for her two youngest siblings, Ariel and Joey, whom he'd helped obtain a "humanitarian pardon" from federal authorities. The only other papers she might have signed, he said, could have been related to her own citizenship application.

In hindsight, these stories seem to reflect expectations by the Zahau family, which they either formed on their own, or were based on what Rebecca had told them with the hope of gaining more approval for her live-in relationship with Jonah. The ring he'd given her was not a promise or pre-engagement ring, Jonah said, it was just "a gift" he'd picked up on a work trip to Toronto.

"I think the mom, and the father, and perhaps Mary, had an extremely strict constructionist Christian view," Jonah said. "Her father took the Bible, every word, as literal. It may be that Rebecca looked forward a little too much just to make them a little more comfortable that this was going somewhere, and it wasn't a casual relationship. There was never a bad side to her, but she certainly tried to present a very different view to that part of the family than that maybe she lived."

As for her family's claims that she was modest about nudity and the way she dressed, Jonah said Rebecca was again different from how her family saw her, both privately and publicly.

"No way would I say that her comportment or clothing was modest," he said, noting that she always wore whatever was most flattering to her figure, including skintight workout clothes, such as a sports bra with a bare midriff.

"She was in very good physical condition, she was very proud of that. It was important to her to exercise, maybe compulsively so, and she took that seriously," he said, noting that it was also something he admired. "I try to stay fit myself."

While they were in Coronado, Rebecca typically got up after Jonah, who rose early with Max when the child stayed with them. She would come down and help with breakfast, whipping up a protein fruit shake for Jonah while he made pancakes.

Her days were relatively unstructured. In the morning, she took Ocean to the dog park on the Coronado Cays, or rode her bike around town with him. Then she either showered and took the kids to the zoo, or she worked out at one of their two gyms, then went for a run. She and Jonah worked out together if they didn't have the kids, and in shifts when they did.

Their one routine was to eat lunch together. Afterward, she and Jonah might hang out at the house and play with the kids, or Rebecca might walk into town with Cindy, or take her somewhere. She and Jonah often went out for dinner, with or without the kids, but they also cooked at home if they were alone.

Rebecca liked to go to bed earlier than Jonah did. If he wasn't around, she went to sleep between 9:00 and 10:00 P.M. When the kids were there, they usually stayed up until at least eleven o'clock, which was Cindy's curfew, because Jonah said he "didn't like to go to sleep until she walked through the door."

Rebecca and Dina managed to avoid any conflicts at the most recent family get-togethers, a beach-bonfire birthday party near the Hotel del Coronado for Max on June 7, and a July 4 gathering by the hotel pool.

But that all changed a week later, when Max went over the banister.

Chapter 23

The day Max was hospitalized, Dina was pretty agitated as she sat with Jonah at the boy's bedside in the ICU. Rebecca was supposed to be taking care of Max, and then this happened?

Trying to ease Dina's mood, Jonah told her she should be grateful that Rebecca had been there to administer CPR and call 911, and also that they lived in Coronado, where the paramedics had arrived so swiftly.

"You should get down on your knees and thank her for saving Max's life," he said.

"Of course I'm grateful to her," Dina replied.

The wording and the timing of these statements are key, because they go to the identity and motivation of whoever painted the message *SHE SAVED HIM CAN YOU SAVE HER* on the hallway door.

According to the Zahaus, only a small circle of Max's family members knew from Jonah that Rebecca had "saved him," which they contend points to Adam as her killer. They also believe that Rebecca was optimistic about Max's chances for recovery on Tuesday night, and had no reason to kill herself.

But Jonah disagrees. He said his scientific and medical background helped him recognize early on that Max's condition looked bad—and that she hadn't actually saved him—but he didn't share that with anyone, because he "didn't want to extinguish hope." By Tuesday, Adam still "had no awareness of the gravity of Max's condition that night, or the early-morning message that I left for Rebecca, because he was sleeping. I was not in touch with him, and he wasn't at the hospital, so this whole theory that this was some sort of revenge just doesn't hold up."

Memories vary about the content and timing of Max's grim prognosis by his doctor, Bradley Peterson, which is also essential to understanding what Rebecca and others in that small circle were thinking on Tuesday night.

As of 4:20 P.M., Max's CT "was not worse, and looked even a little better," said Dr. Peterson, who subsequently ordered a magnetic resonance imaging, or MRI, to "get a better look at his brain and spinal cord."

Peterson had administered hypertonic saline to try to shrink Max's brain swelling. But he was worried from the first day of treatment, because he knew Max had required thirty minutes of resuscitation and epinephrine. That was a long time to be down without a heartbeat, he said, and Rady doctors generally don't even try to treat kids under those circumstances, because they know it's hopeless.

When Peterson gave his deposition six and a half years later, he couldn't remember exactly what he said to Jonah and Dina that Tuesday night, and the medical reports don't note specifics. He only recalled that he spoke more with Jonah, who seemed "reserved and sad," and that Dina had seemed "more upset than the father."

But typically, he said, he tries to convey to parents what he's thinking, but nothing too definitive until he has clear test results. "You say things and then people hear them differently," he said. "They hear them in the way they want to hear them . . . I think I would have told [Dina], 'I've got some bad information here.

We've got to get some more information. We're not quitting yet,' kind of like that."

Nina's recollection, based on what Dina told her, was that Peterson said, "I don't know if he's ever going to walk or talk again."

But according to Jonah, Peterson said the best prognosis was that Max "would never walk or talk again," which prompted Dina to scream at the doctor, "You're wrong, you're wrong!"

After that, Jonah said he took Peterson into the hall, out of Dina's earshot, and scolded him for speaking to her in such blunt terms.

"I just like to tell it like it is, I've been doing this for a long time," he said Peterson replied. "I don't think anyone should have any false hope."

Looking for a second opinion, Jonah subsequently sought out another ICU doctor, Francisco Recalde, who was at Rady on a fellowship rotation. Asked to talk to Dina, and "be a little more gentle in presenting the medical facts and not hypothesizing," Recalde spoke to both parents at 10:38 P.M. Afterward, however, Dina was still clinging to the idea that Max was going to pull through.

Based on their volatile history, it's not surprising that Jonah and Dina have different accounts of what the doctors said that night. In addition to the recent trauma, Max's health and welfare had been a point of dispute between them for some time.

Max had hit his head at Dina's house a couple of weeks before his fall. Jonah said they were concerned he might have a concussion, but Dina never took him to the doctor.

Conversely, during their heated divorce battle, Dina made a report to Child Protective Services (CPS) in Arizona in February 2009. She alleged that Max had come home from Jonah's with a bruised leg, claiming that Jonah had hit him with a watch after he made a fuss about going to get a haircut.

Maxfield stated his dad caused the injury on purpose, the CPS report stated. *Dad has a real bad temper, but not in front of people. It is a concern that dad will start taking his anger out on Maxwell* [sic] *now that mom is not around to beat on. Dad is "very smart," and knows how to handle situations . . . Dad has guns and an attack dog that will bite.* As the reporting party, Dina *indicated fear of harm to self because* [she] *filed a report.*

After a six-month investigation, Dina's allegation was found to be unsubstantiated. Jonah said he didn't even learn of the report, which he said "was spurious on its face," until after Max was dead.

"The story was so stupid that it probably got the attention that it deserved," he said recently. "I will never forgive her for having done that."

It wasn't until Wednesday, the day Rebecca was found dead, that Max got the MRI that Peterson ordered, and that the family really started to learn how bad Max's prognosis was: Even if he were to come out of his coma, "he would be a vegetable," Nina said.

After hearing how Rebecca died, Jonah said Peterson became more "circumstantially" concerned. "She wouldn't have done this if she hadn't felt guilty," the doctor told him, prompting Jonah to admonish him "not to let his imagination run away with him and not play detective."

When Max's test results came back Thursday, Peterson told Jonah and Dina there was no way Max could have had CPR within two minutes of being injured, because the damage was too great.

Asked by Dina what could have caused the injuries, Peterson suggested that Max could have been suffocated, because his symptoms were similar to those after a drowning. They simply didn't match Rebecca's account of how he got them.

Dina and Nina were shocked. Who would want to harm such a beautiful, loving little boy? Did Rebecca lie about giving Max CPR or make up a story to cover up what really happened?

"I don't know," Nina said later. "Maybe she was in the back-yard, maybe she was distracted. Maybe she found him, didn't know how long he'd been lying there. I do think she knew more than what she was telling, because that's the feeling I got." But whatever she might have been hiding, Nina said, "she took those secrets with her."

After listening to Dina's theories that Rebecca was somehow involved in Max's fall, the staff at Rady notified CPS in San Diego.

Jonah didn't know anything about this CPS report either, until a Coronado police detective came to Max's room to take photos of the boy.

"I asked what precipitated that and he mentioned that Dina was asking a lot of questions and they wanted to have their ducks in a row," Jonah recalled.

Fearing what was coming, Dina brought a shaman Thursday night to Max's hospital room, where the mood was somber.

By the next morning, Nina said, "I looked at my nephew and I knew he was gone."

Nina had agreed to take a polygraph exam at 8:00 A.M., but with Max in such grave condition, she couldn't face it.

"I was an absolute wreck," she recalled later. "I don't even know how many hours I'd been up."

So she sent a message to Special Agent Sonia Ramos, telling her, essentially, that it was the worst day of her life and she couldn't make it. Ramos responded with condolences, saying they would contact her if they needed to reschedule. But they never did.

"Polygraph tests are consensual and Nina canceled the appointment. She was under no legal obligation to undergo the polygraph," said sheriff's lieutenant Justin White. He didn't respond to the question why Dina wasn't also asked to do one.

Max was deemed brain dead two minutes before midnight on Friday, July 15, but the official finding still had to be confirmed by another doctor, who was not on duty at the time.

That declaration came at eleven-thirty on Saturday morning. For the next eighteen hours, they kept the boy's body alive to clean his blood and donate his organs. Max's liver and kidneys went to three recipients.

After the procurement, Dr. Jonathan Lucas, the same pathologist who did Rebecca's autopsy, did Max's on July 18.

Chapter 24

Once the investigators finished their work at the mansion, the property was released to Jonah on Saturday through a local security company that Medicis had hired to respond to threats and "create a distance" between its CEO and the reporters who were following him around. An ex-cop from the security firm also collected Ocean from the kennel.

But after returning to the mansion twice after Max's fall, Jonah could never face going back again. He put the place up for sale and made sure that Ocean was adopted by a family in Phoenix.

"I have a belief that Ocean was somehow involved with Max's fall," Jonah said. "It was Rebecca's dog. It was good that he be with a family that would love him and take care of him."

Over the next few weeks, the sheriff's crime lab analyzed the fingerprints and DNA swabs collected from the scene.

Before the steak knife was processed for fingerprints, which involved a superglue mist-and-bake to release fumes that coated the prints, a lab tech swabbed a red stain on the bottom rivet of the handle for DNA. After the printing process, the rest of the knife was swabbed for DNA.

Rebecca's DNA turned up on that knife, which investigators

believed she used to cut the rope into several pieces. It was also
found on knots in the lengths of rope that were tied around her
ankles, wrists, neck, and to the bed frame. Rebecca's prints were
found on the doorjamb leading into the guest room, on a balcony
door, on the chef's knife, and on the bed leg where the rope was
anchored.

In those same areas, they found no identifiable DNA or prints
linked to Adam Shacknai, Nina Romano, or Ariel Zahau, who
were all specifically excluded. Apparently, they didn't look for
Jonah's or Dina's prints or DNA because the SDSD had determined that their whereabouts were accounted for at the time of
Rebecca's death.

Other evidence items were taken to the San Diego Regional
Computer Forensics Laboratory (RCFL), which duplicates data
on computers and devices without disturbing the original, then
examines the copies for relevant information and browser activity.

These items included Rebecca's Samsung cell phone, which
was found on the guest room floor and showed no signs of physical damage, an iMac desktop computer, and a Hewlett-Packard
laptop from the computer room. Each computer had a registered
user, indicating that the iMac was Jonah's and the laptop was
Rebecca's.

Investigators initially believed that someone tried to access
one of the computers at 3:02 A.M. on Wednesday, July 13, but
they later determined that it was an automatic update.

They did, however, find that someone had accessed a series
of pornographic sites on Rebecca's laptop the previous night, in
the early-morning hours of Tuesday, July 12. The session started
at 1:34 A.M., and ended a couple of hours later.

The laptop's browser history showed no searches or access to
any porno or other suspicious sites in the previous weeks and

months. Nor did it show any searches using the terms "suicide," "rope," "knots," or "hanging." The laptop also had no stored documents relating to suicide.

Previous browsing activity focused mainly on sites for online banking, Facebook, hair salons, athletic clothes, Scottsdale-Phoenix nightlife, spas and resorts, and some Southwest Airlines booking and ticketing pages.

Investigators reviewed security video, obtained by a search warrant, of people going in and out of Rady Children's Hospital and the adjacent RMH, from 2:00 P.M. on July 12 until 9:00 A.M. on July 13.

Several sources said the footage shows Dina walking in and out of Rady before midnight on July 12. However, asked to comment on claims that this video had been tampered with, Lieutenant White said obliquely that the RCFL "was unable to download the requested video."

The investigator who analyzed the video noted in his report that the card reader for the hallway leading to Jonah's room at RMH wasn't functioning that night. Jonah had to walk through the outdoor patio area and go through a side door to get to his room. One camera monitored the building's single entrance point at the front door, but there were several exits, and some didn't have cameras. Jonah said he took the circuitous route to avoid the media, who were posted in and around the hospital.

Either way, the time-stamped video appears to support the timeline Jonah gave investigators. Because the cameras in the two buildings were three to five minutes out of sync, he was seen leaving the hospital's main entrance at 12:28 A.M. and entering RMH at 12:25 A.M., then heading through the hallways and patio to get to his room. Either way, his whereabouts were captured on camera just before 12:30.

He showed up next at 5:49 A.M., walking in a hallway toward

a doorway leading to the lobby and cafeteria, where he said he went to get coffee. A minute later, he was seen on his way back, walking through the patio toward the hallway near his room.

At 6:53 A.M., he was wearing different clothes, walking toward the exit of the RMH, then standing by the elevator en route to the hospital.

When detectives examined his pass into Rady's parking structure, it showed that he had last entered on July 12 at 4:53 P.M.

Chapter 25

Neil Nalepa was driving to the gym on Thursday, July 14, when he got a call from an ABC News reporter who was speaking so quickly he couldn't understand what she was saying. Neil asked her to slow down.

"Have you been watching the news out here in California?" she asked.

"No," he said.

As she explained that his ex-wife had been found dead at the Spreckels Mansion the day before, Neil proceeded to have a panic attack.

He had no idea how the reporter had gotten his number, but the calls kept coming—to him, his father, and even his aunt in Texas, who didn't have the same last name.

Thinking back, he remembered texting Rebecca about a week earlier, asking if she was okay.

You can always talk to me, he texted.

I know, she replied.

Rebecca added that she thought of him sometimes when she wanted to talk, but she didn't call out of pride. She said she was busy and was getting ready to go visit her mom in Missouri.

He texted back some days later, asking, How's your mom doing?

She never texted back and he'd wondered why. It was unusual for her not to respond, especially when it was only six or seven o'clock on a weeknight. Now he knew the answer.

When Neil sat down with Detectives Mark Palmer and Hank Lebitski the night of July 17, they asked for his whereabouts in the hours before Rebecca was found dead. Neil said he was in a lecture and microbiology lab at Scottsdale Community College on the morning of July 12, and was at his gym by 5:00 A.M. on July 13, before going to another lecture.

But the detectives seemed just as interested in the childhood molestation that Rebecca and her sisters had suffered because it provided an insight into her adult state of mind.

Neil said the molestation seemed to have had a lasting effect, because he saw pain in their eyes. "It looks like it had to be instilled in them, not like just the onetime thing," he said.

"Three daughters who were molested and they don't discuss it," Lebitski said. "It's huge. Stuff like that changes a person and a lot of times it breeds insecurity."

Neil didn't see it that way. "Rebecca was the farthest thing from insecure," he countered.

"But she went out on you. That comes from insecurity."

"I have a different view. It comes from learning that you get things from guys. This is what guys like, then you know how to get things."

In fact, Neil said, Rebecca used to complain that *he* was insecure.

The detectives said her "cheating" behavior signaled that she wasn't in love with him as much as he was in love with her.

"What is she missing in her life? . . . The fact that she's not dealing with the molest[ation] as a kid. What's she chasing, what's she running from? What's causing her to act out? You're married, she's out with a guy. What was she missing with you?"

"Money," Neil said. "She was raised poor. She didn't want to have to ever wonder when she was going to eat again."

Looking for other factors that would back the suicide scenario, the detectives asked if she's ever exhibited mental-health problems, or sought therapy. Neil said they went to marriage counseling a few times, but that was it.

"Was there any depression? Problems sleeping?" the detectives asked.

No, Neil said, noting that she could sleep twelve hours straight when she had the chance. Despite his nursing training, he apparently didn't know that sleeping for such long periods can be a symptom of depression.

"We're trying to understand what happened to her," the detective said.

"I would like to know too," Neil said.

Asked if he knew anyone who would want to hurt her, Neil said, "I haven't met someone who didn't fall in love with Rebecca. You meet her and you just go, *wow*. So, it's hard to imagine that someone would want to hurt her."

Had she ever expressed fear of anything or anyone? "No, she was never in fear," he said, not even when his DEA agent brother and their family were threatened by a cartel leader who had been arrested in 2010.

"Would there be any reason why you'd want to hurt Rebecca?"

"No."

"Did you participate in this?"

"No."

"I got to ask the question. You know that, right?"

"No, I don't. I'd love to clear myself and that's fine."

"You're not in any trouble."

"I had nothing to do with this," Neil said. "I actually wanted to call and I wasn't sure what to do. I was wondering why I found out by the news, and didn't hear something sooner."

Although they told him several times that they hadn't yet settled on a suicide scenario, the tone and direction of their questions—only one day after Rebecca was found dead—indicated that they were already going in that direction, noting that "the forensics so far is leaning toward the suicide."

But Neil couldn't see it. "Rebecca wouldn't commit suicide," he said.

"Why do you say she wouldn't?"

"We've been through a lot and she's had a lot of pain in her life, and she's dealt with it, she's not ever—she loved life. You know what I mean. She would never take her life. She would just deal with whatever she's got going on, even if it meant she would deal with it in an enclosed way where she introverted."

"How would she handle it if she was losing everything? This money and this lifestyle?" the detective asked.

"She didn't have it, she couldn't lose it. It was his, right?" Neil said.

"She was living it, though."

As they worked the good cop/bad cop routine on him, Neil started crying, saying repeatedly that he didn't accept the suicide scenario.

Palmer explained that they had been looking at half a dozen people in Rebecca's life, including "anyone and everyone who had motive, but more important, opportunity."

"We have been able to eliminate just about everybody," he said, adding that there was "evidence that we can't divulge that we can't ignore."

"If it's a murder, we have to look at all the players on the board and you're on the board," Lebitski said.

"I'm aware," Neil replied.

Others "on the board" included Jonah, Dina, and Ariel, the

last of whom had already left town by the time Rebecca was dead.

"Do they think Rebecca had anything to do with [Max's fall]?" Neil asked.

"We don't know," Lebitski said. "More than likely, it was an accident. So that's three people out of the six that have been eliminated. And also Jonah's brother. He was in the guest house the night it happened. He found her."

"We've pretty much eliminated him," Palmer said.

"He has participated in our investigation, one hundred percent. Passed the polygraph, volunteered a statement, gave us all the DNA we wanted. Not a scratch on him. Cooperated."

As for the others, he went on, "Jonah can account for his time. I don't think Dina participated. I don't think she's big enough to do everything that was done. She has no marks on her body . . . and Rebecca wasn't sexually assaulted."

Neil was clearly struggling with her death, trying to imagine what might have been going through his ex-wife's head, and questioning why, if she were in trouble or in emotional pain, she hadn't reached out for his help.

"We had our problems, but every time I was there, she came back. Every time I accepted her, I listened to her. I don't think that there's anything she would have gone through that she wouldn't have known she could call me," he said. "It makes me feel, as a husband, that I failed. Either way, it's scary to think either that she was in the emotional state to do this, or the fear she felt as someone was doing it, not that I'd wish that upon her either. With suicide, there's no closure, it seems."

To be thorough, the detectives didn't overlook the possibility that Ariel could have been involved somehow in the week's tragic events, or might have some insight into Rebecca's death.

A group of sheriff's investigators traveled to St. Joseph, Missouri, where they took her fingerprints and a DNA swab. They also interviewed her—with Pari, Doug, Snowem, and Timo present—at the Northwest Missouri Children's Advocacy Center on July 20. By that point, the authorities were publicly offering support for the suicide scenario.

"There are documentations of incidents throughout the country where people have secured their feet and hands as well, to commit suicide, so we have to keep an open mind," sheriff's sergeant Roy Frank told KFMB-TV that day.

"Some of the psychologists will tell you, once that decision is made, there is an urge of self-preservation, and this is one way to preclude oneself from stopping an attempt to end their life," Coronado police Lieutenant Lou Scanlon said.

A few years after Michael Berger and Rebecca broke up, he emailed her to offer to return some photos of her in Nepal that she'd left at his house.

She wrote back from Arizona, saying that she would like them back, she wanted to talk to him, and she'd always loved him. But after he sent her the photos, he never heard anything more from her.

In July 2011, he was on a camping vacation in Utah, back from his studies in China, when a former karate student called with news of Rebecca's violent passing. Michael's first thought, and his brother's too, was that Neil was involved.

It took him four days to get his mind together and call the sheriff's department, describing himself as "the former boyfriend of Rebecca."

"I just got this news a couple of days ago, and . . . ," Michael said, his voice breaking, "I just wanted to see if I might offer some help. It's been really upsetting, because I was very close with her. It's just been really shocking and I want to do all that I can."

"What kind of help can you offer?" Detective Palmer replied.

A number of people had called in, saying they were this and that to Rebecca. Some panned out, some didn't. Palmer was skeptical by nature anyway, but this was the first he'd heard of Michael Berger since the investigation had begun eight days earlier.

Michael gave Palmer the short version of the abduction by her estranged husband, Neil, in Glendale, and encouraged the detective to call police there to back up his story.

"She was in constant fear of him, he had an abusive history, and he had abused her physically and emotionally," he said. "She was constantly threatened by him."

Palmer said he would be in touch. But as they hung up, Michael felt that the detective had been dismissive with him, just like the Glendale police.

After hearing nothing for several days, Michael called again, but still got nowhere. It was all very disheartening.

Michael wanted to tell the detectives that he didn't believe Rebecca committed suicide, that she would never have killed herself in such a degrading and revealing state—while naked, and bound with ropes. It didn't gibe with the woman he had known and loved so deeply.

Although she had a submissive personality, she seemed classy and wholesome to him, and had never shown any interest in rope-tying play or bondage. He couldn't even fathom how she'd done this to herself.

"How is that physically possible? She was smart, maybe she could have studied how to tie these knots, but being able to plan exactly how you're going to swing off that balcony? I don't see that. It's just so unlikely, so improbable," he said. "She was more [culturally] Asian to me. She was shy. She would not have done it nude like that."

To date, Michael has never felt the same love for anyone else, and hopes that by conveying his experience and observations that "maybe some justice will come as the result of it. Because I don't accept the way things are portrayed about what happened, and [the SDSD's] portrayal of her."

Chapter 26

Nina Romano and her son flew home to Tracy, California, on Saturday, July 16, returning the next day with her husband to help Dina pack up the Coronado house and head back to Arizona for Max's funeral.

Max was buried in Mt. Sinai Cemetery in Phoenix on July 20, a week after Rebecca's death.

To honor his son, Jonah renamed the private philanthropic organization he'd established in 1997 as Noah's Family Foundation to make it the Max A. Shacknai Foundation. The private organization, set up to help children's welfare causes, doesn't accept more than the occasional private donation from friends; the rest comes from the Shacknais.

Later in the year, Jonah also formed MaxInMotion, a not-for-profit foundation that gives scholarships to young athletes who want to participate in competitive soccer and hockey, as well as wheelchair soccer and basketball.

On Saturday, July 23, Rebecca's family and friends braved a heat wave to attend her memorial service and bury her remains at St. Joseph Memorial Park, near Missouri's northwestern border with Kansas.

Jonah, who paid for Rebecca's funeral and burial costs, caused a stir by showing up with an armed bodyguard, a former Secret Service agent hired by Medicis after its computer server was inundated with death threats and accusatory emails. The bodyguard was asked to wait in the car during the private service, but there was clearly concern that Jonah's safety was in danger, even in a small town halfway across the country.

Several hundred people attended the memorial, many of them Calvary Chapel members and Burmese refugees like the Zahaus, who arrived in buses from all over the country. A dozen or so of Rebecca's former coworkers and college friends came as well.

As Jonah sat in the front pew between Rebecca's parents, Snowem explained to him that the attendees were chanting in Burmese around the open casket as part of the ritual mourning ceremony.

Snowem watched her mother try unsuccessfully to take Jonah over to see Rebecca one last time in the open casket, where Rebecca was dressed in a dark dress with sequins or some type of sparkly sheen, and covered with a tribal blanket.

But Jonah didn't want to go, which made a poor impression on the Zahaus and raised their suspicions about his true character as the death investigation progressed.

It had been only a few days since he'd buried his son, following the organ donation. He'd already gone with Rebecca's family to the funeral home in San Diego to identify her body as it lay on a slab, so he didn't see the purpose of looking at her body again, especially when it was on display like that.

"It's not that I was standing in the back of the room," he said, "and I certainly wasn't averting my eyes disrespectfully."

Many of the buses and vans drove away after the service, leaving a smaller group to gather for the burial. Despite Snowem's claims that she saw no expression of sadness or grief on Jonah's part, he said he was actually in a "state of shock and deep sorrow" as he stood with Rebecca's parents at the graveside.

Her headstone reflected her full name, REBECCA "HNIANG-SINMAWII" ZAHAU, "SPRINGTIME BEAUTY" . . . GRANDDAUGHTER, DAUGHTER, SISTER AND FAVORITE AUNT.

She was the beauty of every season, her family wrote in a statement. *If you ever met Rebecca, you could not help but love her.*

Jennifer Watson, a college friend who came to the funeral, later told Detective Tsuida that none of Rebecca's friends believed she would have committed suicide because of the humiliation it would cause her family.

"She was a very sweet, just a person you can totally confide in, you can trust. She was a very dependable, sweet, genuine person," Jennifer said. "If she was going to take her life, I think she would have taken pills, nothing . . . so horrid."

In the days after the funeral, Rebecca's sister Mary and Jonah continued to console each other by text, sharing how much they missed Rebecca. Mary said she kept waiting for her to call: 'n everything will be okay.

Me too. I really need her now, Jonah wrote on July 28.

After the funeral, Snowem's feelings toward Jonah began to change. In a phone interview a couple of weeks later, she told Detective Angela Tsuida that she was concerned by Jonah's behavior during and after the service, which laid the groundwork for distrust that only worsened over time.

Snowem was put off by his rather abrupt denial when she asked if they'd secretly gotten married and brought up the papers that Rebecca said they'd both signed. Snowem also didn't like Jonah's perfunctory delivery of Rebecca's belongings in a couple of boxes, which she said he plonked down, unemotionally, on a desk right after the funeral.

"These are all I could find," she quoted him as saying.

This surprised Snowem, because Rebecca was not the tidiest person, and often left papers and personal items strewn around.

When Snowem looked in the box, she wondered why it contained no personal notes or paintings, such as the one of Max playing soccer, which she'd planned to give him as a gift. Or the white horse galloping in the wind, with his hair flying, the orchids, and the birds she painted. These were the keepsakes that Rebecca's family wanted.

Tsuida told Snowem that Jonah was likely in shock after losing his son and girlfriend just a few days apart.

"That's more than I would expect any person to be able to handle," she said. "I don't even think it has sunk in to him yet." To her, his being in "robotic mode" signaled that he was trying to keep moving forward with busywork "to just keep him from basically losing it."

Jonah explained recently that those first boxes contained financial paperwork pertaining to Rebecca's house and bank accounts, which Mary had asked, with some urgency, that he bring right away, along with Rebecca's guitar. He subsequently sent eight more boxes by FedEx, filled with her more personal effects, drawings, sketches—and lots of shoes. But they arrived in mid-August after Snowem had returned to Europe, so she was unaware of them.

Although she lived in Germany, Snowem said she and Rebecca had stayed in regular phone and email contact, and they were closer to each other than they were to their sister Mary.

"Angela, you don't know my sister. If you knew her, you would know that she would not do such a thing to herself," Snowem said. "Not this way, you know? I know her too well."

Snowem said the Zahau family had trust problems with the sheriff's department and investigation, because their only official notification of Rebecca's death had come from Jonah, with only a few more details from Adam. Snowem described this failure as "suspicious."

Tsuida explained that death notification was the medical examiner's duty. Hers was to process the death scene.

"When somebody else has a responsibility to notify the family, I just assume that that's being done, so I can do my job. So, if that wasn't, I apologize. I can't provide any excuses or reasons why that was not done."

But moving forward, Tsuida said, she wanted to better understand Rebecca, and learn who might have been angry with her or have a motive to kill her.

Snowem's first thought was *Of course, Dina,* given all the financial support she received from Jonah because of Max, which was immediately in jeopardy after his accident.

"The doctors even said that there was no hope, that's what Jonah told me," Snowem said, "which really surprised me, because Becky did not know that it was hopeless."

When she and Rebecca spoke and emailed after Max's fall, Rebecca said, essentially, "Everything's hopeful. Thanks for your prayers," and that they could talk more by phone on Wednesday.

Snowem said several other possible suspects also came to mind, including Adam. "It had to be someone in the family who knew that she was going to be alone, who knew that the doors were probably not even locked," she said.

Rebecca always laughed when Snowem asked why they never locked their doors in Coronado. "No one would rob you here," Rebecca replied. "No one is going to come in. Everyone leaves their door open."

She said Jonah was another possible suspect, because it had to be hard to lose a son.

"I just hope and believe," she said, pausing to sigh, "or want to believe, that it is not him, [but] someone else."

That said, to her, "This so much seems like a revenge for me. I might not be a detective or whatever, but I'm not stupid either, and I know my sister. She was happy with her life. She always had hope, of even the weirdest situation. She was so strong inside, and I could imagine her probably trying to fight back, or a struggle, even on that night."

When Tsuida pointed out that Snowem hadn't mentioned Neil, she said the thought had crossed her mind. But despite his inability to take care of Rebecca properly, to be a good husband, and to finish anything he started, Snowem said, "He loved her. He really loved her, you know? And because of his faith and belief in God, I knew that it couldn't be him."

Besides, he was in Arizona at the time, she said. "Of course, Neil was still hoping that she would come back to him one day, and now she's not."

Asked about the molestation that Neil had described, Snowem said it had happened multiple times at their parents' house, where visitors would put the girls in their laps and touch them inappropriately. She didn't mention whether this was in addition to the touching at the dean's house, or if those details were wrong.

"Like nowadays, you would probably sue them, and they would be sent to some kind of a psychiatric [facility]," she said. However, once the sisters grew up and looked back, they laughed about it, because they'd been too naive to know what was going on at the time.

Tsuida explained her reason for asking, noting that men sometimes fall in love with children they molest "and it almost becomes an obsession, even years down the line. You know, in his mind that might mean, like, 'Okay, you know, Snowem's mine now. She's going to be mine forever.'"

Asked if there was any particular person who might have been obsessed with Rebecca, Snowem said they were all old or had died by now.

"It is like a closed case for not only us kids, but for my family, my mom and dad as well," she said. "It is nothing that traumatized any of our lives, and I think that Becky would be able to say the same, and Mary and me as well."

Snowem said Rebecca never had issues with depression. In fact, she admired her sister's ability to stay so upbeat, positive, and hopeful. Instead of being unhappy, Rebecca would simply go to sleep. Snowem assumed that Rebecca needed a lot of rest because of all the long-distance running and bodysculpting she did.

To her knowledge, bedtime was the only time Rebecca got naked, and if she had guests, she would sleep in a T-shirt. "Never, ever in public," she said, which was why she thought Rebecca was killed by "someone who caught her in her sleep, in her bed."

When Tsuida asked if Rebecca had any boating, knitting, or crocheting knowledge that would help her tie knots, Snowem said no.

"Did she want to get married to Jonah?" Tsuida asked.

"Yes, she said they were getting married," Snowem said, but there was no exact date, and no rush, "because she had enough of that." Rebecca told their parents, "I just want to wait and see first how things go," possibly until the older kids left for college, so she and Jonah could start a new life together.

But after mulling that for a moment, Snowem reconsidered. "I actually don't even know or even remember Becky saying anything like they wanted to get married."

When Tsuida asked about Rebecca's desire to have kids, Snowem said they used to laugh about that too, because neither one of them wanted children.

"We were both like, 'Oh, no, us and kids? Never.' That was something between me and Becky. We said, we cannot imagine ourselves to be moms. And it stayed that way."

Snowem said they laughed again later, when she reminded Rebecca of those conversations. "Do you remember when you said that, and now you have three kids?"

"Yeah, I know," Rebecca replied.

When Rebecca was still with Neil, she had a miscarriage, bleeding so heavily at work that she had to go to the hospital,

Snowem said. But in the end, she was happy she didn't have a child with Neil. Rebecca's parents were angry at him for being such a bad husband that she had to run away from him, and that her life had to end this way.

Toward the close of the interview, Tsuida asked who stood out the most as someone who might harm Rebecca. Snowem came back to Adam, and perhaps even Jonah, though she didn't want to believe it, to seek revenge for Max's injuries.

Two weeks earlier, she said, she'd been mourning with Jonah. But after thinking more about it, if he had to be a suspect, then so be it. She didn't know much about him, but based on his seemingly cold behavior, she wondered how he truly felt about Rebecca.

What might "make him snap in his mind"? Had he insulted Rebecca in some way, or scolded her about what happened to Max?

All she knew was that Rebecca had loved and treated Jonah and his kids the best way she knew how, even when the rebellious teenagers acted out. And she found herself wondering, "They meant [a lot] to her, but now that she's dead, was it all in vain?"

Chapter 27

After a seven-week joint investigation by the SDSD and the Coronado Police Department, the agencies called a news conference to announce their findings on September 2, 2011.

Still hoping to write a book on the case, I asked to attend. However, I was told I couldn't come because I didn't have a press pass, which was only available to working media.

My hinky meter immediately went off, because I'd previously been admitted to other news conferences, such as the one following the arrest of sexual predator John Gardner, who ultimately pleaded guilty to raping and murdering teenagers Chelsea King and Amber Dubois. I'd also had a two-hour face-to-face interview with Sheriff Bill Gore for a book on that case, *Lost Girls*, which had painted a positive view of the SDSD.

What was so different this time? Were they wary of having a seasoned investigative journalist examine their findings?

Gore told reporters that his department "normally wouldn't comment on this type of investigation," but was doing so because of the "national and even international media coverage."

"Were these deaths the result of criminal conduct? Was Max's death a homicide?" Gore asked rhetorically. "The answer is no, it was a tragic accident. Was Rebecca's death a homicide? Again, the answer is no, it was a suicide . . . The conclusions presented today are based on good methodical investigative work and science. Science is our best witness in this case. Science is not biased and it does not lie . . . There's really no other logical explanation for what happened to her."

Sheriff Gore and Coronado police commander Mike Lawton outlined their theory of what happened to Max, based on the forensic evidence and an evaluation by a local biomechanics expert, Mark Gomez.

They said they believed Max was running down the hall on the second floor, where he frequently played, and "something caused him to trip." It could have been a ball, or the dog, but whatever it was caused him to fall over the railing near the top of the staircase. Max grabbed for the chandelier as he went down, which twisted him around so that his back smacked into the railing below. As he landed in the alcove next to the stairway, he went down to his knees and hit his head on the floor. Gore didn't mention the Razor scooter that first responders found lying on Max's leg.

Deputy Chief Medical Examiner Jonathan Lucas, who did both Max's and Rebecca's autopsies, said the cause of the boy's death was a contusion to the upper cervical spinal cord. The injuries to his forehead, under his right eye, and the midline fracture of the frontal bone indicated that he struck the carpeted floor face-first.

If these were the only injuries, Max could have survived, he said, but the fall caused his spinal cord to hyperextend and bend his head backward, which explained why paramedics found him without a pulse and not breathing.

Although they got his heart started again, the lack of oxygen to his brain caused irreversible damage. "He died of that brain damage five days later," Lucas said. "There was no evidence of a struggle," and the toxicology test detected "no alcohol, medications, or drugs."

* * *

Moving on to Rebecca, Sergeant Dave Nemeth said Rebecca listened to Jonah's voice mail at 12:50 A.M., indicating "Maxie's grave condition," then decided to "take her own life."

She went to the garage and found the rope among the boating items, leaving a space on the otherwise full shelf. Returning to the mansion, she either removed her clothing or was already naked, painted the message on the door, cut the rope into sections, placed the T-shirt around her neck, fashioned her bindings, leaned forward over the exterior balcony railing, and went over headfirst.

To show that this was possible, they played a videotape of a female deputy as she tied bindings—in front of her while seated—in a figure-eight fashion around her wrists. She pulled one hand out of the loop, put the bindings behind her, then inserted that hand back through the loop, tightening the slipknot by pulling down on the end of the rope. When Rebecca was found, Nemeth said, "the rope was still grasped in her fingers."

Fingerprints found on the entry door and its doorjamb, the balcony door, the chef's knife, and the bed leg where the rope was anchored were all Rebecca's, he said. DNA profiles taken from the bindings and the steak knife "were only from Rebecca."

The V-shaped impressions in the dust on the balcony floor, right outside the door and just short of the railing, were "consistent" with her feet and ankles being bound, as she hopped toward the railing, then leaned forward and went over it, "as if the toes had slipped backward."

The eleven-inch disturbance in the dust along the railing corresponded to the width of her petite hip bones, and the half-inch area cleared of dust was consistent with the rope rubbing where it went over the edge.

Without naming Snowem, Nemeth said a witness who had

seen Rebecca in January told investigators that Rebecca had lost weight, seemed stressed, was not sleeping well, and wasn't exercising, which wasn't normal for her, because she was a "health nut. She exercised a lot."

Rebecca also told this person "about problems she was having at the time," which were described in a journal entry on her cell phone. The detectives didn't release any further details about the journal.

"We received information from witnesses that Rebecca was distraught over Maxie's injury," Nemeth said. "No one witnessed this event. We don't know exactly how this event occurred. We don't know in what order things were done. The only person who can answer that, unfortunately, is deceased. Based on the evidence we received during the course of this investigation, this is the best conclusion we could come up with."

Lucas explained that Rebecca, like others who have bound themselves before committing suicide, tied her ankles together and wrists behind her so she didn't change her mind "midway through."

The "scattered abrasions on her back and her legs" were consistent with her body hitting the "large plants against the exterior of the house," he said. "There was no evidence of a struggle or a sexual assault, and there were no other significant injuries."

Lucas said it was easy to pull Rebecca's hand through the loose wrist binding. "I personally removed it and it was just a simple matter of slipping her hand out."

"I'll be the first to admit that this was a unique and unusual case," he said. "We have to look past the unusual appearance of the death and focus on the facts and the evidence."

Although Nemeth conceded that a message had been painted on the door, he said they weren't going to reveal what it was. There was also no discussion about the T-shirt gag stuffed into Rebecca's mouth.

The historic Spreckels Mansion in Coronado, California, was built by the county's wealthiest man, John D. Spreckels, in 1908. Rebecca Zahau's boyfriend, Jonah Shacknai, bought it for $12.75 million in 2007.
AUTHOR PHOTO.

The beachfront mansion, where Rebecca spent summers with Jonah and his three children, is surrounded by expansive, well-groomed homes. PHOTO BY SAN DIEGO COUNTY SHERIFF'S DEPARTMENT (SDSD).

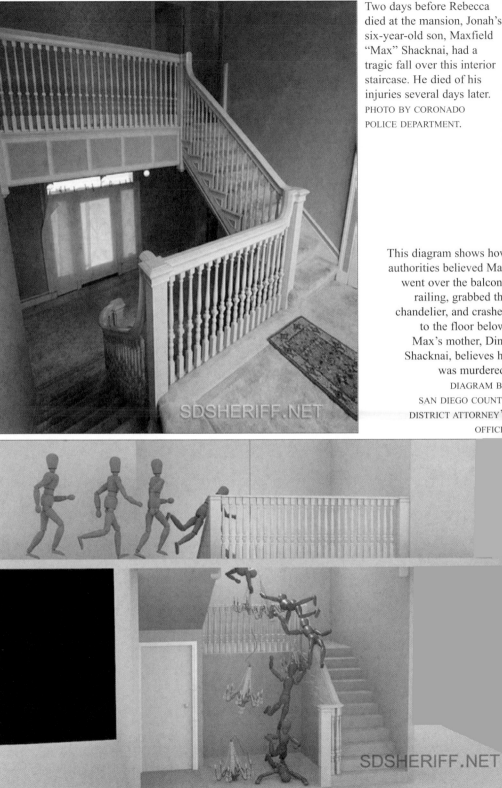

Two days before Rebecca died at the mansion, Jonah's six-year-old son, Maxfield "Max" Shacknai, had a tragic fall over this interior staircase. He died of his injuries several days later.
PHOTO BY CORONADO POLICE DEPARTMENT.

This diagram shows how authorities believed Max went over the balcony railing, grabbed the chandelier, and crashed to the floor below. Max's mother, Dina Shacknai, believes he was murdered.
DIAGRAM BY SAN DIEGO COUNTY DISTRICT ATTORNEY'S OFFICE

The beautiful ocean view from the Spreckels Mansion.
AUTHOR PHOTO.

The historic Hotel del Coronado, a local landmark, where famous films,
such as *Some Like It Hot*, were shot, is right down the street from the mansion.
AUTHOR PHOTO.

Jonah's brother, Adam Shacknai, said he cut Rebecca down from this exterior balcony after finding her hanging by a red nylon boating rope. PHOTO BY SDSD.

Adam was a considered a "person of interest" but was cleared after being questioned by SDSD detectives and taking a polygraph exam. POOL PHOTO BY NELVIN C. CEPEDA/*THE SAN DIEGO UNION-TRIBUNE.*

This cryptic message was painted on the door to the guest bedroom, where Rebecca's hanging rope was anchored to an antique-replica bed. PHOTO BY SDSD.

The rope was anchored to the left leg of the bed, went out the French doors, then over the balcony railing, from which Rebecca allegedly fell nine feet and two inches. PHOTO BY SDSD.

Investigators found two knives, a tube of black paint, and two paint brushes on the guest room floor. The same paint used to write the message on the door was also found on Rebecca's body, but on the backs of her hands, not her fingertips. PHOTO BY SDSD.

During the autopsy, the forensic pathologist preserved the knots taken from Rebecca's wrists, placing them on cardboard rolls. He said one side was loose enough to slip out of, while the other was tighter. PHOTO BY SDSD.

Before quitting her job six months before her death to take care of Jonah and Max, Rebecca worked as an ophthalmic technician at a Lasik eye center in Arizona.
PHOTO BY DWIGHT SMITH.

While separated from her husband in 2005, Rebecca dated and briefly lived with martial arts instructor Michael Berger in Glendale, California.
PHOTO BY MICHAEL BERGER

Shown here in 2005,
Rebecca was described
by friends and family
as a happy, loving,
athletic woman who
enjoyed body sculpting,
running, and hiking outdoors.
PHOTO BY MICHAEL BERGER.

After Rebecca disappeared
in April 2005, Michael reported
her missing to Glendale police.
She later told him that her
estranged husband, Neil Nalepa,
had kidnapped her.
PHOTO BY MICHAEL BERGER.

The Zahau family initially hired attorney
Anne Bremner to help them reopen
the criminal case into Rebecca's death
after the SDSD ruled it a suicide.
PHOTO BY THAI TAI STUDIO.

To this day, Sheriff Bill Gore firmly
believes Rebecca killed herself,
saying the SDSD's investigation was
based on science and forensic evidence.
AUTHOR PHOTO.

Rebecca's sister, Mary Zahau-Loehner, testified during a civil trial in 2018 that she believed Rebecca was murdered.

POOL PHOTO BY NELVIN C. CEPEDA/*THE SAN DIEGO UNION-TRIBUNE*.

Rebecca's mother, Pari Zahau, on the stand. She was so emotional that the family's attorney, Keith Greer, had her wait in the hallway outside the courtroom to avoid hearing the graphic details of her daughter's death.

POOL PHOTO BY JOHN GIBBINS/*THE SAN DIEGO UNION-TRIBUNE*.

Forensic specialist Lisa DiMeo testified that she believed Rebecca was sexually assaulted by a steak knife handle and that Rebecca tried to cut herself free from the bindings using a chef's knife, shown here. POOL PHOTO BY JOHN GIBBINS/*THE SAN DIEGO UNION-TRIBUNE.*

DNA expert Suzanna Ryan testified that DNA was missing from at least a dozen places where one would expect to find it, which was conistent with attorney Greer's theory that those areas had been wiped clean. POOL PHOTO BY NELVIN C. CEPEDA/*THE SAN DIEGO UNION-TRIBUNE.*

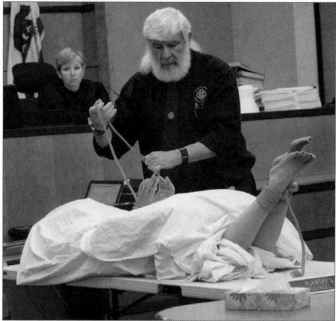

Knot expert Lindsey Philpott demonstrated on a mannequin, covered by a sheet, how the ropes around Rebecca's ankles were tied into complex knots. POOL PHOTOS BY NELVIN C. CEPEDA/*THE SAN DIEGO UNION-TRIBUNE.*

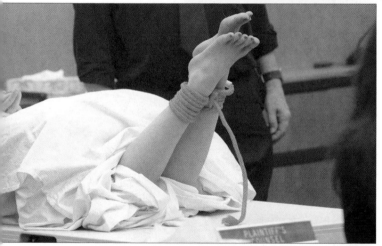

Dr. Cyril Wecht, a renowned forensic pathologist, testified that he believed Rebecca was hit over the head four times, manually strangled, then pushed over the balcony railing. POOL PHOTO BY NELVIN C. CEPEDA/*THE SAN DIEGO UNION-TRIBUNE.*

Forensic kinesiology expert James Kent demonstrated how Rebecca would have held the chef's knife to try to cut herself loose from behind, as attorneys Keith Greer and David Elsberg observed. AUTHOR PHOTO.

Adam, who has denied killing Rebecca, showed the jury how he held Rebecca's body against his own while cutting the rope above her head—as he stood on a patio table with a broken leg. POOL PHOTO BY NELVIN C. CEPEDA/*THE SAN DIEGO UNION-TRIBUNE*.

Adam's primary counsel, Daniel Webb, a former U.S. attorney and a high-profile corporate lawyer, repeatedly told the jury there was no physical evidence linking Adam to Rebecca's death.

POOL PHOTO BY NELVIN C. CEPEDA/*THE SAN DIEGO UNION-TRIBUNE.*

Forensic technician Denys Williams (now retired) testified about processing evidence items— including the steak knife, which had Rebecca's blood on the bottom portion of the handle— for fingerprints and DNA.

POOL PHOTO BY NELVIN C. CEPEDA/*THE SAN DIEGO UNION-TRIBUNE.*

Jonah Shacknai, who has since remarried, testified it was "inconceivable" that his brother would do physical violence to anyone. POOL PHOTO BY NELVIN C. CEPEDA/*THE SAN DIEGO UNION-TRIBUNE.*

Jonah was asked to demonstrate how he would tie up his boat at a dock, using the same type of red rope that was used to bind Rebecca's wrists, ankles, and neck. POOL PHOTO BY NELVIN C. CEPEDA/*THE SAN DIEGO UNION-TRIBUNE.*

Superior Court Judge Katherine Bacal said the sheriff's investigation raised as many questions as it answered and that it was reasonable to ask, "Who murdered Rebecca Zahau?"
POOL PHOTO BY NELVIN C. CEPEDA/*THE SAN DIEGO UNION-TRIBUNE.*

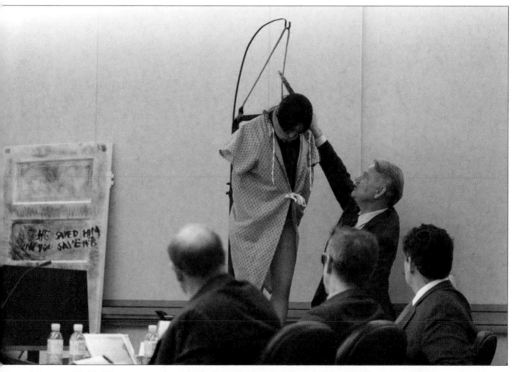

Attorney Keith Greer caused a stir during closing arguments by stringing up a lifelike nude mannequin, made to look like Rebecca, complete with painted toenails and marks corresponding to her injuries. POOL PHOTO BY NELVIN C. CEPEDA/*THE SAN DIEGO UNION-TRIBUNE.*

Greer gave a victory sign to media and Zahau family advocates after the jury verdict, finding Adam responsible for the wrongful death and battery of Rebecca Zahau, was announced. POOL PHOTO BY NELVIN C. CEPEDA/*TH SAN DIEGO UNION-TRIBUNE.*

After the verdict, Greer, Mary, and her husband, Doug Loehner, told reporters that they would continue to fight to get the criminal case reopened. POOL PHOTO BY NELVIN C. CEPEDA/*THE SAN DIEGO UNION-TRIBUNE.*

This case has always drawn tremendous media attention, as evidenced by the throng of reporters and news cameras at the postverdict news conference. POOL PHOTO BY NELVIN C. CEPEDA/*THE SAN DIEG UNION-TRIBUNE.*

When video of the news conference was posted on the sheriff's website, the hour-long question-and-answer session with
reporters after the presentation was missing. And because the
autopsy report wasn't released until later that day, reporters were
on their own to discern any omissions or discrepancies.

Dr. Lucas's written autopsy findings dovetailed with the sheriff's conclusion that Rebecca had committed suicide because
the balcony had no foot imprints other than hers: *[T]here was no
evidence that the decedent was bound against her will . . . no
sign of a physical struggle at the scene or on her body, and . . .
no toxicological evidence that she was sedated.*

The ensuing news stories quoted one notable critic, the na-
tionally renowned forensic pathologist Cyril Wecht, who had re-
examined the controversial deaths or murders of JonBenét
Ramsey, Anna Nicole Smith, and President John F. Kennedy.

After reading the autopsy report, Wecht questioned why further investigation wasn't done, saying it was premature to call
Rebecca's death a suicide in light of injuries such as the four
subgaleal hemorrhages under her scalp, which Lucas did not
question.

Lucas's response: "Because there was evidence that she went
over the balcony in a nonvertical position, she may have struck
her head on the balcony on the way down."

Wecht disagreed, saying he saw no evidence of that. He also
noted the suspicious presence of sticky tape residue on Rebecca's legs. "Are we to think she first bound her legs with duct
tape, but took it off to use rope instead?"

In a subsequent news release, Lucas offered explanations
for questions that had come in: The one-inch span and positioning of tape residue "would have been unusual for evidence
of leg binding." The blood on Rebecca's inner thighs was either from her menstrual period or spotting from her intrauter-

ine birth control device, known as an IUD. And the blood on her big toes appeared to have been from small scratches caused by the foliage—a green leafy tree and a tall, somewhat neglected cactuslike succulent, apparently a *Euphorbia ingens*, below the balcony.

Still, the overall suicide findings were enough to send out waves of shock and surprise, not just to Rebecca's family, but to the community at large. As I looked back years later, it was remarkable how few details of the investigation were initially released to the public, and how many questions were left unanswered.

Although this orchestrated public relations presentation was designed to squash public debate and speculation, the official conclusions only resulted in criticism and challenges—that ultimately went all the way to the courtroom—for many years to come.

After the news conference, Jonah Shacknai issued a statement thanking the SDSD, the first responders, and the medical team at Rady Children's Hospital, "who worked tirelessly to try to save Max's life."

While the investigation is over, the emptiness and sadness in our hearts will remain forever, it read in part. *Max was an extraordinarily loving, happy, talented, and special little boy. He brought joy to everyone who knew him, and we will miss him desperately. Rebecca too was a wonderful and unique person who will always have a special place in my heart. Nothing will ever be the same for our families after these losses, but with today's information providing some much-needed answers, we will try to rebuild our lives and honor the memories we carry with us.*

Jonah clearly wanted to move on, but the Zahaus would not accept this outcome. They expressed disbelief. Sadness. And soon, indignant outrage.

* * *

"My sister did not commit suicide," Mary Zahau-Loehner told NBC. "She was murdered . . . She would not have exposed herself, knowing that everybody would see her that way."

"There was no search on the internet for this type of suicide," she added. "There was nothing on her computer, nothing that even showed that she even looked for this type of binding . . . I mean, I love my sister and she was smart in a lot of ways. But Becky was not smart in that kind of sense."

Although Mary had reached out to Jonah for mutual comfort early on, she, like Snowem, had begun to view him and his relationship with Rebecca differently. Recalling that she'd never seen him be affectionate toward her sister, she wasn't even sure whether he'd ever truly been in love with Rebecca.

Rebecca's mother Pari spent her days crying and praying, while her husband, Robert, remained stoic and silent. Pari couldn't understand how the authorities could have reached this conclusion.

"Why would they say that?" Pari told the *San Diego Reader*. "That she committed suicide? Our family is hurting. We're a poor family. We can't pay for investigators. My husband says nothing. All his feelings are trapped inside. But we know for sure, she wouldn't ever kill herself. And she was very modest. It is our Asian way. She would never do a thing like that, and never without clothes on. But nobody will listen to us."

When Robert died in July 2013, his family believed it was from a broken heart. Deep in grief, the Zahaus remained upset for years that they weren't consulted in any meaningful way before the authorities made up their minds. When they did talk to them, Mary said, Detective Tsuida said it may look like it was a homicide, but there were "no signs of foul play."

"In the entire investigation they talked to me only once, to ask me a few questions, but basically to convince me that it was a suicide. It bothers me," Mary told the *Reader*. "Why isn't our family asked about *who* Becky was?"

The sheriff's timeline for Rebecca's death also didn't make sense to them. Jonah's call came shortly before 1:00 A.M., and if the time of death was estimated to be between 1:00 and 3:00 A.M., why was there still food in Rebecca's stomach?

Depending on what and how much a person eats, it can take four to six hours to fully digest a meal, and after having little appetite at the Fish Market, Rebecca may not have eaten anything substantive even after she got home around 8:00 P.M. Yet her stomach contained "2 cc of thick, green material."

"You are trying to convince me that my sister came up with this elaborate plan in less than two hours?" Mary asked.

Sheriff Gore had this response: "Sometimes family members hear what they want to hear."

Chapter 28

The Zahaus were determined to find a different agency to investigate Rebecca's death as a homicide, but they needed help—because they had no way to pay for it. The family launched the first of several online fund-raising campaigns to subsidize a private investigation into Rebecca's death, but none of them raised much.

Hearing of their plight, attorney Anne Bremner stepped in and offered to help the family pro bono.

"This was a family of little means," she said. "That didn't stop me from seeking justice for them. It's sad when the criminal justice system fails families and they have to seek counsel and investigate the cases involving their loved ones."

Bremner went on TV to explain why she and the Zahaus believed Rebecca was murdered, and accused Jonah Shacknai of having undue influence over the investigation because of his wealth. Those statements triggered a cease-and-desist letter from Chicago-based attorney Dan Webb, one of the nation's most prominent corporate litigators.

In the letter, which Bremner released to the media, Webb warned her to stop making "inaccurate and utterly unsupported statements" about the facts surrounding the deaths of Max and

Rebecca that were not only "highly insensitive," but also defamed Jonah, his client.

What is most concerning are recent false statements you have made that Mr. Shacknai, because of his business success, has somehow improperly influenced the investigations and conclusions of four different, and independent, California law enforcement agencies, he wrote. *Mr. Shacknai was not advancing any particular outcome regarding Rebecca Zahau's cause of death, because he had absolutely no knowledge of what happened the night she died.*

Jonah recently explained that Bremner and her client, author Ann Rule, were both sent letters warning them that they had an obligation to determine the truth of the facts before making public accusatory statements, or they could be sued.

"It's horribly offensive and upsetting that anyone would imagine that I had anything to do with Rebecca's death, which, in fact, was a suicide," he said.

But in Bremner's mind, sending those letters only raised more questions. "I thought that was weird," she said. "It was my opinion, why do that, unless Jonah had something to hide?"

Also, she said, "They don't have full surveillance of him at the hotel [that night]. It could be argued that it was a concocted alibi for him."

Jonah's response: "I think we can say I hold Anne Bremner in very low regard and don't take anything she says at face value. She's proven herself to be bombastic and sensational with no genuine interest in this case other than her own self-promotion."

Calling Jonah's remark about her "beyond insulting," Bremner countered that she reached out to help the Zahaus get to the truth of what happened to Rebecca, but made no money from it.

Private citizens, such as Pri Goslin, of La Jolla, also stepped up to help, posting a petition on change.org to request that California Attorney General Kamala Harris open a new criminal investigation. Goslin's petition accused the authorities of racial discrimination and urged Harris to open an independent investigation that encompassed the Zahaus' outside experts.

Perceived as an investigation biased against minorities, in particular Asians, the manner in which the San Diego Sheriff's Office has handled this case reflects poorly upon San Diego, Goslin wrote.

Calling the sheriff's evidence "flawed," she claimed that detectives prematurely decided that Rebecca had taken her own life within forty-eight hours of her death, "regardless of the bizarre circumstances" and all "evidence pointing elsewhere."

The petition drew 1,562 supporters, but did nothing to persuade authorities to change their findings. In 2020, Harris became the first woman and second person of color to be voted vice-president-elect.

Neil Nalepa also posted his own petition online calling for a review: *It is my believe [sic] that not only did Rebecca and her family not receive justice that day, but the public was also asked to swallow this information and believe it as well.*

Realizing that the Zahaus and the media weren't going to go away quietly, Jonah sent a letter to Kamala Harris on September 19. He requested that Harris's office review the SDSD's and Coronado's "investigatory methods and conclusions" in this case—not because he didn't believe it was a suicide, but to help the public accept the integrity of the investigation and to bring "clarity, dignity, and, ultimately, closure" to Max and Rebecca's deaths.

The heartbreak of these losses, as anyone might imagine, is unbearable, Jonah wrote. Although he and his family had been trying to grieve in private: *[T]he unrelenting and often vicious speculation and innuendo in certain media outlets continue to bring further pain to everyone who has been touched by these tragic events.*

Sending his deepest sympathy to Rebecca's family, Jonah said he understood all too well "the limitless pain" they were going through because he, too, had lost a child. Although he was satisfied that the authorities' findings were "sound, scientific, and supported by a thorough and competent investigation," he acknowledged that the Zahaus and others were not.

He accused "certain media outlets" of exploiting the unanswered questions for ratings, saying this had only fueled more speculation and caused more pain, as well as "unfounded rumors and accusations."

The state AG's office responded to Jonah's letter within two days, declining his "invitation" to review the investigation. It said such an inquiry would be done only under "very narrow circumstances," such as a conflict of interest, a request for assistance or exhaustion of resources by local law enforcement, and allegations of "gross malfeasance by the investigative agency."

That same week, ten news agencies from the San Diego and Phoenix areas joined to ask the court to unseal search warrants from the case.

Right before a hearing on the matter, however, the court unexpectedly released several warrant affidavits, revealing new details of who was where and when in the hours before Rebecca's death, and that the sheriff's polygraph examiner had found Adam Shacknai to be "truthful" during his test.

The words painted on the door also leaked out, though sheriff's officials still would not, or could not, explain their meaning, let alone why Rebecca would have left a message written in the third person and with such an angry, taunting tone. Her family insisted that it looked and sounded nothing like her writing.

"You can speculate endlessly about the note on the door," sheriff's lieutenant Larry Nesbit told *The Daily Beast*. "It is somewhat cryptic. It is not clear-cut—I will say that . . . It could mean any one of several things."

* * *

After submitting a request for all the sheriff's investigative case files under the Crime Victims' Rights Act, Anne Bremner began to compile a team of experts, including pathologist Cyril Wecht, to come up with new evidence, witnesses, and theories. But unable to take the case any further on her own from Seattle, she enlisted the help of attorney Marty Rudoy in Sherman Oaks, California.

The SDSD subsequently released some case files to them, but as tensions in the war of rhetoric escalated, the agency also sent a letter in late October, warning them not to release any portion "to the public, to the media, or anyone else, unless there later develops a law enforcement necessity to do so."

If the Zahaus publicly released documents "piecemeal" and portrayed the department or its investigation "in a false light," the agency threatened to "correct the false portrayal by opening the entire investigation for public scrutiny."

Not knowing what evidence the sheriff was holding on to, Bremner and Rudoy saw this as "an implied threat in the letter that they would release information hurtful to the victim and her family," Rudoy said. "It has chilled our willingness to release relevant information to the media that would help the public determine what happened in this case."

Instead, Bremner and Rudoy enlisted the aid of Phil McGraw, whose afternoon TV show, *Dr. Phil,* frequently features victims and others involved in high-profile crime cases, especially those involving mental-health issues.

In turn, private investigator Paul Ciolino, of Chicago, was hired to do interviews and examine evidence collected by sheriff's investigators.

"I was one of the first people to say this is bulls—t," Ciolino said recently of the suicide finding and "the crime scene as presented by [Jonah's] brother," who, in Ciolino's mind, was "the guy who committed this murder."

First of all, he said, the patio table Adam used to cut Rebecca down was unstable. With only three working legs, it likely would have collapsed under Adam's weight, coupled with the deadweight of Rebecca's body, because "she's not cooperating."

"A world-class gymnast is not going to climb on this table and hold their balance while doing all these activities," he said, "holding up a one-hundred-pound woman and cut[ting] through a ski rope with a knife, without falling, crashing, or otherwise really having some sort of accident where you're going to leave injuries or marks on the person."

He also didn't believe Adam's story, that he flew across the country to support his brother at the hospital, but then went to the mansion to rest, and yet still had time to watch porn on his phone.

"That would never happen in most families," he said. "If it was me, I'd say, 'bro, get up, let's go to the hospital, I need you there.'"

Ciolino faulted the sheriff's department for not doing a more thorough job of processing the scene for DNA, with Adam in mind as a suspect.

"The so-called interrogation of this guy was horribly lacking, and it was inexcusable not to [seize] his phone," he said, adding that there was a reasonable explanation for why Adam's DNA wasn't found on the rope or knife, which he admitted to touching.

"They didn't look hard enough there, because there's a thing called touch DNA, and if you handled it, then your DNA is going to be on there," he said, unless, of course, the killer was wearing gloves.

The sheriff's video re-creating how Rebecca could have tied herself up didn't convince him, either.

"She's not Houdini and there's not a chance that she practices anything like that before," he said. "It's absurd that you'd think this girl did this." No educated, world-traveled, semiprofessional woman like Rebecca would commit an "over-the-top suicide" like this one.

"The rope thing—it's ridiculous. Naked—I don't care how hot she was. Women do not display their bodies when they commit suicide like that. They may if they're in the bathtub and overdose. They don't want people to be gawking at their body like that, and this woman displayed no prior signs of suicide that I'm aware of."

The sheriff's department "bum-rushed this thing for whatever reason, and they wanted their results to be the only ones looked at," he said. "They did an investigation that would show that it was a suicide, and they didn't want to hear anything else."

But he said he didn't believe Jonah "had anything to do with it. I think Jonah was too busy dealing with his son's tragedy. The motive is [Adam] sexually assaulted her, she said no, and then now we have a problem. The quickest and easiest way to solve that problem is to kill her."

The suicide findings also generated rampant speculation online about who, how, and why Rebecca had been murdered in what looked to many to be a ritualistic killing. Armchair detectives flocked to internet forums and blogs to discuss their theories and suspicions and to raise unanswered questions based on the scant evidence that authorities had released.

How did Rebecca become an expert in such complex knot tying and know exactly how long to cut the rope to hang herself, but not touch the ground?

How exactly did she get herself over the railing with her ankles bound together and her hands tied behind her back?

Why was the lividity spread across her back and not in her feet, where it would be if she'd been hanging vertically for hours?

Why were investigators photographed by the media taking a picture frame and a rolled-up rug out of the house, and yet they weren't cited on the list of evidence items taken from the mansion?

Why were items that detectives found in the guest house—makeup wipes, clear liquid on a nightstand, and a pair of women's panties—not tested?

How did investigators know for sure that Adam had slept there that night?

Fueled by the continued public interest in the case, KFMB-TV reporters staged several "unscientific reenactments" of the hanging scenario, which sheriff's detectives never even attempted. They used a punching bag the same weight as Rebecca's body, then added weight to more than compensate for the mass of the mattress and bed frame, which was identified by the original manufacturer as a queen-sized "Imperial 61" antique replica.

Based on those experiments, they said, the bed at the mansion should have moved as much as five times farther from the wall if Rebecca had truly flung herself over the railing.

Anne Bremner also hired Maurice Godwin, a forensic crime scene expert from Fayetteville, North Carolina, to examine the death scene evidence, and he, too, concluded that Rebecca was murdered.

The fact that he saw no "drag or brush pattern" on the carpet from the bed frame was a red flag, because it indicated that the bed was lifted off the carpet and placed down manually as part of a staged suicide scene.

Godwin also didn't see any clear impressions of heels and toes in the two areas of the balcony floor, where detectives said Rebecca had been standing and then hopped to the railing. In fact, he said, he didn't see a print of her left foot at all. He believes the assailant lifted her from the bedroom to the balcony, set her down for a minute while he got a better grip—allowing only her right big toe to touch the ground near the railing—then picked her up again to push her over.

Even Michael Macceca, the criminalist who made a diagram of the prints on the balcony, testified that he didn't see two clear sets of heel and toe prints on the balcony. He said he plainly saw prints in a V-shape just outside the French doors, but no definitive set near the railing.

"I don't think that's a heel," Macceca said.

Godwin said he also found two additional sole prints, with ridges a quarter-inch apart, that investigators missed because one of them was partially underneath Officer Langlais's boot mark. He said the print matched the ridged sole of an EVA (ethylene vinyl acetate) copolymer flip-flop, and he found others in front of the French door, indicating that a third person stood behind Rebecca on the balcony, and stepped on top of her foot impressions.

"I do think it was a murder," he said recently. "In my opinion, I don't think that somebody would strip naked and tie a cord around their neck to hang themselves over the death of a child. That's unrealistic to me, and it's way out of character for what a female would do to kill themselves. I just don't think it was a suicide at all. There was somebody else in that room that night with her, and I think some of the evidence shows that."

Attorney Marty Rudoy suggested that the dirt and sand on the soles of Rebecca's feet were more consistent with the garden soil than the dust on the balcony, noting there were also no muddy footprints on the bedroom carpet.

This led him to offer yet another possible murder scenario: Her killer manually strangled her in the garden. Then, after calculating the length of rope needed, he hoisted her up. This theory would explain why her neck wasn't broken in the fall, and why she wasn't decapitated.

"The person who wrote the message [on the door] knew that no one could save her, because she was either dead already or going to be dead within a few minutes," Rudoy said. "I think the sheriff wanted to end the speculation with suicide, because it's real convenient for the community."

According to the owner of Websleuths, an estimated 90 percent of people posting on the website's forums on the case thought Rebecca had been murdered. As of 2019, Websleuths had more than 137,000 members all over the world, and more than 12 million posts.

"Websleuths members, in general, have a lot of common sense," said owner Tricia Arrington Griffith. "Early on, first looking at this case from a common-sense way made it just impossible to come up with any other conclusion . . . It just seemed like there was no other answer.

"I think it will go down as one of the weirdest cases in American crime," she said. "It's just too wacky," with too many holes in the "suicide" scenario.

Griffith said she tried to remain neutral, but some members advocated the "suicide" theory in such a confrontational and personal way that she felt she had to remove their posts, and shut down some threads altogether.

She couldn't prove it, but she believed that some of these people were Shacknai family members, their friends, or part of Adam's defense team, posting as "anonymous," or under a fake name, to try to sway public opinion.

"Why are they so bent on disrupting?" she wondered. "This is just a discussion. They were so vicious."

Similar threads were found on Reddit, Tapatalk, and in the comment section below news articles about the case. Some of those advocating the murder scenario named Jonah, Adam, Nina, and Dina as possible killers, and ascribed various motives to different scenarios, while others suggested wild conspiracy theories based on scant details that had come out online, some of which didn't accuse people by name:

Max and Rebecca were both killed in an outside hit because of hatred, jealousy, or revenge related to Jonah's business dealings.

Rebecca and Max were both murdered, but under unrelated circumstances, by different people with separate motives.

Jonah killed Rebecca, with or without Adam's help, or hired a hit man to do it, because he blamed Rebecca for his son's injuries.

Dina or Nina, together or acting alone, killed Rebecca, with or without Adam's help, after a confrontation to get more information about Max's fall went awry, because they blamed her for his injuries.

Adam killed Rebecca, alone or with Jonah, for revenge for "allowing" or enabling Max's fall.

Rebecca was murdered, and her bindings looked like bondage porn. If people believed that a deranged killer was out to get Jonah and his loved ones, then more people would have sympathy for him, rather than see him as a suspect.

The killer has yet to be identified, and we may never know who killed Rebecca, but her injuries simply don't fit with suicide.

Jonah, Adam, Dina, and Nina were all cleared by the authorities. Adam and Jonah both proclaimed their innocence, saying

Rebecca killed herself. Dina said she believed Rebecca and Max were murdered, but Adam was not involved. Dina, who denied killing Rebecca—as did her sister, Nina—didn't respond to repeated attempts via email, letter, and through various associates to interview her for this book. Neither did Nina.

Some of the speculation about Jonah's involvement may have stemmed from small-town scuttlebutt over previous clashes with his neighbors and local preservationists over his proposed modifications to the Spreckels Mansion. Also, as a self-made pharmaceutical tycoon, his success and wealth made him a target for conspiracy theories.

Although the mansion was never listed on the National Register of Historic Places, its city designation as a "historic resource" in 2006 enabled the owner to get tax breaks under a state law known as the Mills Act. In exchange for an assessed value of only $5 million, the owner had to agree to maintain the architectural integrity.

Shortly after Jonah bought the historic home for nearly $13 million in 2007, he applied for a permit to change the interior and exterior. As he explained to the mayor over coffee, he believed the house had deteriorated so much that it needed to be restored.

After Jonah's first proposal was rejected in 2008, he returned with a scaled-down version in July 2010. He acknowledged that his previous attempt had been "extraordinarily controversial," drawing considerable vitriol from the locals.

"Every time there was a hearing, they kicked up a lot of dust," he said of the ten to fifteen activists who lobbied to maintain the status quo. "I'm sure they were sincerely motivated."

Jonah told the Coronado Historic Resource Commission that although he lived much of the year in Arizona, he'd been a homeowner in town for more than a decade, and intended to relocate his family there in four or five years. Offering to surrender his tax benefits, he said he didn't expect to be treated any differently than someone who had lived there for thirty years.

Among the proposed changes or additions to the main house: a new seven-hundred-square-foot master suite, replacement or repairs to all wood-framed windows, a new series of French doors, awnings over the front windows to restore a historic feature to the mansion, and a thirty-inch stucco wall just inside the front sidewalk.

As Jonah handed out booklets to the commissioners, some were put off by his approach, which they saw as patronizing and condescending.

"This was such overkill that it was almost like, 'The way I'm presenting this to you yokels, of course you're going to approve it,'" Coronado businesswoman Kris Grant said, describing the sentiments of two members who confided in her.

Jonah also irritated neighbors such as Jeff Allison, who complained that Jonah accepted the tax break and the rules that went with buying the house, but then immediately expected the city to make exceptions for him.

"I thought he was as arrogant as hell. It was his way or the highway," said Jeff, whose wife, Marsha, claimed to have heard a scream the night Rebecca died.

Jonah's permit was approved by the commission in the summer of 2010, and formally granted by the city council that December—with the exception of the master suite addition.

Within two months, Jonah submitted another permit application, this time asking to modify the guest house and caretaker cottage. Approved by the council in May, the permit allowed him to connect the top floor of the main house with a bridge to the caretaker cottage, replace and modify other windows, add an outdoor staircase leading to the terrace, add more French doors, and upgrade the garage door.

Rebecca had video on her computer of one of the applications being approved. However, the remodeling work had yet to start by the time of her death.

The home was more like "a run-down beach house you'd find in OB," Sheriff Gore said, referring to the lower-scale neighborhood of Ocean Beach. "That house was a mess . . . not what you'd think of *the* Spreckels Mansion. The bathrooms had mold around the tubs."

Chapter 29

Gearing up for a two-part *Dr. Phil* show that aired November 14 and 15, 2011, the Zahau family had Rebecca's body exhumed for a second autopsy, subsidized by the producers.

After telling Jonah the family didn't even want the first autopsy, Mary Zahau-Loehner said it was difficult to do a second one.

"I feel like my sister hasn't rested yet," she said. "I don't feel like I have an answer for her, as far as what happened. But when we did exhume her, it felt like day one again."

The show featured the coffin being dramatically pulled from the ground, still adorned with flowers, and shipped to Dr. Cyril Wecht's forensic pathology lab in Pittsburgh.

"The findings lead me to express grave and serious doubts about the conclusion that the manner of death was suicide," Wecht concluded.

Again, he pointed to the four subgaleal hemorrhages under her scalp, which he said indicated blunt-force trauma. He also noted the absence of severe injury to the neck and spine, saying that "if [the] body had just plummeted down [nine feet over the balcony], then the cervical vertebrae would have been dislocated from the base of the skull."

Based on the spatial relationship between her nearly sixty-four-inch height and a balcony that was thirty-six inches high, he said her center of gravity was too low for her to simply bend over the railing and fall. The prospect of a woman plummeting over a balcony naked also didn't make sense to him.

"In all of my autopsies, I can't remember a case where a woman commits suicide, nude, in an outdoor environment. Women just do not do these things," he said. "I lean very strongly toward it being a homicide."

All of this "cries out for an explanation" and further investigation, he said, calling for the manner of death to be changed to "undetermined" rather than "suicide."

Attorney Anne Bremner also poked holes in the SDSD investigation, accusing the agency of ignoring important leads and failing to do proper testing and analysis of DNA and other evidence, such as blood found in the master bathroom shower.

"They didn't look at a pair of woman's underwear in a garbage can in the guest house. They didn't look at black gloves at the scene," she said, referring to a pair of garden gloves found on the living-room coffee table, one of which had two different DNA contributors on it.

Rebecca's death, she declared, was "a homicide masquerading as a suicide."

In a written statement, the SDSD said that neither it, nor the ME's office, had seen the second-autopsy findings or other objections discussed on the show:

If Dr. Wecht or Miss Bremner would like to share information they believe is pertinent with our investigators, we would be glad to meet with them, rather than hear their results on television, presented as entertainment.

After months of investigating the case, the Zahaus' attorneys, who also included Marty Rudoy's partner, David Fleck, sent a request to the state AG's office in January 2012, asking for a new criminal investigation into Rebecca's death. The request was denied, saying the attorneys needed to first approach the sheriff's office, and if refused, they should go to the district attorney.

Denied by the SDSD, the Zahaus' attorneys submitted a confidential request that April to the DA, Bonnie Dumanis, offering several of the reasons cited by the AG that would allow for a new investigation into Rebecca' death, including a conflict of interest and "gross malfeasance" by the SDSD.

In a twenty-four-page report, with just as many pages of attachments, the attorneys listed a number of instances that posed a conflict of interest by the county government agencies investigating this case.

The attorneys cited a report that on the same day in November 2011 that they'd been scheduled to meet with Gore, the sheriff allegedly met with Jonah Shacknai later in the day. The attorneys acknowledged that they were unable to confirm the meeting occurred, but they were concerned that the sheriff may have had a special relationship with Jonah nonetheless.

They also accused Gore, who formerly headed the FBI's San Diego office and was one of the special agents in charge at the Ruby Ridge siege in 1992, of having a conflict of interest with Jonah's attorney, Dan Webb. Webb, who later went on to represent Adam Shacknai at the Zahau trial, had also represented one of Gore's FBI colleagues and codefendants in the legal battle that erupted after Ruby Ridge, and filed court papers with Gore's attorney.

Finally, the Zahau attorneys' letter underscored that the sheriff's and ME's offices had jointly concluded that Rebecca's death was a suicide, a finding that was based on circular reasoning of each other's "flawed analysis of the situation."

But DA Dumanis denied the request to conduct a new investigation.

Asked about these claims recently, Jonah described them as "completely fabricated." He said he had no reason to meet with

Sheriff Gore in November 2011. In fact, he didn't remember ever meeting him face-to-face, even though Gore recalled meeting with Jonah once out of the office.

"I'm sure I've never met him in person," Jonah said. "We talked about having a cup of coffee someday, because I truly felt awful that he has taken so much criticism and been abused over this investigation, when to me, he's always been earnest, forthright, and sympathetic to the losses our family took on."

Chapter 30

The Zahaus weren't the only ones who were upset by the findings by the SDSD and Coronado police. Still convinced that Rebecca had more to do with Max's fall than she'd admitted, Dina Shacknai hired her own team of experts to look into the biomechanics related to her son's physical injuries.

When she was refused investigative documents and autopsy photos concerning Max's case, Dina filed a lawsuit against the County of San Diego and its chief medical examiner, seeking to force their release in March 2012.

Dina forwarded the materials to Dr. Judy Melinek, a forensic pathologist in San Francisco, who had worked at the chief medical examiner's office in New York during 9/11, and Robert T. Bove Jr., an injury biomechanics expert in Philadelphia, who had worked with the Central Intelligence Agency (CIA).

After studying the evidence independently and also in collaboration, Melinek and Bove both disputed law enforcement's conclusion that Max's death was an accident.

First, Max weighed only forty-four pounds, not fifty-seven as the autopsy report stated, and he stood forty-five inches tall. Because his center of gravity was below the railing, they said it was highly unlikely that he could have thrown himself over it or had worked up enough momentum to be thrown, even with the four-inch boost of standing on his scooter.

Melinek's report concluded that the boy had been assaulted and was the victim of a homicide, meaning that "he died at the hand of another," and that the evidence supported "Rebecca Zahau's direct involvement." This was based on Rebecca's "apparent suicidal death" two days after the fall, "inconsistencies in her verbal reports about the incident," her comment that "Dina's going to kill me," her statement to Nina that Max had fallen from the upstairs bedroom, and the multiple planes of injury on the child's body.

Melinek noted that the pattern of bruising on Max's back, which looked like the number seven, lined up with the protrusions on the wooden railing and ornate legs beneath it, known as balusters, as if he'd been pushed against them. She cited a statement by an unnamed witness who claimed that Rebecca "had a quick temper and knew jujitsu," would put this person "in a hold," and require a "tap out" to be released.

Bove said he ruled out the accident scenario because it was inconsistent with Max's injuries, but he couldn't say exactly what happened to the boy, either. He also wouldn't take a position on whether the incident was intentional, who was at fault, or the nature of the "initiating event."

He noted there was new damage on top of the banister railing and the "corner spindle" where the staircase descended from the second floor, as well as some white paint flakes near the corner, which reportedly had not been there the day before Max's fall. The right front wheel and frame of Max's scooter also had several corresponding "white transfer marks" on both faces of the wheel, the largest of which was two inches long.

The location of this damage, he said, didn't fit with law enforcement scenarios that Max had fallen while running down the hallway or while riding his scooter into the second-floor railing, and then tumbled over the top of it. By the same token, he said, neither scenario was consistent with the scooter landing on top of his right shin.

The chandelier, Bove said, had been hanging by a gold-colored metal chain of oval-shaped links, one of which broke apart. Investigators found a single broken link on the landing between the first and second floors, not on the first floor, directly below where the chandelier had been hanging. This indicated that the chain broke where it attached to the top of the chandelier, and the link fell as Max swung from the chandelier.

Melinek said she couldn't tell from photographs alone whether that "link would suffer metal fatigue with a yank produced by a forty-four-pound falling child," or if it would require the "assistance of a greater weight."

But if Max had toppled over the banister and grabbed the chandelier on his way down, why didn't he have any cuts on his hands? Also, given the injury to his basal ganglia, the lateral bruise across his back, and the subgaleal hemorrhage on his head, why didn't he have any brain bleeding?

Max's toxicology report showed that he had a "presumptive positive benzodiazepine screen," but Jonah said that turned out to be a lab error that wasn't reflected in the autopsy report.

The autopsy report also showed that the boy's stomach contained 30 cc of black liquid, "consistent with charcoal," which is typically administered if a patient may have ingested a toxic substance, because it helps block poisons from being absorbed into the bloodstream. Jonah had no idea why Max was given charcoal, but said it may have been "part of the organ donation process," because he'd received "dozens of medications every day."

Like Jonah, Dina started her own nonprofit organization to honor her son's memory. In July 2012, she launched Maxie's HOUSE, an acronym for Hope, Outreach, Understanding, Safety, and Education, the purpose of which was to protect the emotional and physical well-being of children who, like Max, lived in "blended" families under shared-custody arrangements.

"Maxie's legacy reminds us of how undeniably important it is that every child has the right to be safe in their own home, wherever that home is," Dina said at a news conference.

Jonah said he never supported the premise of Dina's organization, because it stemmed from the claim that Rebecca had done something to harm Max, which he believed was "completely flawed."

"The whole intellectual basis was kind of a fraud, and she herself in time retreated from that point of view," he said recently.

By 2019, the website for Dina's foundation was no longer active.

While Dina's experts were looking into Max's death, Jonah hired his own consultants to do the same. The report he commissioned, issued in August 2012 by Kroll Inc., supported the findings by local law enforcement that Max's fall was an accident.

The evidence is consistent with an accidental tragic fall, with no evidence of foul play, malice or other non-accidental occurrence, the Kroll report stated. *Although no police investigation is perfect or error-free, and while aspects of any police investigation can benefit from 20/20 hindsight, we have identified no legitimate reason to question the findings and conclusions of law enforcement in this case.*

During the investigation, Jonah said, he purposely had no contact with Kroll to ensure the assessment would be conducted independently. The consulting firm, based in New York, is headed by William "Bill" Bratton, the former head of both the Los Angeles and New York Police Departments.

In a case of dueling consultants, the release of Kroll's assessment supporting the law enforcement investigation, coincided with Dina's submission of her experts' refutation of the same findings to the Coronado Police Department. In doing so, she asked the agency to reopen the investigation into Max's death as a homicide.

Hoping to gain public support, she also promoted her theories to TV hosts David "Dr. Drew" Pinsky and Jane Velez-Mitchell on HLN.

"The experts . . . were so thorough in their investigatory process, and they have presented us with science," Dina told Velez-Mitchell. "Max couldn't have gone over that railing like that."

The only other known people at the mansion when the incident with Max occurred, she said, were Rebecca and her teenage sister, Ariel. Why didn't authorities check to see if Ariel's hair was wet to confirm she'd showered? Disputing the law enforcement theories, she said Max was not a risk taker, and wouldn't have, for example, ridden on the dog's back, somehow getting thrown over the railing.

Coupled with the media reports on Dina and Jonah's domestic violence reports to police, the case took on some of the same "he said, she said" tone as their volatile divorce. Trying for balance, Dr. Drew also spoke with Coronado Mayor Casey Tanaka, who defended Jonah as "a very patient and rational person" who didn't "throw his weight around" during the permit process to remodel his historic home.

Despite Dina's pleas and media promotion, Coronado police refused to reopen Max's case, standing firmly by their original conclusion that his death was a tragic accident.

"The word 'suffocation' brings to mind somebody putting their hand over somebody else's mouth," Commander Mike Lawton said. "What it really means is loss of oxygen. And that could happen by striking one's head and cracking one's vertebrae. But to assume it was suffocation in the way the public sees it, as foul play, we found no evidence of that."

*   *   *

A couple of weeks later, Dr. Melinek and Dr. Wecht appeared on *Dr. Phil* for further discussion, as the case continued to pique the public's curiosity.

Given the injury to Max's cervical cord, Melinek said she agreed with the authorities on one thing: "It is incredibly unlikely that Maxfield would have been able to clearly articulate the word 'Ocean' after the fall," as Rebecca had claimed, because the cord would have needed to be intact for him to be able to talk.

"Max could not have said much of anything, I think he was immediately unconscious," Melinek said, adding that Rebecca seemed to be deflecting blame from herself and onto the dog.

"There are major inconsistencies and problems in her statements that implicate her, but there's nothing on the body to suggest she intentionally did anything to Max," she said. "I can't say for certain that this was murder, as opposed to an involuntary manslaughter."

Wecht differed with Melinek's interpretations, saying he found inconsistencies between her report, her comments to him personally, and then on the show.

He said he had no problem understanding how Max might have leaped or jumped over the banister when a dog, scooter, and soccer balls were involved; it wasn't like Max was a monkey swinging from the chandelier or an acrobat performing in the Cirque du Soleil.

Max hurtled over the banister somehow, and "would have been hanging on for dear life, then [the chandelier] swings and it hits the banister and down he comes," Wecht theorized. "I find nothing inexplicable about that at all."

Wecht saw Max's fall as accidental, but offered a caveat. "Having said that, and having expressed my opinions previously about expressing great doubts concerning Rebecca Zahau's death," he said that he joined Dina, Mary Zahau-Loehner, and

Anne Bremner "in strongly, strongly pleading, begging" the sheriff and medical examiner to reopen both cases.

"Their adamant refusal to do so and intellectual arrogance, their dogma[tic] insensitivity is beyond all understanding," he said.

"We want both cases reopened," Bremner said, "because you've got to know what happened to Max to know what happened to Becky."

Stifled by the authorities, Dina privately demanded $15 million from Jonah. If he didn't pay up, she would file a lawsuit against him in Arizona alleging that he'd negligently entrusted Max's care to Rebecca, Jonah said.

When he refused, she went ahead with the lawsuit in July 2013.

"The whole premise of the lawsuit was Max was murdered by Rebecca," he said, adding that it was ultimately dismissed with prejudice because the claims were "utterly frivolous" and "based on imagined facts that were proven not to be true."

In lieu of a settlement, Jonah said, his insurance company, which also represented Dina, made a $40,000 donation to Sharp Coronado Hospital, where Max was initially taken by ambulance, and $35,000 to an Arizona State University scholarship fund in memory of their son.

The lawsuit was subsequently sealed, so it doesn't appear in court records.

Dina eventually gave up the idea that Rebecca was involved or responsible for Max's fatal injuries, but the mystery of how or why he fell persists.

During a deposition in 2017, Dr. Bradley Peterson explained why Max's injuries weren't consistent with a supposed fifteen-foot fall.

Under that scenario, Peterson said, he would have expected to see a more severe neck or spinal cord injury and brain hemor-rhaging. He wasn't sure if Max might have had a heart attack, but there was no visible trauma to explain why his heart had stopped beating. The MRI of his spinal cord was normal, and his airway wasn't crushed.

Before Max was declared brain dead, the doctors explored whether Max's chest could have been struck during his fall, causing his heart to stop, a condition known as commotio cordis. But neither that, nor the possible diagnosis of Long QT syndrome, was borne out.

According to his autopsy report, Max's official cause of death was *anoxic/ischemic encephalopathy due to resuscitated cardiopulmonary arrest due to cervical spinal cord contusion due to blunt force trauma of head and neck.* This series of medical events caused a lack of blood flow, and thus oxygen, to the brain.

But Peterson was still confused about these perplexing contradictions all these years later. "It didn't make sense to me," he said. "I still don't understand why he had a cardiac arrest at the scene . . . Now, maybe there's some crazy outlier someplace, but the facts as we know and think about them did not fit together with the trauma."

Chapter 31

In May 2013, the Zahaus' attorneys filed a lawsuit against San Diego County, the sheriff, and the chief medical examiner to force the release of all investigative materials from the case. They specifically requested clean copies of 911 calls by Adam Shacknai and attorney Paul Pfingst, because Adam's had "an unexplained eight-second gap," and they wanted to compare it to Pfingst's.

The Zahaus' attorneys had been running their own private investigation at a loss since the beginning, working largely pro bono. After another online fund-raising campaign raised only one percent of its $535,000 goal, they couldn't afford to keep going.

They handed their research and theories over to San Diego civil attorneys Keith Greer and Frederick Gaston, who filed a wrongful death lawsuit two months later in federal court, accusing Adam Shacknai, Dina Shacknai, and her sister Nina Romano of conspiring, carrying out, and concealing a scheme to assault and murder Rebecca Zahau.

Based on the evidence they had at the time, the vaguely-worded suit claimed that Rebecca died by manual strangulation or by being hung from the balcony, a wrongful death in which the three defendants "participated in some manner." Rebecca's mother, her father's estate, and her sister, as executor of her father's estate, sought $10 million in damages.

In an amended complaint filed a year later, the allegations became a bit more specific and accused Dina of being the ringmaster:

> Dina, whose uncontrolled anger had been documented, had made public, demeaning statements that Rebecca had caused Max's death; she was jealous of Rebecca's relationship with Jonah, and a witness had seen her at the mansion that night. Nina had publicly acknowledged that she had visited the house as well.

> After the two women attacked Rebecca, Adam woke up from his Ambien-aided sleep and stepped in to help. Using his nautical abilities, he tied up Rebecca and anchored the rope around the bed leg.

> Black paint was found on Rebecca's breasts, on or near the nipple as if tweaked or pinched, which was consistent with the pornographic state of mind that Adam admitted to police. As the strongest of the three, he choked her to death. Dina instructed him to paint the message on the door, which was done by someone his height. While Dina and Nina sat on the bed to try to keep it from moving, Adam lifted Rebecca and threw her over the balcony.

In October 2014, a federal judge conceded that the allegations were specific enough to proceed to trial, but he refused to accept jurisdiction for the case. Greer refiled the lawsuit in state court, where the case was assigned to Judge Katherine Bacal.

The allegations continued to evolve as Greer filed a series of amended complaints. To explain the sticky residue on Rebecca's legs, the November 2014 version alleged that the defendants first restrained Rebecca with tape, gagged her, then tied her up with ski rope, removing the tape and disposing of it off-site.

The March 2016 complaint stated that as Rebecca tried to run away, Adam hit her in the back of the head and strangled her before throwing her body over the railing.

The lawsuit was headed to trial when Keith Greer dropped a surprise bombshell in April 2017. Calling a news conference, he announced that he was dismissing Dina and Nina from the lawsuit, and apologized for accusing them of wrongdoing. This came in the wake of a $100,000 settlement that Nina's insurance carrier had issued to the Zahaus, even though neither she nor Dina had wanted to settle the case.

Greer said Dina had been his "number one suspect," but the notion had never felt right to him. After reviewing the hospital videotape, he saw that Dina had been there, as she'd claimed all along. In addition, cell phone records and witnesses backed Nina's claim that she'd been at Dina's house all night after leaving the mansion.

Greer admitted that his initial theory had been "flat-out wrong," which left him with only one defendant.

"Boom," he said. "Adam did it alone."

Greer's allegations changed again in further amended complaints, which accused Adam of attacking then killing Rebecca to keep her from reporting the assault.

In the final version, filed in February 2018, Rebecca's fifty-eight-year-old mother was now the sole plaintiff. The allegations against Adam Shacknai consisted of battery, conversion (the civil equivalent of the theft of Rebecca's clothes for malicious purposes), and wrongful death.

Greer and Gaston had both kicked in some money, the Zahaus paid what they could, but funds were running low, and trial experts needed to be paid. Mary launched yet another online fund-raiser, this time on GoFundMe, but it earned less than twenty percent of the $50,000 target.

As the case moved forward before Judge Bacal, the attorneys submitted several dozen motions in limine to exclude evidence and expert witnesses the other side wanted to present to the jury.

Adam's lawyers fought successfully to keep out evidence painting him as a masturbating sex addict who took Ambien. They argued that mention of the drug would be prejudicial and post a "substantial danger of confusing the issues and/or mis-leading the jury."

In several publicized incidents, Tiger Woods, U.S. Representative Patrick Kennedy, Roseanne Barr, and Charlie Sheen have cited the Ambien defense after crashing cars, tweeting offensively, or ravaging a hotel room. Lesser-known people have successfully used the same defense after committing murders they said they didn't remember, because the drug can trigger a dissociative or disconnected state, which can be exacerbated by alcohol.

According to drugs.com: *Some people using Ambien have engaged in activity such as driving, eating, walking, making phone calls, or having sex and later having no memory of the activity.*

The defense also prevented Greer from citing the theory that Adam had deleted Rebecca's last voice mail; from raising the issue of Medicis Pharmaceutical's declining stock prices; and from alleging that Jonah, because of his "wealth and influence as the founder of a large pharmaceutical company," had undue sway over the investigation, which resulted in the suicide findings.

In addition, the defense fought to preclude Greer from bringing a naked mannequin into the courtroom, which he argued would give "the jury a better understanding of what and where Rebecca's injuries are" and "a better sense of what Adam Shacknai saw the morning of July 13, 2011, when he told the 911 operator that a woman had 'hung herself.'" The mannequin was actually an $8,000 sex doll made to look like Rebecca, with the same long black hair, black-paint marks, painted nails, ligature marks, and abrasions.

The defense also worked to keep Greer from discussing Adam's polygraph exam; from offering his theory of how the wicker chair was overturned—that Adam "aggressively confronted" Rebecca; and from showing KFMB-TV's video reenactment of the bed moving during the hanging.

Despite the defense's objections, however, Greer was able to proceed with a number of his most important witnesses, even though the judge narrowed the scope in some instances.

Greer also won the fight to keep the witchcraft book out of court by arguing that it was irrelevant. During his deposition, even Jonah said the book wasn't his or his children's. Jonah said he didn't know where it came from, and there was nothing, based on Rebecca's "behavior—the way she was—that would link her to [it]."

According to Bill Garcia, a private investigator who worked for Dina's insurance company while she was still part of the lawsuit, it was actually her book, which she'd left behind in that room while she was still with Jonah.

Hearing this, Jonah said that made sense. "There was a period of time when Dina was fascinated with witchcraft," he recalled, adding that he couldn't say Rebecca had never looked at the book, but he'd never seen her do so.

Trying to head off ridicule for his evolving stories of how Rebecca was killed, Greer asked that the defense be prohibited from referring to the now-dismissed defendants or to the "plaintiff's contentions that had been withdrawn or supplanted based on development of new evidence or new interpretation of evidence." However, Greer lost that battle, because the defense brought them up at trial. But it didn't faze him. Greer continued to offer more new scenarios at trial, and even after the proceedings were over.

Chapter 32

A ttorney Dan Webb, a former U.S. attorney who had represented Jonah in some previous corporate matters, as well as the defamation allegations against the Zahaus' first attorney, Anne Bremner, was brought in *pro hac vice*, or just for this occasion, to lead Adam's defense team.

Adam said he'd been working with lawyers in the San Francisco office of Webb's international firm, Winston & Strawn, when Webb, the firm's cochairman, was brought in shortly before the trial was scheduled to start "almost as a favor" to Jonah "to see if we could get this dismissed." Adam's home insurance policy with Travelers was supposed to pay most of the expenses, with Jonah's help as "backup."

But legal observers speculated that Webb and his team of corporate lawyers were far too expensive for the typical home insurance policy to afford, and that Jonah was likely footing a much bigger portion of the bill, which Greer estimated at $5 million. Some also wondered whether Jonah paid or helped pay for Adam's house, which Jonah has denied. Records show a mortgage is associated with the 3,572-square-foot property, which was purchased for $151,000 in January 2012.

According to Jonah, Adam's insurance company "made an

exception" to allow Webb's firm to work on this case under a negotiated rate, because it never thought the lawsuit would make it to trial. Jonah agreed to pay the difference between that rate and the firm's normal fee.

When the case proceeded to trial, Jonah said, the carrier ended up paying "the overwhelmingly large portion" of the firm's fee, and he paid the rest, in an estimated ratio of eight to one. Jonah wouldn't give specifics, but said the total was "several millions of dollars," and that Greer's $5 million estimate wasn't too high. He noted, however, that Webb, as a senior partner, only came in to argue one pretrial motion and then the trial itself. The firm's junior partners did the rest of the work at much lower rates.

Dan Webb didn't respond to a request to be interviewed for this book, but his national reputation is well known, and his résumé long and impressive. While still working for the federal government in 1990, he served as lead special prosecutor during the Iran-Contra affair's trial of Admiral John Poindexter, President Reagan's national security advisor. After switching to the private sector, Webb represented corporate giants, including Philip Morris, Verizon, and Microsoft. He also defended businessmen and elected officials in white-collar-crime and corruption cases.

During the Zahau trial, President Donald Trump asked Webb to lead his private defense team in Robert Mueller's investigation into Russian election interference, but Webb declined, citing "business conflicts." His firm was already representing a number of clients in related matters, including some who have since been sent to prison.

More recently, Webb was named a special prosecutor for the fifth time in his career, to investigate the dismissal of charges against *Empire* actor Jussie Smollett, who was accused of staging and falsely reporting a hate crime against himself.

* * *

With Adam's trial slated to start with jury selection on February 27, 2018, Webb and Greer engaged in a round of settlement negotiations.

According to Jonah, who consulted with Webb and Adam, but wasn't part of the phone discussions, Greer was the one to broach the subject of a settlement.

"My clients would be happy to get out of this, but obviously they want to get paid," Jonah quoted Greer as saying.

"What do you have in mind?" Webb replied.

Greer disputed that account, saying that it was Webb who opened the discussion by suggesting that he might be able to settle for "up to a million."

Greer said he countered with $5 million, half the original $10 million figure in the lawsuit. When that didn't fly, he said he'd see if his clients would accept $3 million.

Although Travelers' settlement ceiling was $600,000, the company refused to settle the lawsuit initially, because, like Adam, it was "extremely confident in the outcome," Jonah said. That meant Adam would've had to come up with the money himself, which Greer rightly assumed he couldn't do, and expected Jonah to cover the rest.

"Jonah's got a lot of money, he can afford this," Jonah said Greer told Webb.

Under standard practices, Jonah said Greer would have gotten 40 percent of any settlement, plus trial expenses. But Greer said he had a different arrangement with the Zahaus, which would have given him only a "fraction of that," however he wouldn't disclose details because of attorney-client privilege.

Either way, any settlement would depend on both clients agreeing on an exculpatory statement. As the attorneys traded proposed language back and forth, one version said the Zahaus still thought Rebecca was murdered, but there was little direct evidence to establish that Adam—or anyone else in the Shacknai family—was involved.

Greer said he "really put the pressure on" the Zahaus to take $3 million, and consider it "as a war chest to continue this fight . . . [and] as a tool to right this wrong" rather than to risk going to trial.

"You win, it's a hollow victory," he told them, because they would only get an annual $20,000 or $30,000, which they would have to garnish from Adam's wages. "But if you get this money, you can go head-to-head with Jonah," work to get a new sheriff elected, and keep searching for new evidence after being constantly outmatched by money, experts, and staff available to the other side.

Negotiations broke down, because "there was never client consent on either side" to either the amount or the statement, Greer said. The Zahaus refused to say Adam wasn't culpable, and despite Jonah's urging, Adam never wanted to settle, convinced that he would be vindicated in the courtroom.

"It was against my advice not to settle the case for what, in essence, was pennies on the dollar from what they originally wanted in their lawsuit, just to avoid the public spectacle, the publicity, and the hardship," Jonah said.

Judge Katherine Bacal was a no-nonsense woman who spoke slowly and deliberately, as if she were a teacher talking to misbehaving schoolchildren. She repeatedly thanked the jurors for being on time, handing out candy and doughnuts to them.

But she kept the attorneys on a tight leash, scolding them if they stepped over any line she put down, and kept the trial moving quickly. That said, the defense disagreed with a number of her rulings.

Born and raised in Tucson, the married mother of three was working toward a doctorate in European history when she decided to switch to law. Rising to partner twice, while specializing in securities and international law, she was elected president of the Lawyers Club of San Diego. In 2008, she was appointed to the bench by former Republican governor Arnold Schwarzen-egger, and held her seat in the 2010 election.

Judge Bacal got through jury selection quickly, in one day, by distributing a questionnaire to the pool of forty to sixty potential jurors. Greer thought the voir dire was typical, though shorter than he'd expected, while Jonah thought it was so fast and lim-ited that it could have been a point of appeal.

Dan Webb "was very unhappy with the process before it even started and found it irregular in his experience," Jonah recalled.

The attorneys chose an ethnically diverse mix of men and women: six of each gender on the jury, with four alternates. Based on facial features, their ethnicities appeared to be six white, three Asian, four Latino, and three blacks (all men). A few of the sixteen appeared to be of mixed race.

In civil court, a verdict does not have to be unanimous—only nine of twelve jurors are required to agree. The standard of proof—that a defendant is more likely than not responsible—is also lower than in criminal court, where a defendant must be found guilty beyond a reasonable doubt.

Also, a win for the Zahaus wouldn't legally equate to Adam "murdering" Rebecca, only that he was responsible for her death. Nor would he go to jail for it.

Chapter 33

A line to watch opening statements started forming outside Bacal's small courtroom as soon as the Hall of Justice in downtown San Diego opened at 7:30 A.M. on February 28, 2018.

I joined the media and a few retirees as we filed in to claim the few remaining seats about ninety minutes later. Most of the wooden benches in the gallery behind the defense table were already filled with attorneys and staff for the Shacknais, who had flown in from all over the country. That whole side of the courtroom smelled like money, power, and confidence.

Most of the print reporters and producers for TV news shows, including *Dateline* and *20/20,* sat on the other side, behind the two pool cameras, one each for print and broadcast outlets.

As a sole practitioner facing half a courtroom of people on the opposing team, Keith Greer was full of bluster, though he looked a little shell-shocked, often shuffling papers at the plaintiff's table as he searched for the right file. This was his first wrongful death case, but he was a showman all the way. Well-groomed and friendly, Greer loved the news cameras, while the defense adhered to a strict policy of not talking to the media.

Greer made up for his lack of experience with gumption. He seemed to genuinely care about his clients. However, he made no secret of the fact that he'd contributed nearly five years of his time and effort, worth at least $1 million of uncharged attorneys' fees, to get to this point.

During his opening statement, Greer set the stage for the sympathetic Zahau family, who had tragically lost their daughter, as Adam sat stone-faced at the defense table, surrounded by his high-powered dream team. Rebecca's sister Mary sat next to Greer at the plaintiff's table.

Greer had been talking for only a few minutes when he stopped to ask a man in the gallery to take Rebecca's crying mother out of the courtroom. Still overcome with grief nearly seven years after her daughter's violent death, the sweet, gentle woman spent most of the trial mopping her eyes with tissue in the hallway or restroom.

"Rebecca was a very energetic person," Greer continued. "She cared about people. She was very bright . . . Her life ended needlessly and early."

The Zahaus felt a great distrust of the authorities for the way they characterized Rebecca and dismissed her death as a suicide when her injuries were more consistent with murder, he said. The evidence would show that Rebecca was hit over the head four times, manually strangled, then thrown over the railing—after she was sexually assaulted with the handle of a steak knife, which left a blood smear on her left inner thigh as it was extracted from her.

The location of the black paint on her body was telling—on the sides of her nipple, "like it was pinched," and on the back of her hands, not her fingertips. The "deep bruise" on her ribs likely came as she was trying to flee from her killer's grasp, when she was hit on the right side of her head. Rebecca was then tied up with knots in "a very nautical way." Adam was a tugboat captain, while she had no "experience with ropes or bindings at all."

Rebecca's center of gravity was below the height of the balcony railing, he said, another indication that she couldn't have hurled herself over it, especially with her ankles and hands bound.

She left a trail of menstrual blood as evidence that she had paused outside her bathroom door, then stood with a striped bath towel on a different floor of the house—in the hallway outside the guest room, where several more drops of her blood were found, "confronting what we allege is Adam Shacknai."

The next morning, the "evidence shows [Adam] didn't run over to help her, he called 911," Greer said, by which point Adam had already masturbated to porn on his cell phone "in a demented sort of way."

Other than making these sexual inferences, Greer didn't explicitly describe a motive for the killing, saying only that a confrontation had gone awry after Rebecca showered. Often using the phrase "whoever murdered her," Greer only obliquely accused Adam of murder.

He said the Zahaus' experts would show that the note on the door was painted by one of the few people who knew that Rebecca had tried to save Max by giving him CPR, and that person was between five feet ten inches and six feet tall. Adam, who is five feet eleven, was in that closed circle of people.

Although authorities found Rebecca's DNA in certain key areas in the guest bedroom, Greer said, the notable absence of any DNA on other items indicated that someone had wiped away crucial incriminating evidence. He said Adam apparently didn't shed DNA, because none was found on the knife he'd used to cut Rebecca down, even though "we know he used it vigorously."

Giving the opening for the defense, Dan Webb pounded the jury with the mantra that Adam's fingerprints and DNA were nowhere to be found, and yet Rebecca's DNA and fingerprints were everywhere.

"How can her DNA be on the rope if she's unconscious and hit on the head four times?" he asked rhetorically.

Rebecca was the one who knew her painting supplies were stored in that guest room, and that the red rope was kept in the garage, not Adam.

Adam had no past problems with the law, nor had he ever harmed anyone. Although Greer described the slipknots on Rebecca's bindings as nautical, Webb said they were commonly "used by huge numbers of people."

"There's nothing to connect this knot to Adam Shacknai," he said, and absolutely no evidence that "Adam had anything to do with her death whatsoever."

Webb said it was impossible to selectively wipe away Adam's DNA without losing Rebecca's as well. There was simply no evidence of a sexual assault, he said, "no vaginal damage, no semen, nothing."

Webb closed by noting that the sheriff's investigation concluded Rebecca had committed suicide, because the evidence showed that "no one killed Rebecca."

But just in case the jury still wanted to believe it was a murder, he said, if someone *had* killed Rebecca, it wasn't Adam Shacknai.

Chapter 34

Most of the media dispersed after the openings, leaving the daily coverage primarily to the two pool cameras. Some days, a couple of reporters came for only part of the day due to limited staffing and early deadlines. I stayed for the duration.

As Greer presented his fourteen witnesses and experts, defense attorney Dan Webb was joined by David Elsberg, who flew in from his own firm in New York, Selendy & Gay. Together, they did most of the cross-examination, while half-a-dozen more junior associates and staff took notes, scurried around with files, or put exhibits on the overhead screen.

Clearly the underdog, Greer set out to win the jury's heart by describing the Zahau family's modest beginnings and hard-scrabble life as political refugees.

As Mary Zahau-Loehner took the stand, it soon became clear that she was the head of the family now, and that her widowed mother had to depend even more on her eldest daughter for financial and emotional support after losing the money Rebecca used to send each month.

Neither of her parents was very educated, Mary said. After they joined her in Missouri, Pari stayed home to take care of her older husband, Robert, who was in ill health until his heart and spirit gave out.

When Mary and her sisters were young, "we had a lot of hardship. So we were going to work very hard so our parents didn't have to live like they did when we were growing up," she said. Since the family had fallen back on tough financial times, Pari had been forced to go to work at a pork-packing plant to pay bills.

As Greer led Mary through the calls and texts she'd exchanged with Rebecca after Max's fall, she said Rebecca had never seemed depressed or suicidal. She was focused on staying strong to support Jonah.

Greer asked Mary about the molestation, knowing that it was better to mention it proactively before the defense brought it up as a risk factor for suicide.

"We didn't talk about it that much and we didn't let it affect decisions that we made in life," she said, noting that they'd talked more about other challenges they'd faced, and how they'd managed to survive them all.

As Webb began his cross-examination, he didn't go easy on Mary, even though she'd lost her sister in a violent death. In fact, he went on the offensive, trying to taint the family's credibility by highlighting the stream of allegations against Dina Shacknai and Nina Romano that had been withdrawn or proven false.

"Everything that was done was done under the instruction of our attorney," Mary said, explaining that the authorities wouldn't share their rationale or investigative findings, which "didn't leave us any option but to start from scratch."

"We have evidence that my sister was murdered," she said. "It's pretty obvious that she was murdered."

Yet, when Webb tried to pin Mary down on that evidence, she couldn't produce it. "I don't know off the top of my head, but my attorney should have the list.

"The sheriff's department had lied to us the whole way and

we had no choice but to start our own investigation," she said. The three initial defendants were the only people who had a "strong motive" to kill Rebecca, and they were either at the mansion, or were seen there by a witness.

"We didn't have enough evidence to exclude any of them," she said.

Mary said she "begged the detectives to retrieve" Jonah's voice mail, but they didn't try until it was too late. As a result, there was no way to confirm or disprove what he said in his message, and yet "they used that message as a reason why my sister committed suicide."

Webb's questions aimed to make Rebecca seem like less of a model wife or girlfriend and more of an unstable, impulsive woman who slept around as she moved from state to state. He painted her as someone who was so stressed in the months before her death that she lost weight and sleep. He also confronted Mary with the texts that she and Jonah exchanged the morning Rebecca's body was found, discussing why she might have killed herself.

After the break, Mary was better prepared to answer Webb's earlier question about the evidence: Rebecca had been taped and bound "and she didn't do that herself"; they had a witness who described a woman fitting Dina's, not Nina's, description at the front door; and "they [the sisters] could not prove that they were not there and we asked for it."

"My sister said Dina was going to kill her," she said. "My sister and Dina did not have a good relationship."

Pari Zahau took the stand the next morning. But after watching her struggle to answer Greer's questions in broken English, the defense set out to find a translator for their cross-examination. That was no simple matter, however, because her Burmese dialect, known as Chin-Zahau, was spoken in only a small region of the country.

Pari described Rebecca as a kind, loving daughter—a good girl, who sang church hymns with her mother, tried to make her laugh, sent her money every month, and tried to call her weekly.

"When she died, we are so empty and crazy," Pari said, crying as she pulled her sweater tighter around her.

"Did you ever feel concerned, think that Rebecca would kill herself?" Greer asked.

"No, no, never. She is very sweet girl. She is very strong. No suicide. No, no, no. They killed her, my daughter."

Through the translator, attorney David Elsberg asked Pari many questions about Rebecca's life, jobs, friends' names, marital affairs, sexual abuse, where she lived and when. Pari's frequent reply was "don't know" or "don't remember" as Elsberg tried to illustrate that Pari didn't really know her daughter—or many details of the case, for that matter.

Asked if they'd ever discussed Neil's reported physical abuse, Pari said, "No, but based on her voice, I can feel there might be some issue between her and Neil, but I encouraged her with God's words."

"Do you believe that more than one person had something to do with Rebecca's death?"

"Yes, I believe."

"Other than Mr. Shacknai, do you believe someone had something to do with her death?"

"I believe it might be more than one person, but the detail will be discussed by my attorney."

"Who else?"

"I cannot point their name," she said.

Moving on from Zahau family members, Greer brought up his first expert witness, Lisa DiMeo, a forensic specialist who used to work for the sheriff's crime lab.

Because Rebecca was on her period and had no other bleeding injury, DiMeo said the red "caked material" on the steak knife handle had to be Rebecca's menstrual blood, mixed with a whitish vaginal discharge. There was no blood on her fingers, yet the red stain reached the second rivet on the knife handle, so DiMeo believed someone sexually assaulted Rebecca with the knife, leaving behind a blood smear on her inner thigh.

Based on the unusual pattern of Rebecca's fingerprints on the chef's knife blade, DiMeo said she believed that Rebecca had tried to cut herself loose from the bindings around her wrists behind her.

Also, she said, fingerprints and other evidence appeared to be missing or wiped away on items such as the paint tube, where the only identifiable print was on top of the cap.

"I know of no other explanation for that," she said, adding that no prints were found on the doorknobs either, though she acknowledged that "not everybody leaves prints all the time. You can damage fingerprints easily."

In a lengthy cross-examination, Elsberg tried to shred DiMeo's believability by questioning her about a sexual harassment lawsuit she'd filed while working at the crime lab, the stress of which resulted in her attempting suicide. In the end, she lost the job she loved, where she'd worked with several of the defense witnesses.

"You don't have any bias against the sheriff's department?" Elsberg asked.

"No," she replied. After the SDSD lost the lawsuit, she was offered a job in the county jails or on patrol, but she wasn't interested. "I said, 'No way.'"

Elsberg tried prompting her to say that she hadn't seen any evidence proving that Rebecca was murdered. But based on the totality of evidence, including the way Rebecca was bound, DiMeo said she couldn't say "it wasn't a murder."

"You disagree with the conclusion that it was suicide?" Elsberg asked.

"I would have to say I do," she said, noting that the crime lab apparently missed the unusual orientation of Rebecca's fingerprints on the chef's knife. "I don't think they put it together." She acknowledged, however, that she saw no cutting marks on the rope around Rebecca's wrists.

Without video footage, DiMeo acknowledged that she couldn't prove Adam Shacknai was involved in Rebecca's death. However, she pointed out that he was the only other person on the property that night.

"You didn't see any evidence of injury to Rebecca's vaginal area?" Elsberg asked.

"Traumatic injury, no," she said, but with a small, thin object like a knife handle, "you're not going to see any injury."

Forensic document examiner Michael Wakshull took the stand on day three after a long hearing, with the jury absent, where the defense tried to preclude his testimony.

Wakshull said he used samples of Rebecca's writing and of Adam's signature to evaluate which one was more likely to have painted the message on the door.

When Adam's signature was projected onto the screen, observers could see that it wasn't signed in one fluid motion of cursive letters, the way most people sign their names, but that he actually printed his name in capital letters. Greer tried to underscore the correlation between Adam's signature and the block letters painted on the door, but the defense objected.

"He hand-prints it, rather than upper- [and] lowercase printing," Wakshull said. "It's block printing."

Wakshull said he used the *A*s and *M*s in Adam's signature to determine that Adam was more likely than Rebecca to have painted the message. In particular, he pointed to the long tail on the right leg of Adam's *M*s, noting that Adam's *A*s slanted left, and Rebecca's *A*s leaned right.

"Between Adam and Rebecca, it's more likely Adam, because it's Adam's writing that comports with the writing on the door and Rebecca's doesn't," he said.

Greer's DNA expert, Suzanna Ryan, testified that she found it "odd" there was no DNA in a majority of twenty samples taken from places where she would have expected DNA to be found.

Those twelve examples included the rope and knife that Adam admitted to touching when he cut Rebecca down, the tube of paint and the handle of the brush used to print letters on the door, the balcony railing that Rebecca went over, the footboard of the bed where the rope was anchored, and several doorknobs in the guest bedroom.

In addition, Ryan pointed out that some areas had only partial prints or an insufficient amount of DNA needed for conclusive test results. After the trial, Ryan said that if these areas were retested today, using more advanced DNA technology, some might show more conclusive results. Those items included one of the paintbrushes, male DNA found on a doorknob in the guest room, and the black garden gloves found in the living room.

Asked why Adam's DNA wasn't found on the rope where he cut Rebecca down, Ryan said that perhaps the analyst didn't swab the portion of rope that Adam touched, noting that the knots were swabbed, but other areas were not. Also, only one area of the T-shirt was swabbed—the part that was in Rebecca's mouth—even though Adam said he'd pulled out the cloth before starting CPR.

"Maybe Mr. Shacknai doesn't leave a lot of DNA behind when he touches an object," she said. "Sometimes you can touch something and leave no DNA," and other times you can leave "a lot of DNA." Or, "it could be that whoever touched [these items] is not a good shedder."

Good DNA results depend on proper collection, storage, and analysis, she said. DNA can degrade over a number of hours, and exposing evidence to heat and sunlight will only degrade it further. Results may also change if "the sample has been removed prior to when the DNA was collected."

"You're talking about wiping it clean," Greer said.

Yes, she said. "It can be fairly easy to remove DNA by wiping it down, handling it too much, especially smooth surfaces."

On cross by Webb, Ryan conceded that it would be impossible to selectively wipe away Adam's DNA and leave only Rebecca's.

She also said she didn't think DNA could be lifted from a nylon rope like this one, because it would have sunk into nooks and crannies. However, skin cell DNA has been known to rub off one body area and be transferred to another surface "during packaging and transport."

Also, she said, "If someone was wearing gloves, I wouldn't be able to see that person's DNA. It doesn't mean that absolutely someone else wasn't involved."

On day five, before the jury was brought in, the defense objected to Greer's knot expert using the mannequin to demonstrate how the bindings were tied on Rebecca's ankles, wrists, and neck. Webb even objected to draping the mannequin with a sheet during the demonstration, saying he didn't want it to look like a body.

In a practice session for the judge, Greer carried the giant doll, draped in a white sheet, into the courtroom and laid it facedown on a table, exposing just the calves, hands, and forearms.

When he started bending the legs into a right angle and manipulating the wrists and feet, I instinctively gasped. The doll was so lifelike—complete with the same bright reddish-orange toenails noted in Rebecca's autopsy report—it was creepy.

When Greer was finished, he picked up the mannequin and carried it over to a wheelchair, his arms slumping with the weight, as if he were carrying a dead body. The bailiff wheeled the doll out of the courtroom and into the judge's chambers until she could make a ruling, which was ultimately in Greer's favor.

Once the jurors were seated, Greer's expert, Lindsey Philpott, used the draped mannequin to conduct a powerful reenactment of the intricate knot tying on Rebecca's limbs, exposing only the arms or legs at any given time.

Based on his analysis of photos and the actual knotted ropes in the evidence locker, he said the knots on Rebecca's body were far more complicated than those depicted in the sheriff's video, which the jury watched for comparison purposes.

"They are not similar," he said. For starters, the type of rope used in the video was "more flexible and could be maneuvered more readily." Also, the loops in the rope around Rebecca's wrists were much tighter, and they were also tied behind her back in the opposite direction from what was shown on the video. This would have made it more difficult to extricate her hand from the bindings, as the woman did in the video.

The knot's ability to slip along the rope was crucial, he said, so it would constrict the loop around the neck. "You need to know what you're doing to create it," he said, or it wouldn't work effectively.

The series of knots he tied in his demonstration, which he described as "nautical," appeared far too elaborate for any novice to make, but he said seamen were required to practice to retain their licenses. As part of his lengthy bio, Philpott noted that he was a trained master mariner.

*   *   *

On cross, the defense debated what type of knots Philpott had tied, throwing around various names for the same knot—two successive half hitches are the same as a clove hitch, for example.

Webb got him to admit that some of the knots, on their own, were very simple. So simple that even birds, gorillas, and children could make them, which meant they weren't restricted to maritime use.

However, Philpott emphasized that it was the totality of all the knots and their positions on Rebecca's body that made the bindings so complicated.

But why investigators found only Rebecca's DNA on the rope, and none of Adam's, was another mystery.

On day six, the jury was shown video depositions by Ariel Zahau and Dina Shacknai. This emotional testimony offered insight into Jonah's, Dina's, and Rebecca's states of mind and their views on Max's condition the night Rebecca died.

No one explained why these and other depositions were played for the jury rather than having the witnesses testify in person or present any analysis of what was said, presumably because the witnesses could not be cross-examined. But on its face, Dina's statement supported the Zahaus' claim that Rebecca had no reason to kill herself out of guilt that night.

Dina said she went home to sleep for a few hours on Tuesday morning, then returned to the hospital, where she stayed at Max's bedside throughout the night—leaving only to get a Diet Coke, or walk to the parking lot with her sister.

"There was no negative news that day," Dina recalled. "They explained to me his numbers were very good."

That night, when Dr. Peterson bluntly announced, "I don't know if he's going to walk or talk again," Dina said she replied, "Well, he *is* going to walk and he *is* going to talk."

Dina said she left the room in tears, and Jonah was so upset by Peterson's remark that he wanted to have the doctor fired, but she urged him not to. "You catch more bees with honey and they're taking care of our son," she said.

After they paged two other doctors, Dr. Recalde came in to try to reassure Dina, but she was "fine" by then.

"It was a very positive night," Dina recalled.

Ariel said that she and Rebecca were close, often talking on the phone, but she acknowledged that Rebecca "would never tell me about her problems."

"Did Rebecca tell you that Jonah was mad at her and you for what happened to Max?"

"No."

Ariel was asked why she texted her sister's cell phone the day that Rebecca's body was found, saying that it wasn't "her fault."

"Because it wasn't," Ariel said.

"Did Rebecca think it was her fault?"

"She just thinks that if she had been there with him, that he would not have fallen."

"That's what you think?"

Ariel conceded that was her own opinion, and that Rebecca had never said so directly to her.

On day seven, Dr. Cyril Wecht took the stand. Still feisty as he approached his eighty-seventh birthday, the forensic patholo-gist said he'd personally conducted twenty thousand autopsies, supervised forty thousand others, and had performed a couple hundred second autopsies.

Wecht not only gave crucial testimony that differed sharply with the county ME's office, but his latest conclusions were even more definitive than those he'd discussed on *Dr. Phil* in 2011. That, he explained, was because subsequent evidence had convinced him that Rebecca was murdered.

"I had argued strongly for the case to be reopened," he said. "I did not have the complete picture that I have since obtained."

But he noted that he'd expressed doubt about the suicide findings from the beginning, "and had already mentioned the manual strangulation back in 2011."

Based on the subgaleal bruises on Rebecca's head and the location of the ligature marks on her neck, he believed she was hit over the head with a blunt-force object, "manually strangled," then "dropped to a hanging point . . . in a staged hanging."

If Rebecca had hung herself, he said, the nine-foot fall from the balcony should have left her at least partially decapitated. However, the cartilage in her neck was only fractured, and there was no injury or dislocation of the spine.

"Cricoid fractures are rarely seen in cases of hanging," he said.

Because Dr. Lucas didn't shave off her thick, long hair, he said, Lucas was unable to make a proper determination that her scalp had no lacerations. Her hair also would have acted as a cushion, "so that connotes a blow of some significance," which would have rendered Rebecca unable to fight back, because she either had "a diminution of consciousness, [or] quite possibly unconsciousness."

As he'd said in 2011, the tape residue on her calves still raised questions for him. "Why would you use tape and then use ligatures?"

Wecht said rigor mortis usually starts to form two to three hours after death, so he estimated her time of death to be 3:45 or 4:45 A.M.

Wecht's cross-examination was one of the most dramatic portions of the trial as Adam's lawyer aggressively challenged the pathologist's claim that the first two pages of his second-autopsy report from 2011 had innocently gone "missing."

When Webb implied that the pages had conveniently disappeared because they would have conflicted with Wecht's testimony, the pathologist indignantly retorted, "I have withheld nothing."

Webb also confronted Wecht for airing his findings on national TV, then changing his conclusions once he was paid to testify as an expert witness.

But Wecht handily fended off the efforts to attack his professionalism, accusing the attorney of being disingenuous by asking why Wecht had or hadn't done certain tasks that he knew Wecht would never be asked to do.

"That's not how it works, and in all due respect, I think you're fully cognizant of that fact," he snapped.

Up next was kinesiologist James Kent, who built on Wecht's testimony as he cited mathematical calculations to explain why a self-induced "longdrop" hanging should have caused far more serious injuries.

The expected outcomes "don't match what we're actually seeing in the autopsy findings," he said, adding that it was far more likely that someone lowered Rebecca over the railing.

"It's not magic," he said. "She didn't have wings."

At five feet three and a half inches tall, her center of gravity would be at thirty-two inches, yet the balcony railing was higher than that. So, she wouldn't be able to lean over it naturally.

"Once she falls forward, her hands are behind her," he said. "She really has no ability to propel herself forward . . . She has no way but to sit there at that point . . . The alternative is that someone brought her out here and positioned her like that and pushed her forward," by picking up her feet and flipping her over. But "something still had to lower her down."

"I believe she was pitched over headfirst," Kent said, but "regardless of how she went over, she went headfirst."

If she'd gone over on her own volition, he said, she should have had abrasions and scratches on the front of her thighs and body from the spiny foliage below, not just on her back. She also would have been partially or completely decapitated.

Based on the height of the message painted on the door, he said, the author should be between five feet ten inches and six feet tall. For Rebecca to do it, "she would be writing at eye level or higher to accomplish this, which is not a natural position. It's not at a comfortable height for a short person."

On cross, David Elsberg tried to persuade the judge to let an Asian female staff member, who was five feet three inches tall, stand next to the door to illustrate how she, as a stand-in for Rebecca, would paint the message.

Clearly annoyed, Judge Bacal denied the request, saying the defense could only ask a witness under oath to do such an act, "not you or someone you brought with you." Part of the issue was that the door, when it was hung in a doorway, would be higher than when it sat on the courtroom floor.

The judge grew testy with Elsberg again as he approached the witness and crowded next to him with Keith Greer, asking Kent to hold the exemplar chef's knife behind him. Kent tried to line up his fingers to match the pattern of Rebecca's prints along the blade the way DiMeo had described, as if he were trying to cut toward his body, but it was a very awkward position.

"You're not going to stand over the witness, and you're not going to argue with him," Bacal barked. "We're not going to do that in this courtroom."

"May I pass that knife around to the jury?" Elsberg asked.

"No!"

The next morning, on March 14, Greer told Bacal that his first witness had heard a woman screaming for help the night of Rebecca's death, but she was now a seventy-nine-year-old widow, suffering from a lot of pain.

Marsha Allison also claimed she was foggy from her medication, he said, and was not well enough to come down and testify. The defense, however, claimed that Marsha was *not* unavailable, because their private investigator had seen her out and about, driving her car.

Because Marsha had been subpoenaed to testify, Bacal called her on the speakerphone, with the jury absent, to assess her ability to testify that day.

"I live by myself. I can't get around a lot," Marsha said in a shaky, weak voice.

Told that the defense had seen her driving her own car, she replied, "I'm not dead yet, don't rush me off already."

Asked why she couldn't come down, Marsha said, "I have fibromyalgia," and started to cry.

"How is your fibromyalgia today?" Bacal asked.

"It's not good at all. I have bad days," she said, adding that her friend was coming to take her to the doctor. "I'm nothing but a nervous wreck. My body is shaking. I just can't do it."

With that, the judge declared Marsha unavailable, saying she didn't want a witness crying in the courtroom. Instead, the jury watched a video of her deposition in 2017 and listened to one of her recorded interviews with detectives from 2011.

Later in the trial, Detective Troy DuGal testified that he'd suggested to Detective Tsuida that they "role-play" the scream scenario—to try to re-create the cry for help and determine if it was even possible for Marsha to hear someone screaming from the mansion's rear balcony while she was sitting in her front room. But that never occurred, he said, because it wasn't a high priority.

Keith Greer left Adam Shacknai's testimony until the end of his case, calling him to the stand as his last witness on March 19.

Until then, Adam had been quiet, sitting at the defense table with a straight face. I never saw him smile, but he always held the courtroom door for me if we arrived at the same time. As he walked through the halls, I recognized the boyish bouncing gait of tennis players from my high school days. Based on his appearance alone—he always wore a jacket, tie, dress slacks, closely cropped brown hair, and dark-rimmed Hollywood-looking glasses—he didn't fit the preconceived image of a tugboat captain.

Greer started off asking him about Mary Bedwell, his girlfriend of twenty-five-plus years. Adam replied vaguely that she was in her early seventies, as if he didn't know her specific age, they lived in separate houses, and they never planned to marry.

It didn't take long for Greer to go on the attack as he set out to paint Adam as a sexual deviant whose relationship with this much older nurse wasn't normal.

"She prescribe you medication?" Greer asked.

"No, sir," Adam replied.

"You don't remember her prescribing you medication? How about May 9, 2011?"

"Not impossible, but I don't have a recollection."

Greer didn't mention any particular drug, but Adam's use of Ambien the night Rebecca died had already been debated in the pretrial motions and had been reported online.

"She's not really your girlfriend, right?" Greer asked.

Breaking with court protocol, which requires all comments and questions to go through the judge, Adam spontaneously called out to a woman sitting in the gallery behind his attorneys.

"Mary, are you my girlfriend?"

"Yes," the woman replied. Mary was also wearing glasses, her face framed by her shoulder-length hair, a wavy mix of white and ash-blond.

After Greer said he might call her as a witness, the judge asked Mary to leave the courtroom, over Webb's objections.

Webb pointed out that Mary wasn't even on the plaintiff's witness list. "She has a right to be here," he said.

Once she was gone, Greer continued to question Adam about their unusual relationship, and why he'd never introduced her to his parents.

"My parents are pretty culturally rooted in our religion," he said. "She's a Christian . . . I'm Jewish, she's not Jewish."

Asked if he'd known what Rebecca's religion was, Adam said, "I do now from the testimony," but not before. "I knew she wasn't Jewish. I didn't care, but I knew."

Greer asked Adam how he and his brother got along. Did they always have "each other's backs"?

"Yes," Adam said. "He always looked after me. He always extended himself to me."

Was Jonah doing that now? Greer asked. "Is he looking after your back by taking care of your defense in this case?"

Adam replied that Jonah was "helping . . . just like he's done since the day I was born."

Asked if he felt Rebecca was responsible for Max's death, or if Jonah said that he blamed her for Max's accident, Adam said no.

"What did he say to you about his feelings about Rebecca and Max's accident?"

"He did mention that she did save Max," Adam said, using words similar to the phrase painted on the door, without any prompting.

"That was your understanding, as of July 12, 2011, that Rebecca had saved Max's life by being there and giving him CPR?"

"Yes."

Greer asked if Adam had found Rebecca attractive. "I was not attracted to her," Adam said. "She was my brother's girlfriend."

"Did she ever flirt with you?"

"No."

In a series of confrontational and accusatory questions, Greer tried to poke holes in Adam's story that he never went into the main house after saying goodnight to Rebecca in the driveway.

But Adam didn't break. He said he didn't hear her shower running, he didn't attack her, and "she never attempted to flee, because I was never in the house."

"Did you hit her four times in the head?"

"I never hit Rebecca on the head or anywhere else. I never tied Rebecca up."

"Did you insert the steak knife handle into her vagina?"

"Most certainly not."

Greer asked if it was the "sexual excitement" of what Adam had done to Rebecca that made him want to pleasure himself that morning.

"I never did anything to Rebecca Zahau, and it had nothing to do with Rebecca Zahau," Adam said.

"What was it that got you excited?"

"Nothing, I woke up a little early, feeling fitful," he said. "I was trying to fill up a little time."

"What were you looking at while masturbating?"

As he'd told investigators, Adam replied, "I was looking at some pornography on my iPhone." No, he had not masturbated in Rebecca's presence, he said, and, yes, he believed he showered again that morning, but he couldn't remember if it was before or after he masturbated.

"To clear off any residue that may be on you because of what you did to Rebecca Zahau?" Greer asked, moving on to the next question.

Asked about the knots he used to tie tugboats to the dock, Adam said he didn't know if they were the same type of knots used to tie up Rebecca's wrists.

"I'm not really sure what I saw tied on Rebecca. I didn't really get that great a look at it," he said. "It was some kind of knot."

"What did you do to loosen the rope?" Greer asked.

"I was more getting my fingers under something to feel a pulse. I didn't do anything under the ropes. I did have to pry underneath to get at the pulse."

As Greer played the 911 tape for the jury, he stopped it frequently to question Adam about what he'd been doing at those junctures. For many people in the courtroom that day, including me, it was the first time hearing the call.

Afterward, he asked Adam about the initial text and call he made to inform Jonah that Rebecca had killed herself, but omitted specifics. "Is it true that, because the guilt you were feeling, you couldn't even share that?"

"No."

"You were prepared to answer that question pretty good, huh? You still think Rebecca committed suicide even after you saw evidence that the knife was inserted inside her?"

"I do, sir."

As Webb began his cross-examination, he got the obvious denials out of the way up front.

"Did you ever, at any time, participate in the murder of Rebecca Zahau?"

"Most certainly not."

"Did you ever at any time of the evening of July 12, or early-morning hours, leave the guest house and go into the main residence?"

"Most certainly not."

After reviewing Adam's social history and education, Webb asked, "Has anyone ever accused you of being violent?"

"No, sir," Adam said, provoking an objection from Greer, presumably because Adam was on trial for wrongful death.

Asked if he volunteered the information about masturbating that morning because he wanted to tell the whole truth, Adam said, "With some embarrassment and hesitation, yes, sir."

* * *

Greer went back on the attack on redirect.

"Were you wearing gloves when you cut Rebecca down?" he asked.

"No."

"Why didn't you remove the ropes from her wrists so you could do chest compressions properly?"

"I didn't know that wouldn't let me do it properly," he replied.

Asked how high off the ground Rebecca's feet were, Adam said he didn't recall, only that "it looked like I needed a table and I went and got one."

"This isn't burned into your brain?" Greer asked, moving on. "You felt comfortable, you wiped down the place really good?"

Webb objected, so Adam didn't answer the question.

"You didn't ask for a lawyer because you were worried you'd look guilty?" Greer asked, noting that attorney Paul Pfingst had called and come looking for him.

"I didn't answer the call, [because] I didn't know him," Adam said, conceding that he called Pfingst the next day and told him he didn't want a lawyer.

Right before the afternoon break, Webb announced he was submitting a nonsuit motion, arguing that there wasn't enough evidence against Adam to proceed. Webb described it as a "kill," as in a case killer.

Holding up the thick document, Judge Bacal said wryly that she was "highly skeptical" she could read it over the break, which usually lasted about twenty minutes, so she directed the defense to proceed with their first witnesses, who, in this case, were sheriff's detectives.

It was remarkably unusual to see detectives and forensic techs testifying *for* a defendant in a death case, because in a criminal trial, law enforcement always helps *prosecute* a suspect.

*   *   *

I ran into Adam's girlfriend, Mary, in the ladies' room, where we had an innocent chat about our respective hairstyles. She seemed quite normal and sweet, not the type of woman who would date a sexual deviant. I gave her my card, hoping that she or Adam would talk to me down the road.

Partway through the trial, KUSI, a local independent TV station, hired me to give my analysis, which I did eight times. As we discussed Adam's testimony, one of the anchors described him as "arrogant." Other observers called him "cocky."

Later, when I interviewed Mary for this book, I asked for her reaction to those descriptions. She agreed that Adam "acted pretty arrogant at the courthouse," but said that was "because I thought we were supposed to not talk to people." This was at his attorneys' advice, she said, but she "didn't realize Keith [Greer] was shucking and jiving. Adam['s attorneys] put on a good case, and [Greer] put on a good show."

To her, the trial had a circus atmosphere, just like in the old days, when Barnum & Bailey sent out a showman before each performance to work the crowd into a frenzy.

"When the circus came to town, it was all over."

Chapter 35

The defense called its first witnesses, sheriff's detectives Angela Tsuida, Troy DuGal, and Sergeant Todd Norton, to defend their work and their agency's findings, knowing that juries typically trust law enforcement testimony. Only this case was anything but typical.

Because of a scheduling issue, Tsuida was called out of order, before Adam testified and before Greer rested his case. The media was prohibited from photographing her face because she was now working undercover.

As lead detective, Tsuida said she and her team were initially notified that this was a "suspicious death," so they approached the investigation as though it was a homicide.

"Because in my career, I've never seen a situation like this," she said. "It was very odd."

As a result, she said, they treated Adam as a "person of interest," which, in general, meant "we're looking at them as a potential suspect."

Asked if she considered whether surfaces might have been wiped down, she said, "That's something we always consider," but no one on the team saw any evidence of that in this case.

This time, it was Greer whom the judge admonished, scolding him for talking to his client while David Elsberg was questioning his witness.

"Counsel, you will not make remarks while opposing counsel is asking questions," Bacal said.

Greer had made repeated objections during Elsberg's direct examination of Tsuida, and he was even more fired up after lunch, when he began his cross with increasingly combative questions.

"You're aware this is getting a lot of public scrutiny," he said. "Do you feel you need to bend over backward . . . to save face?" The defense's objection saved Tsuida from having to answer, but Greer made his point.

Greer tried to undermine the defense's case by implying that the investigation was shoddy and superficial, and that detectives were single-mindedly biased toward only one outcome: suicide.

As he listed the various contributors cited in reaching that conclusion—such as Rebecca's weight loss, the child molestation report, and other "risk factors" for suicide—Greer asked Tsuida if the detectives had done "further investigation" into each one. But regardless of the question asked, Tsuida wouldn't budge from her position that they had weighed all the evidence in a comprehensive manner.

"Not just this one factor, no, again it was the totality," she said.

Greer prompted her to admit that Rebecca hadn't shown many of the most common signs or behaviors that precede suicides, such as alcohol and drug use, suicidal threats or attempts, self-harm, or mental illness.

"Not that I'm aware of, no," she said, adding that each of those was just one factor. "Again, it was the totality."

As Greer highlighted areas where the investigation didn't go, Tsuida acknowledged that no fingerprint analysis had been done on Rebecca's phone. Adam claimed he wasn't in the house, she said, but it also made sense that the phone's owner would be the one answering it.

"Unless they were bound and gagged at the time, right?" Greer quipped.

Greer also cited a list of places where no DNA was found, asking her in each example if that "cause[d] you any concern?" Tsuida answered "no" to every question.

Taking a cumulative approach, he asked, "If you get six or ten things without DNA, would that cause you concern?"

"I can't give you a number," she said. "Again, it's the totality."

He also pointed out that investigators didn't test for DNA on certain evidence items, or to see if the steak knife handle showed any trace of Rebecca's vaginal fluid.

"That's why we test multiple items," she said. "You would think you would leave DNA. You would think you would leave fingerprints. But you don't."

Tsuida acknowledged that they also didn't collect the athletic tape they found at the house to determine whether it matched the residue on Rebecca's legs. Nor did they look at the tipped-over chair. And they never discussed why the steak knife handle had blood on it when the only source was Rebecca's menstrual period.

Toward the end of her testimony, Greer raised a whole series of questions, which the detective either said she couldn't answer or told Greer he should ask a different witness. The implication being that the detectives were, essentially, passing the buck, or hadn't properly investigated these issues.

"I cannot tell you what the source of the blood is that got on the knife," Tsuida said. "That's something I cannot answer." But she noted that it was only "an assumption that this knife was inserted into her vagina," meaning it was Greer's theory, not theirs.

The team did try to figure out what the phrase on the door meant, she said. Their conclusion was that Rebecca was referring to her 911 call when she wrote, *SHE SAVED HIM,* and to God when she wrote, *CAN YOU SAVE HER.*

Asked about department policy concerning the sharing of information or status of an investigation, Tsuida said, "We leave it pretty general."

"But it was more than just open, closed, right?" Greer asked. "You never gave Jonah Shacknai any details about the case, under penalty of perjury?"

"I'm not saying I never shared any information," she said.

Judge Bacal took the weekend to review the defense's motion before issuing a tentative ruling on Tuesday, March 20.

The defense had a "gotcha" moment when it presented a sheriff's photo that proved the "stolen" shirt Rebecca had been wearing in the last picture on her camera was actually in a heap of clothes on her closet floor. Because this gray-and-white-striped shirt had never been returned to the Zahaus, they believed Adam had taken it, and that became the basis of the "conversion" count against him.

Based on the discovery of that photo, Bacal said she was ready to grant a dismissal of the conversion charge. But unless she was otherwise persuaded by oral arguments, the wrongful death and battery allegations would stand, as they did in her final ruling.

Despite the lack of fingerprints and DNA linking Adam to Rebecca's death, Greer argued that other evidence tied him to the scene: Adam was the only other person on the property that night, and Rebecca's nipples and buttocks had been touched in a sexual manner by someone with black paint on his hands.

Although the jury was absent, Greer presented his case in **more definitive terms that Rebecca** was murdered after Adam sexually assaulted her. Rebecca had no paint on her fingertips, while Adam had admitted to an "act of pleasure" the next morning, which was the "climax after sexually abusing this girl."

Bacal supported the plaintiff's case by noting a few points of evidence from prior testimony, as well as a few others that weren't discussed. This showed that she was not only listening carefully, but she was also reading the investigative reports sent to the jury as exhibits.

She noted, for example, that the pair of women's panties found in the guesthouse had never been tested for DNA, that the guest house wasn't secured until 10:00 A.M., and that the search warrant wasn't served there until 6:30 P.M.

"There is eyewitness testimony that connects Mr. Shacknai to the scene," Bacal said, noting that Adam said on his 911 call that the victim was "in the guest house," where he was staying. He also admitted to pulling or loosening the ropes around Rebecca's wrists, yet the ropes showed none of his DNA. The front door and the back door to the kitchen weren't locked, and if both French doors to the balcony were open, someone had to touch those doorknobs, yet no fingerprints were found.

Because of the sexual assault allegation, the defense asked that the actual steak knife be brought from the evidence locker to the courtroom for witnesses to examine.

Next up was retired forensic evidence tech Denys Williams, who testified that she took DNA swabs, hair samples, and fingernail scrapings, processed the scene for fingerprints, and took more than twelve hundred photos, including views of Adam's body and aerial shots of the mansion from a helicopter.

Showing her the steak knife, attorney Krista Enns asked, "Do you recall seeing blood on this knife?"

"Yes," Williams said, but "not very much. I didn't examine it."

She recalled seeing only "a little red stain" up to the first rivet, not to the second, as Lisa DiMeo had testified, and only on two sides of the knife, while Greer claimed it was on all four. However, she acknowledged that she had not taken a photo that would support her recollection.

Williams said she assumed that the blood came from the injury on Rebecca's middle finger, which was still oozing when she photographed it. The investigative reports showed that Williams swabbed the knife handle for DNA, processed it for prints, then swabbed the entire knife for DNA.

The surface of the wooden paintbrush proved too porous to collect prints, she said, but she was able to check the paint tube for prints, and she found two of them: one on top of the cap, and one on the tube itself—testimony that conflicted with Greer's claim that the body of the tube had been "wiped clean."

Starting his cross, Greer asked, "Have you seen rope burns before, ma'am?"

"Not in maybe fifty years," she replied.

"Isn't that a rope burn?" he asked, referring to the oozing finger injury she'd described earlier.

As Greer had Williams demonstrate on a replica how she would hold the steak knife, he asked, "Isn't it true that the wound would not be touching the knife?"

"I don't know, it doesn't seem like it would," she said. "It doesn't make contact for me, the way I would hold the knife."

Referring to the blood on the lower portion of the handle, Greer asked, wouldn't that be consistent with the knife being inserted into her vagina?

"I didn't see any evidence of that," she said.

The next witness was Linda Wright, a latent fingerprint examiner, who testified that she saw no "indications of wipe down" in the guest bedroom.

Wright explained that fingerprints were found on the paint tube, where a person would squeeze to get the paint out, but they were deemed inconclusive because the prints overlapped in five areas. Only the cap clearly showed Rebecca's print.

"If it was wiped down, we would not see these [other] ridges," she noted.

There were also fingerprint ridges on the steak knife handle, she said, but none was identifiable. That evidence was deemed inconclusive, but it was nonetheless inconsistent with a wipe down, as was the fact that Rebecca's fingerprints were found on the chef's knife and bed frame. Same for the door frame, which had prints and smears that she didn't try to process. When someone wipes down a surface with fluid, they can leave identifiable streaks, Wright said, but she saw no evidence of that either.

Prints are fragile, she said, and it's not unusual for people to touch things and leave no trace, especially if they've just washed and dried their hands. If someone wore gloves, he would leave no fingerprint ridges, but the fingertips of latex gloves leave impressions with identifiable textures of their own, and she saw none of those either.

On cross, Wright acknowledged that doorknobs are a good place to check for prints, and the fact that there were none found on the doorknob "could be" consistent with a wipe down.

Shelley Webster, a criminalist who did DNA analysis at the crime lab, said this case generated four or five times more testing samples than usual.

Tests for DNA in the vagina or mouth should show significantly more DNA and epithelial cells than in the rest of the body, but similar levels to each other, she said. Rebecca's oral swab had six hundred nanograms of DNA, while the swab of the knife handle showed a much smaller amount, with only thirty-five nanograms—testimony that flew in the face of Greer's sexual assault theory.

"Is this consistent with the knife being inserted into the vagina?" Dan Webb asked.

If that was the case, "I would expect to see more DNA in vaginal fluid," Webster said.

Because the amount of DNA in the oral and vaginal swabs should be about the same, she said, she, too, believed that the blood on the knife handle was more likely transfer blood from Rebecca's finger injury.

To process a knife for fingerprints, she explained, the techs first spray a mist of superglue on an item, then place it in an oven, which releases a vapor that affixes the print. The DNA swab of the entire knife comes after that.

Webster wasn't asked whether the DNA could have been degraded by the print processing or the heat. However, she later said, "When we swab, we still obtain DNA," even after the superglue misting.

"Was Adam's DNA found on any of the items you tested?" Webb asked.

"No."

Outside of the trial, sheriff's lieutenant Justin White said in an email: *Performing these techniques does not interfere with the DNA collection process. DNA is left behind in many different quantities. Every situation is unique and different.*

Under cross-examination by Greer, Webster said the superglue misting could leave a white residue on it, such as the steak knife handle.

Although the actual knife handle no longer showed any red stain, Greer put photos on the screen that depicted the red color, and also backed his claim that the white residue was on all four sides of the handle.

Webster acknowledged that she didn't know exactly where the knife handle was swabbed for DNA, but the first swab showed seventy nanograms, twice as much as the later swab. But either way, the swabs taken from blood on the towel and carpet showed higher amounts of Rebecca's DNA than the knife, which, again, conflicted with Greer's sexual assault theory.

Asked why Adam's DNA wouldn't be on the ropes that he admitted to touching when he cut Rebecca down, she said, it "may not be the same area I tested. I was focusing on the knots."

Later on, she said, "Sometimes people don't leave a lot of DNA when they touch something," adding that dirt, mud, heat, and bacteria can all damage DNA, and smooth surfaces may not retain it as well as others.

The jury was also shown excerpts of videotaped depositions by Max Shacknai's physician, Dr. Bradley Peterson, Rebecca's ex-boyfriend, Michael Berger, and her ex-husband, Neil Nalepa, without any comment or interpretation from either side, and not all on the same day.

Neil's deposition helped put a face to Rebecca's stories about him, and to provide context to her accounts of his abusive treatment. Although he denied hitting her, he seemed like quite an eccentric character. Some of his claims not only conflicted with her accounts, but with Michael Berger's as well, such as Neil's statement that Rebecca had never moved out or lived elsewhere while they were in California.

Michael's deposition also conveyed a number of false or misleading statements that Rebecca had made to him: First, she wasn't married; second, she was going through a divorce; third, she'd been abducted by Neil, only to tell police she hadn't; and finally, she'd gone to Portland to get some space, when she was really back with Neil. Michael said Rebecca had acted impulsively, but only after the abduction, and when she was being pressured by her parents and sister Mary to get back with Neil in their "arranged marriage."

It became apparent that the defense was presenting these statements as a way to raise questions about Rebecca's character, to highlight her troubled past, and to underscore the stories of victimization she'd told the men in her life. This also bolstered the defense strategy to paint Rebecca as a woman who slept around on her husband in cities across the nation.

But the lies she told and the discrepancies between all of these stories didn't become evident until Neil's deposition was played—a week after Michael's.

"During that time period, when you guys were first living in California, do you know, did she see other men?" Krista Enns, one of Adam's attorneys, asked Neil.

"That's why we moved to Oregon," he replied.

"Because she was seeing someone else?"

"Yes."

"And do you know when she started seeing that person?"

"I have no idea. Toward the end of—it was shortly before we moved to Oregon."

"You and she ever talk about her relationship with him?"

"No," he said.

"So, did you, like, follow her or did you just ask her?"

"No, I called her needing something urgent, that, you know, could have been handled. But she was then not able to go. And she wasn't where she said she was, and the story changed. So I just said, 'What are you doing?' And she told me."

"How soon after that did you move to Oregon?"

"A month."

"Were you already planning to move to Oregon before you learned about Mike Berger?"

"No."

"How did it come to her attention that there was a missing person report out on her?"

"The police called me. I believe that's how it happened."

"And then you talked to her and she went to the police department?"

"I put her on the phone with the police department, yes, and she made plans to go meet them."

Finally, on day fourteen, it came time for the long-awaited testimony of Rebecca's wealthy boyfriend, Jonah Shacknai, who was also the defendant's brother.

As he took the stand, his body language conveyed stiffness and anxiety, and he spoke so softly it was difficult to hear him in the gallery. He'd apparently been coached to look directly at the jury when testifying, rather than at the attorney asking him questions, because he kept moving his mouth away from the microphone.

As Snowem had described to Detective Tsuida, Jonah's measured statements about Rebecca made him seem detached and hard to read, but he came off more as an advocate for his brother than anything else.

"Rebecca and I were very close," Jonah said. "I'm confident that we loved one another. We spent all the time together that we could."

But in contrast to Snowem's description, Jonah said Rebecca was a very orderly person, who took it upon herself to reorganize the garage so they could find things—an unstated reference to the claim that she knew where the red rope was stored.

As an indication of her experience in knot tying, he said they enjoyed boating at least once a week with the kids, often towing them in an inner tube around Coronado Harbor. Rebecca cast off and he drove the boat, then as they came in, "she'd jump off the boat and tie the lines so it was secure."

Webb led Jonah through his relationship with Rebecca, coming to the last night he saw her alive.

"She just wanted to give me a long hug and hoped that I could promise her that everything would be okay," he recalled, his voice breaking as he reached for the water.

He then recounted the episode with Dina later that night, saying she got emotional and yelled at Dr. Peterson for saying that Max would never walk or talk again.

"Was what Dr. Peterson told you much different from what you believed based on your medical knowledge?" Webb asked.

"It wasn't a surprise, but it was difficult to hear those words," Jonah said.

Describing the voice mail he left for Rebecca, he said, "I was pretty upset and I basically was crying. I told her what Dr. Peterson had said in a voice message and asked her to call me."

The next morning, when Adam told him that Rebecca was dead, Jonah said, "I couldn't believe it. My son was fighting for his life in the hospital and Rebecca was now gone. It was unfathomable."

Asked if he'd ever seen Adam do anything violent to another human being, he replied, "Never. Never anything. It's inconceivable."

On cross, Greer asked Jonah if he'd ever seen Rebecca "tie ropes in a sexual nature."

"Not with me," he replied.

"Ever seen her tie knots like that before?" Greer asked, showing photos of Rebecca's bound ankles, wrists, and neck.

"No."

Given Jonah's earlier testimony about Rebecca's boating and knot-tying experience with half-hitch knots, Greer asked him to demonstrate for the jury how he would tie up a boat. As Jonah did so, he used a simple figure-eight motion.

"There's no knot in that, right?" Greer asked.

"I think that's how everyone in the world ties down their boat," Jonah said.

Asked if he'd thanked Rebecca for giving CPR to Max, Jonah said, "She said that she gave him a few breaths . . . The boy wasn't saved, but . . . I thanked her for doing her best to save his life."

Greer asked if Jonah recalled saying that he and Adam had each other's backs. "Yes, he's my little brother," he said.

"Are you here today doing your best to save him?"

Webb objected, but Greer's word-play, reminiscent of the message on the door, was left hanging as Jonah stepped down from the stand.

The defense's next witness, document examiner David Oleksow, didn't have much to say about the painted message, other than that he was paid $10,000 to testify that he didn't analyze the lettering because he had no similar samples for a valid comparison.

He said he couldn't compare two different types of writing—such as block letters painted on a door and handwritten letters on a page—especially when each item was created using a different writing implement.

"It's like comparing apples with oranges," Oleksow said.

So, he said, he didn't ask for samples of Adam's handwriting, because it was impossible to conclude whether Adam painted the message on the door, or if it was more likely Adam or Rebecca.

* * *

The next day, the defense's forensic knot consultant, Robert Chisnall, testified about his research into why people self-tie knots in a suicide: to "prevent themselves from self-rescuing" and to "make the act look like a homicide." They may do the latter, he added, to "implicate someone else" for insurance reasons or to "prevent dishonor to the family."

Referring to the plaintiff's expert, who had no training in the forensic science of knot tying, Chisnall said the danger of a "sailor hobbyist's" analysis was that he "could be prone to confirmation," and would identify knots from his own maritime experience. As such, he contended that Philpott misidentified three knots and "made many errors."

Chisnall said self-tied suicide knots tend to be looser, more haphazard, and simple—often leaving a gap between the two wrists—than those used in homicides, which are never loose. The knots found on Rebecca's body not only fit these parameters, they also didn't require any nautical training or particular skill. They were "a very simple knot consisting of two factor knots, and it could slide," he said.

On cross, Greer asked Chisnall to demonstrate how he would tie his own wrists with the same knots that he alleged Rebecca did. Chisnall quickly did so, making it look easy in comparison with Philpott's intricate demonstration.

But asked how many times he had practiced that stunt before trial, Chisnall conceded he had rehearsed it fifty to sixty times. Not so easy, apparently.

Rather than question forensic pathologist Jonathan Lucas about his findings that Rebecca committed suicide, the defense called an outside, "neutral," academic voice to lend credence to Dr. Lucas's autopsy. Dr. Gregory Davis noted that he wasn't paid for his testimony, because it was part of his salaried job at the University of Kentucky College of Medicine.

Calling Lucas's report "one of the finest I've come across in my career," he confirmed its conclusions, and disputed Dr. Wecht's testimony to the contrary.

If Rebecca had been strangled before the hanging, as Wecht suggested, Davis said he would have expected to see a pattern of bruises on her neck, left by the killer's fingers. And if she had been hit on the head four times, he would have expected to see more blood and damage to the scalp.

He said the lesions could have formed on the scalp during the autopsy as the pathologist peeled it back with a scalpel, especially after a hanging, when blood vessels are congested. But in this case, he said, he thought they more likely came from Rebecca hitting her head against objects in the courtyard as she swung down from the balcony.

Although suicidal hangings by naked women, involving bindings, were rare, he said, "we know it's unusual and suspicious, but highly unusual doesn't mean you never see it."

He saw no evidence that Rebecca had been sexually assaulted with the knife handle, but said he'd handled two suicide cases where women had inserted objects into their vaginas—a dildo in one and a pencil or pen in the other.

On cross, however, he acknowledged that he'd never personally seen a case where a woman hung herself while naked, or a suicide by a naked woman who was also bound and gagged.

Asked to estimate the time of death based on the rigor mortis, Davis said he couldn't, because "over time you get rigor mortis, and then it goes away."

The defense's final witness was psychologist Alan Berman, who described a detailed series of factors in Rebecca's past and present behaviors that put her at risk for suicide.

"I am very comfortable with my opinion, to a high degree of certainty, that this death was a suicide," he said.

For me, this was when the trial got most personal. As I listened to Berman run through these risk factors, I couldn't help but relive memories of my husband's suicide, and compare the pre-mortem behavior I'd seen in him with Rebecca's.

Berman said Rebecca's molestation and her reports of being shoved, screamed at, and grabbed around the throat by Neil were clear factors. Sexual abuse can be devastating, he said, producing a sense of shame, low self-esteem and self-worth, distrust in others, and difficulty in relationships, all of which would elevate suicide risks.

"Acting out" via extramarital affairs was Rebecca's indirect way of coping with her issues, he said, which was evidenced by her story to Michael Berger that she'd been "supposedly kidnapped."

"She makes up that incredible story while she goes to spend time with Mr. Nalepa," he said.

The shoplifting incident, he went on, is "an example of how she reacts under intense stress. She has an impulsive reactive reaction to the phone call" about her brother.

Berman also found red flags throughout the journal-style notes on Rebecca's phone. Her remark that "it's my own fault" she was being mistreated is common in those who are abused, he said. The social isolation she described came from having no confidantes or support system outside her religious family, which was even "more of an acute risk factor." Her trouble sleeping, her racing mind, her crying and not knowing why, and her weight loss were all symptoms of depression and anxiety.

After quitting her job, she became financially dependent on Jonah. The notes showed that she felt she loved him more than he loved her, and that "she is struggling with her lovability."

When Max fell and she was the only adult present, she experienced a "moral injury," a feeling that she'd failed to fulfill her responsibility, which "now represented a tremendous threat to her relationship with Jonah," he said. Asked if her thoughts of leaving Jonah changed any of his assessment, Berman said no, because she never acted on them.

When Jonah told her that she couldn't come to the hospital and be part of the family, she felt rejected by the man she loved.

"At this point, she is at a very high and acute risk of suicide," which was the "straw that broke the camel's back," he said. "I believe Rebecca felt tremendous guilt for what happened to Max."

In 2011, a third of the suicides by California women in Rebecca's age group, between thirty to thirty-four, were by hanging. "So, it's common," he said.

On cross, Greer tried to get Berman to concede that Rebecca had many coping mechanisms for dealing with stress, such as eating healthily, exercising, and writing journal entries.

But Berman said people can exercise "for nonhealth reasons as well," and asserted that she chose to put her thoughts into writing rather than to discuss them directly with Jonah, which would have been better.

"She was not a good problem solver," he said, although he acknowledged that nothing was stopping her from repeating her past coping behaviors—having an affair, leaving Jonah, or going to stay with her family in Missouri.

When Greer pointed out that Rebecca had always been able to get a job, even at Starbucks or as a nanny, Berman insisted that the trauma of losing Max would have delayed her emotional ability to do that.

Asked about the message on the door, Berman didn't want to

speculate. "I think she probably had a psychotic break. I don't know."

After Berman admitted he was paid well over $50,000 for his time on the case, the attorneys had no more questions.

"The defense rests its case," Webb said.

"No rebuttal, Your Honor," Greer said.

Chapter 36

After some debate, the defense won its plea to wait until after the weekend to begin closing arguments, saying the attorneys needed the time to assemble numerous binders of material. But the real benefit was that the jury could sit with the defense witnesses' testimony, and not the plaintiff's closing, over the Easter holiday weekend.

Keith Greer and Dan Webb attempted another round of settlement negotiations, but didn't get far because their clients still couldn't agree on wording for the exculpatory statement.

"We couldn't get past the language," Greer said. "It got shut down. No numbers were exchanged."

But by that point, even Jonah didn't support a settlement anymore. After hearing all the testimony, he said, "It was inconceivable that the jury would come back in any way other than a finding for Adam."

And yet, Greer and his clients felt the same level of confidence. "By end of trial, we're thinking we're winning," he said, because they believed that witnesses representing the sheriff's investigation had done a poor job of refuting the premise that Rebecca had been murdered.

* * *

Come Monday morning, April 2, Webb renewed his "very strenuous objection" to Greer's request to use the mannequin as a demonstrative prop during his closing, arguing that it would be "highly prejudicial." Judge Bacal said she would issue a ruling if and when Greer laid the foundation to use it for this purpose.

Before the morning session began, Greer motioned me into a side room, where he showed me the mannequin, and asked if I thought he should use it. I felt uncomfortable being put in that position, so I told him I couldn't give him my opinion, because I was covering the trial, but that it was very dramatic. He was still trying to decide if hanging it up would work for or against him with the jury.

Back in the courtroom, Greer mopped the perspiration from his face as he prepared to deliver his final argument. His eyes red and tired, he seemed jumpy and a bit shaky. Due to the stress and intensity of the trial, eighteen pounds had melted away from his face and waistline, forcing him to make an emergency trip to the tailor.

Both Pari and Mary Zahau sat at the table with him that day as the judge explained to the jury how to interpret evidence, weigh witness credibility, and, depending on the verdict, how to assign a dollar amount to compensate Pari for the harm done to Rebecca.

As Greer gave his latest scenario for how Adam had killed Rebecca, he finally connected the dots with evidence that supported his experts' opinions.

It all started when Adam became aroused by watching Rebecca bathe in the glass-walled shower in the master bathroom. Afterward, something lured her down a level, to the opposite side of the house, and into the hallway outside the guest room, where she stood, wearing just a towel and carrying her cell phone.

"We don't allege this is premeditated," Greer said. "There was a confrontation that went awry."

Rebecca stood there long enough for four drops of blood to fall on the carpet, then tried to run and cried out for help. That's when the neighbor heard her scream, and Adam hit her over the head four times, rendering her partially or completely unconscious.

Greer stopped his story to ask Pari, who was crying again, to step out of the courtroom. "Something no mother should have to hear," he said, continuing on.

Realizing he needed to cover up what he'd done, Adam used his nautical knowledge to hog-tie Rebecca's wrists and ankles together behind her with a single piece of rope, the bindings so tight they left bruises.

But she came to and tried to escape again, holding the chef's knife blade behind her back as she tried to free herself from the bindings around her wrists. Adam proceeded to strangle her to death and, at some point, assaulted her with the steak knife handle.

Then he painted the message on the door, leaving his "signature in a way," lifted her up, then put her over the railing. Even though Adam eventually cut the rope into pieces, her knees were still bent when rigor mortis set in, as they were when the authorities arrived.

Adam was "very bright," has a degree in literature, and "he makes up stories," Greer said. "You couldn't ask for a more creative story here."

Dismissing Berman's suicide risk factors, he said Rebecca had worked through the molestation. "It's one of the things that made her stronger," he said.

Greer repeated Rebecca's story that she'd run out of the store with the jewelry after getting a call from her brother, and he also claimed that she was never charged with the crime of shoplifting, which was not supported by the court records.

Calling her "a fairly centered person, [who was] balanced enough to be Jonah Shacknai's girlfriend for two years," Greer said Rebecca would never have left "her entire family hanging, without her support."

During the morning break, the judge gave Greer a major victory by ruling that he could use the mannequin. However, he waited until after lunch, when the jury was seated, to do the dramatic unveiling.

Walking over to the mannequin, he slowly pulled off the white sheet, then removed the blue cotton surgical robe that was draped over the doll, rendering her completely nude.

I literally gasped out loud from the shock of it. Even more so now that we got the full view, it was impossible *not* to imagine that this doll was really Rebecca, hanging from that balcony.

Jonah, who was sitting right in front of me, shook his head slightly during the disrobing. Investigator Bill Garcia, who attended the trial that day out of personal interest and sat to my left, said he saw the veins pulsing in Jonah's neck and face.

Jonah told me later that he couldn't believe Greer had stooped so low. The defense had done its best to prevent this, but nothing could have prepared Jonah for the trauma of seeing a sex doll, built to resemble his dead girlfriend, hanging nude right in front of him.

"It was so tasteless and disrespectful to Rebecca," he said later. "I thought it was outrageous," and would be a strong part of any appeal, because it was so "disgusting and vulgar that the family and Greer would allow that to be shown." In retrospect, he said, it proved to be "very impactful, clearly, on the jury," but for him, "it was horribly painful."

As Greer replayed snippets of Adam's 911 call, he stopped frequently to offer commentary on what Adam was doing at that moment, documenting his actions and creating plausible deniability for himself. Adam's heavy breathing was a fake panic attack, he said, for the authorities' benefit.

"He knows she's dead," he said.

Holding the knife exemplar, Greer illustrated how Adam didn't need to pull over that table to stand on, because Rebecca's body was low enough to cut her down without it.

"She's right here, right here at this level," Greer said, motioning for the jury.

"What did you do?" Adam could be heard asking Rebecca on the 911 call. "Are you alive?"

"He's distancing himself from this," Greer interjected.

"She hung herself, I just woke up," Adam told the dispatcher.

"How is that relevant?" Greer asked rhetorically. "Not at all. He made this story up and he's selling his story."

Greer noted that Adam was three minutes into the call before he even tried to breathe into Rebecca's mouth, and that was only after the dispatcher directed him to do so.

Finally defining Adam's motive for the jury, he said, it's "one of the oldest reasons in the world. It's sex. Perverse sexual desire, sexual acts."

He said he used the word "assault" because that was the legal term, but he argued that the small, thin knife handle—the size of a light-day tampon—wouldn't cause any trauma to the vaginal walls, which was consistent with the county pathologist's findings.

Why would Adam tell the police that he had masturbated that morning? "Did it happen during that evening? Does it seem like normal circumstances? Your nephew is dying in the hospital. Is that the point in time you're going to be sexually aroused?"

Later in his summation, Greer said, "It all fits together, ladies and gentlemen, everything is just bizarre." Adam lived alone, and he had a girlfriend he "won't even show to his family."

The only man with the means and opportunity for Rebecca's brutal murder, he declared, "was Adam Shacknai."

In determining whether Adam was responsible for Rebecca's death, the jury had to answer two questions: Did Adam touch Rebecca with the intent to harm her? And if so, did that act cause her death?

The battery allegation was for tweaking Rebecca's nipples while he had paint on his fingertips. The Zahaus were symbolically asking for one penny for the paint Adam used to write the message, presumably to show that it had caused them pain. But they didn't claim any economic damages for the value of the paint itself, because it was the pain, not the paint, that had value. They were also asking to recoup the loss of monthly financial support Rebecca used to send her mother, and the loss of her companionship.

"I don't know what amount to put on a mother's loss of her daughter's love," Greer said. "It's priceless and it's not going to bring her back. See the evidence here, see that the sheriff's investigation was wrong. It led to a misleading conclusion."

Prior to this, when the attorneys were debating the wording of jury instructions, Greer had requested that the panel be asked whether Rebecca was murdered and whether Adam was responsible for her death as two separate questions.

But the defense believed that giving the jury no choice would set the bar higher for finding Adam responsible, so it fought to keep the issues conjoined. Blaming Adam would be the jury's only way to communicate that Rebecca didn't die at her own hand, a standard that the defense believed could not—and would not—be met.

Dan Webb's closing argument, which he delivered at a high, fervent pitch from the center of the courtroom, reflected that decision. But he strategically offered the jury the possibility that Rebecca had been murdered by someone else, to give an out to those who didn't believe Adam was responsible.

Webb pounded the same drumbeat as before, that there was

no evidence to link Adam to the death scene or to support the claim that Rebecca was murdered, yet he also repeated the refrain that "if somebody out there did that, it wasn't Adam."

The claims that she was hit over the head and assaulted with the knife weren't true, he said. Investigators found very little blood on the knife, and the pathologist said that the scalpel could have caused the hemorrhages on her head during the autopsy.

"There's been a complete failure of proof in this case," Webb said.

Rebecca was the one who knew best that she had "saved" Max, and it was she who knew where the paint and brushes were stored. Not Adam.

"How would he know that?" he asked. "There's no evidence that Adam Shacknai painted that message."

The Zahaus had filed this lawsuit with one unproven theory, repeatedly changed their stories, and misstated evidence, he said. Dina was the mastermind; now it's Adam. Adam stole Rebecca's shirt; "now we know that's not true." There were no fingerprints on the paint tube; "now we know prints are on the tube."

Webb's suicide scenario essentially lined up with the sheriff's department's: Adam was asleep while Rebecca was in the main house, feeling upset and guilty about Max. After getting Jonah's voice mail, she lost it. She stood in the hallway, dripping blood, as she painted the message on the door. Then she flung herself over that balcony.

The next morning, Adam did what any decent citizen would do. He called the authorities for help in case she was still alive. He voluntarily cooperated with investigators, even when it meant leaving the station without any shoes. But for all his good deeds, his life had been turned upside down.

Why, if someone were trying to stage a suicide, would he call attention to the deed by leaving the victim naked, bound, and gagged? It was more likely that Rebecca had staged her suicide to look like a homicide to protect her religious family from embarrassment.

Law enforcement was thorough in its investigation before determining that Rebecca had killed herself. When they exonerated Adam, Webb asked rhetorically, "did law enforcement become corrupt in California" and hide evidence?

Accused of being a "stone-cold vicious murderer and sexual deviant" since the lawsuit was filed in July 2013, Adam's life has been "a living hell," he said.

Dropping his voice to low, soft tones for dramatic effect, Webb pleaded with the jury to free Adam of the undeserved labels that had only caused "pain and suffering" for him and his family.

Keith Greer had the last word in his rebuttal. He conceded that his theory *had* changed, because "we even learn things in trial, [and see] new connections." But that didn't mean Adam had been exonerated.

"All that happened here was they said the only prints [and DNA] found at the scene were Rebecca's. Someone wiped down the scene and tried to cover up a murder," he said. "We're not putting Adam in jail here, Rebecca is dead. Adam is walking free."

Greer told the jury they weren't going to find any direct evidence of murder, "only what was left behind." The handwriting. The knots. The drops of blood.

"It doesn't make sense that it's suicide," he said.

As soon as the confrontation occurred in the hallway, "that's when Adam's life was ruined." Because he was afraid that Jonah and everyone else were going to find out what he'd done to Rebecca.

"Mary asked me, 'What would her last words be?'" Greer said.

After the defense objected, Greer abruptly stopped talking.

But this was no dramatic pause. The silence hung in the air as he began to pace back and forth, his face scrunched up as if he was going to cry. The only sound in the courtroom was Pari blowing her nose.

"You shouldn't have said that to me, it made me very emotional," Greer said in a low voice to Mary. But even with twelve pages of prepared comments still clutched in his hand, he couldn't go on.

"Please help Rebecca's mother and family, and hold Adam Shacknai accountable for what he did to Rebecca Zahau," he choked out, then sat down at the table.

After the judge explained to the jurors that at least nine of them had to agree on a verdict, one of them was sent home and was replaced by an alternate. With that, the group began its deliberations at 11:30 A.M.

The panel broke for a ninety-minute lunch at noon, but decided to work through the rest of the afternoon without taking a break.

In the midafternoon, they sent a note to the judge, referring to three items that were mentioned in one of the investigative reports, but were not addressed during witness testimony:

> *Is there any more information/evidence regarding these collected items?*
>
> *Tissue with red stains found on a bathroom sink on the mansion's third level.*
>
> *A pair of women's underwear found in a trash can in a guest house bedroom.*
>
> *A pair of black latex gloves found in the crawl space in the basement stairway.*

The judge's unresponsive reply to the note was this: *The jurors have been provided with all the exhibits received in evidence.*

As such, the panel wasn't informed that the panties and bloody tissue were never tested for DNA, or that the "pair of latex gloves" was actually just a single nitrile glove, which is a thinner and more tactile alternative to latex.

Chapter 37

After deliberating for just an hour the next morning, the jury sent word to the judge that it had reached a verdict. Bacal announced that they would wait twenty minutes for interested parties to arrive before the call to order.

The lawyers, court observers, and reporters were all surprised to hear that the jury had reached a decision so quickly—after only four and a half hours of deliberations.

In fact, it was so fast that many observers—the Shacknai brothers and their attorneys in particular—expected the verdict to be in Adam's favor. A quick verdict in civil cases generally signals that the jury has sided with the defendant, while a quick verdict in a criminal trial typically means the jury has found the defendant guilty.

Still, the Zahaus tried to remain optimistic that the jury would confirm what they'd thought all along: Adam had murdered Rebecca.

"To me, it's so obvious," Doug Loehner said, his leg shaking nervously as he sat behind me and members of the media, waiting for the announcement. "You've got to have hope."

As Jonah Shacknai and Mary Bedwell sat in the gallery behind the defense table, Greer approached the opposite side, where his wife was sitting near Doug.

"They have to have found murder," Greer said, almost as if he were trying to convince himself that the jury was going to get it right, despite how it looked. "It fits. Everything just fits."

The jurors' faces were devoid of emotion as they filed in. Sometimes jurors won't look at the defendant they are about to convict, or they smile at the victims or their families. But this jury gave no hints.

"Has the jury reached a verdict?" Bacal asked.

"We have," the blond forewoman said.

As the clerk read the first question, asking if the jury supported the allegation of battery against Adam and the economic loss of one cent for the paint, the forewoman answered, "Yes."

Adam kept a straight face and stared straight ahead, while Greer turned around in his chair, practically exploding with ebullience, and raised his thumb in a victory sign to his people in the gallery.

As the clerk read the second question, asking if the jury supported the wrongful death allegation, the forewoman again answered, "Yes."

With a vote of nine to three on both counts, the jury also awarded the Zahaus $5.17 million for the loss of Rebecca's love, emotional companionship, and financial assistance.

After Greer hugged Mary Zahau-Loehner, they chatted a few minutes before she got up and walked out of the courtroom with Doug, crying with relief.

Okay, I'm not crazy, Mary thought. *I'm not the only one who believes Adam murdered my sister.*

Bacal told the jurors to come back the next morning, when they might be asked to take up "another matter."

Outside, on the courthouse steps, Greer held a news conference for a throng of news cameras and reporters, standing with his arms around Mary's and Doug's shoulders.

A reporter asked if Greer really thought that Max's death and Jonah Shacknai really had nothing to do with Rebecca's death. He also asked what had shown Greer that there was no collusion between the Shacknai brothers.

Greer replied that Max's fall was what brought all these players together, but Adam's "isolation" was a weightier factor than any connection to his brother. "Anxiety of being found out by his brother and the world overwhelmed him," he said.

Through her tears, Mary said she would finally have the time now to truly grieve her sister's death. "The reality that Rebecca is gone is really going to hit me, because all these years, me and my family have been fighting just to prove she was murdered," she said.

But her family's fight still wasn't over, she said, adding that this was never about the money. They still had a hefty outstanding bill to pay for their expert witnesses, and with Adam's modest income, they didn't expect to recoup much of the $5 million settlement.

"My sister was brutally murdered. Just the thought that she knew she was going to die breaks my heart. I know my sister fought. She fought really hard, and the sheriff's department chose not to look at those signs, because it was so convenient for them to close it as suicide, for whatever reason. Maybe I'll never find out. But I know that God knows. I know Rebecca knows. And I know Adam Shacknai knows."

In light of the verdict, she said, "It's still our hope that there will be a criminal investigation and a criminal trial."

Greer shared what he'd planned to say before he was overcome with emotion in the courtroom—his imagined view of Rebecca's last words: "Forgive him. Help my mother and hold Adam Shacknai accountable for what he has done."

Acknowledging there was still a chance for a settlement, he added, "We've done our job . . . It's going to cost six figures to fight an appeal."

But first, he would take the rest of the day to review a thousand pages of financial documents, submitted by the defense, to determine whether he should ask for punitive damages.

Shortly after the verdict was announced, the SDSD released a written statement.

In regards to the criminal investigation, the Sheriff's Department stands by the findings of the Medical Examiner's Office and our investigators. These findings were supported by forensic evidence and medical examinations, it read in part. *We are also willing to meet with the Zahau Family to look at any new evidence that came out of the civil trial.*

Many viewed the quick statement as politically tone-deaf, given that law enforcement expects citizens to respect the justice system and jury verdicts. But it also served as a gut-punch for the Zahau family.

"We're not going to let this issue die," Greer said. "Do we trust a sheriff who's had all this evidence all this time and didn't do anything about it? I don't think he's deserving of that trust."

The next morning, Adam came to court wearing yellow tennis shoes and a brown T-shirt that said STAX in block letters—a record label, originally based in his home town of Memphis, that recorded soul music performers, such as Isaac Hayes and Otis Redding.

But on a day when the plaintiff would either request or waive punitive damages from Adam, his ultracasual music-fan outfit seemed to convey a defiant, irreverent message that he had no respect for the judge or the verdict, and he didn't care who knew it.

After going through Adam's financials, Greer told the court that his clients had decided not to ask for any more damages. He told the media afterward that Rebecca wouldn't have wanted to kick a man when he was down, but he said privately that Adam didn't earn enough to make it worthwhile. As it was, they would be lucky to collect much, if any, of the judgment.

The jury was then discharged. Choosing not to speak to attorneys or the media, they were led out a secret back door as the reporters and photographers rushed toward the elevators to try to chase them down on the street below.

Meanwhile, the political posturing continued, this time at a news conference called by Adam, his girlfriend, Mary, and attorney Dan Webb.

Proclaiming that they were "extraordinarily disappointed and absolutely astounded" by the verdict, Webb said, "In my forty years as a trial lawyer, I have never seen such a catastrophic manipulation of the court system and the judicial process as I've seen in this case." He was confident the verdict would be overturned as they filed an appeal and kept on fighting.

Stepping up to the microphones, Adam was clearly riled up by the injustice of it all. Calling the Zahau camp "posers," he essentially accused the family and their attorney of being grifters.

"They got away with something once," he said. "They got lucky one time. I don't think they're going to get lucky again." Saying they tried to take his money and tarnish his reputation when he was absolutely innocent, Adam threatened to file malicious prosecution and defamation lawsuits against them.

Greer later responded that there was no such thing as "malicious winning," and that someone had to lose a trial to be sued for malicious prosecution.

"God bless the First Amendment," he said, noting that people can't be sued for what they say in court.

Unlike his brother, Jonah didn't feel compelled to speak to the media about the case, or why Adam lost in court. He kept his thoughts to himself until recently, when I asked to interview him for this book.

"I'm not going to comment on his ethics, but [Greer] is a certain style of lawyer with antics and evolving theories—certainly not a regular lawyer that practices at the highest standards," he said. "He behaved like a barnyard animal who would do and say anything in terms of his tactics and demeanor, accusing people of murder, recanting, accusing other people of murder, changing the story to be emotionally evocative, without any factual or evidentiary basis."

Dan Webb, in contrast, "was, and is, a white-shoe lawyer from a very large firm," who was used to following the "rules," and behaving ethically. "I don't think many reputable lawyers would have been used to [Greer's] tactics."

At trial, Greer and Webb were so mismatched that it "worked to Adam's disadvantage," Jonah said, likening the stark contrast to the joke about "the guy who brings a knife to a gunfight."

Hearing these remarks, Greer countered that he liked Webb, whom he described "as a very good lawyer," and from whom he'd learned a tremendous amount. He said they had a good relationship during the trial, "based on professionalism and ethics," making deals and commitments with a handshake. Jonah, he said, was obviously advocating for his brother with such remarks, and was "the wrong one to be casting stones."

"[Webb] has represented a lot of famous criminals, who are in jail, so I can see why they brought in a criminal lawyer in this case," Greer said. "I think the mistake they made was thinking that if they pumped in enough money and brought in enough high-powered attorneys that they could steamroll over the truth. And although I was clearly outgunned, I had the truth on my side. Dan did a great job, but I just think the jury didn't believe him."

Greer acknowledged that he received at least one previous cease-and-desist letter warning him not to make defamatory remarks about Jonah, but he viewed that letter as a trophy. "I'm pretty sure I hung that up on the wall," he said.

* * *

Shortly after the verdict was announced, Sheriff Bill Gore's opponent in the upcoming election started a firestorm on Twitter: When elected Sheriff, I will reopen case, he tweeted.

At the time, Commander Dave Myers, the SDSD's highest-ranking openly gay officer, had nothing to lose—Gore had already told the media that he wanted to fire his campaign opponent, who said he'd been moved into a tiny converted "broom closet" and was prohibited from attending staff meetings.

A former homicide detective, Myers criticized Gore for putting the burden on the Zahau family to bring forth new evidence, characterizing the sheriff's refusal to reopen the criminal case as a matter of pride.

"That's not who we are in law enforcement," he told me. "It's foolish not to look at every conspiracy theory. We need to do anything possible to bring a voice for those who can no longer speak for themselves, to bring closure, especially to murder cases. The best way to get away with homicide is to make it look like a suicide."

The nine-to-three vote by the jury, he said, shows "that there's something there."

Myers said he believed the investigation was "rushed to judgment" after Coronado officers responded to the second 911 call at the Spreckels Mansion. Two days earlier, the same officers had seen Rebecca crying and screaming Max's name as he lay ashen on the floor, so they thought: *Child died, distraught female, she's weak, she's emotional, she just hung herself.*

Myers later claimed that half the sheriff's homicide unit believed the criminal case should have been reopened, because it was "the right thing to do." Max wasn't actually declared brain dead until several days after Rebecca's body was found.

* * *

After getting blowback from his postverdict statement, followed by Myers's tweet, Sheriff Gore announced two weeks later that a new team of detectives would "review" the trial transcripts and any alternative theories that came out during the proceedings. The team would release its findings within ninety days.

However, he underscored that the criminal case was *not* being reopened. This was simply an internal *reexamination* of his department's investigation.

Bill Gore and his family have a long history in law enforcement and politics in San Diego County.

One of Gore's brothers was a local sheriff's deputy and another was an officer with the San Diego Police Department (SDPD), where their father had worked his way up to assistant chief.

While at the SDPD, Bill Gore Sr. mentored a young police officer, Bill Kolender, who rose through the ranks to become chief. Kolender, who later was elected sheriff, delivered the eulogy at Gore Sr.'s funeral.

Before he was sheriff, Bill Gore spent thirty-two years working for the FBI, including stints as assistant director and special agent in charge (SAIC) of the San Diego and Seattle offices. But the Zahau case was not the first time he'd been attacked for his agency's actions in a high-profile case.

Gore headed the bureau's San Diego office during 9/11, when two hijackers—who had attended a local flight school and had lived with an FBI informant—flew planes into the Pentagon. After this embarrassing news came out, Gore contended that the terrorists weren't on the FBI's radar because the CIA didn't share its intel about them.

As one of the supervising SAICs at Ruby Ridge, Gore also came under fire for his handling of the armed confrontation with civilians, one of whom was a woman who was fatally shot while holding her baby. When Dave Myers faulted Gore for not being more transparent and for "taking the Fifth" during the subsequent court proceedings in federal court, Gore said he had just been heeding his attorney's advice.

After his retirement from the FBI, which was mandated at age fifty-seven, Gore worked as a special advisor to District Attorney Bonnie Dumanis until 2004, when Sheriff Bill Kolender hired Gore as his assistant sheriff. Gore was promoted to undersheriff a year later.

When Kolender retired after developing Alzheimer's, Gore was appointed sheriff in a move that some viewed as preordained. Nonetheless, he kept the seat in subsequent elections, though his race against Myers was quite close.

Gore and his department were praised for their handling of the highly publicized search for teenager Chelsea King and the prompt arrest of her killer, sexual predator John Gardner, in 2010. However, the following year, Gore was back in the line of fire for the Zahau case, and has been ever since.

In 2019, he ran into criticism for failing to proactively discipline a sheriff's captain and lieutenant who were arrested by the FBI for engaging in illegal gun sales and facilitating the issuance of concealed weapons permits. He also was blasted for neglecting to reduce an unprecedented number of inmate suicides in the county jails—more than 140 since he took office in 2009, a rate five times higher than state prisons. Gore blamed the opioid epidemic and said today's jail population is much older, sicker, and more mentally and medically unstable.

Then, after the COVID-19 pandemic hit in early 2020, that criticism escalated as hundreds of jail employees and inmates tested positive amid complaints of dangerous health conditions. Gore was forced to release more than two thousand inmates, who weren't charged with a serious or violent crime, with no bail.

*   *   *

The Zahau case is also not the first time the county ME's office has been criticized for its handling of a controversial high-profile death staged to look like something it wasn't.

One of the county's own toxicologists, Kristin Rossum, was fired in 2001 for using meth six months before she was arrested for poisoning her husband with fentanyl and other drugs she stole from the lab, then staging a suicide scene at their apartment. Rossum claimed that her husband, Gregory de Villers, poisoned himself, then sprinkled red rose petals over his own body, because he was depressed that she was leaving him. She was ultimately convicted of his murder.

Her married boss, Australian toxicologist Michael Robertson, was also fired because he'd failed to report her drug use while they were having an affair. He was later charged with conspiracy for helping Rossum try to cover up the murder.

The de Villers family sued the county for negligence and wrongful death. Because Rossum stole meth and drugs from the lab, where she and other employees had easy access to recreational and prescription drugs stored there, I called it a "virtual candy store" in one of my news articles in 2002, and the nickname stuck. I published a book about the case, *Poisoned Love*, in 2005.

The de Villerses' lawsuit resulted in a judgment against the county, which was overturned on appeal, but it forced many changes in the ME's office nonetheless.

"This case certainly got national attention, so I assume a lot of people woke up and smelled the roses," Chief Medical Examiner Glenn Wagner said at the time.

Although the ME's office issued the final determination about the manner and cause of death in the Zahau case, its staff relied on information provided by the SDSD to make that decision. It is rare, if ever, for the two agencies to issue conflicting findings.

Dr. Jonathan Lucas, who did Rebecca's and Max's autopsies, left the San Diego office in 2017 for a $350,000-a-year job heading the Los Angeles County Medical Examiner-Coroner's Office, one of the busiest in the nation.

Chapter 38

After being prohibited from attending the first news conference on this case in September 2011, I started my initial research by gathering search warrant affidavits and Rebecca's autopsy report, which were posted online.

But it was clear that the sheriff's department was still holding back most of its investigative findings, citing privacy issues, even after the case was deemed closed and solved as a suicide. I could only hope that more evidence would come out, or that the matter would end up in court, which would make it safer to write about. So, I waited.

In the meantime, I was constantly asked, "Are you going to write a book on the Coronado mansion *murder*?"

Because Rebecca's death still wasn't a "crime," and I didn't want to get sued, I cautiously responded that I couldn't pursue a book without an arrest, a homicide finding, or some kind of court ruling. Publishers are risk averse, and, frankly, so am I.

Although that changed once the Zahau family filed their lawsuit in 2013, I still had to wait to see if the case made it to trial, got settled out of court, or resulted in a verdict that could lead to the reopening of the criminal case.

* * *

Over the next few years, I often discussed the case with an old friend, private investigator Bill Garcia, who worked for Dina's insurance company before she was dismissed from the Zahaus' lawsuit. Garcia told me that Dina had authorized him to share some information with me.

He and I went back a long way. While married to one of my former editors, he'd offered to go down to Mexico to explore the circumstances of my late husband's suicide in 1999. Naturally, I was distraught, and Garcia helped me tremendously by bringing my husband's Jeep back to San Diego so it could be repossessed. He also hand-delivered a brown plastic box containing a bag of Rich's cremated remains. I still remember how acidic and sharp the shards felt in my hand as I scattered them in a forested area that I thought Rich would appreciate.

In addition, Garcia gave me a detailed investigative report that explained what had transpired in the days before Rich died: After getting his Jeep stuck in the mud while off-roading, he got a room at a motel, where he caused a ruckus by walking around the courtyard naked, yelling with his hands over his head, at 2:00 A.M. The next night, after being moved to a new motel, he drank four beers, then used a taut cord to hang himself over the top of the bathroom door. A maid came in and saw him standing next to the door the following afternoon, but he was cold to the touch.

I was well aware of Rich's mental-health and addiction issues. But even knowing how bad things could get, Garcia's report was still hard for me to read.

Rich had been forced to resign from his county pension fund job after getting arrested for shoplifting while in an alcoholic blackout at the Phoenician resort in Scottsdale, where he was attending an investment conference. In a bizarre coincidence, he was given the same type of plea agreement as Rebecca. They even went through the same diversion program.

Rich was a chronic alcoholic, but he'd been sober and in recovery for a year before he died. However, he was still suffering from depression, and his therapist had informed me—not him—that she'd diagnosed him with borderline personality disorder, and told me not to tell him.

He'd been in the process of switching between antidepressants, but the latest one made his behavior so erratic, aggressive, and scary that I told him to stop taking it and call his doctor for a different medication. I learned a week after his death that he'd never picked up the new prescription.

As our marriage was sputtering to an end, he relapsed again. I could see that he was permanently broken and was never going to be a good partner for me.

After having given him too many chances already, I found him drunk in bed one afternoon, with the sweet cloying smell of alcohol in the air and an empty liquor bottle on the kitchen counter. I was so angry that I was shaking as I packed a bag, and told him to be gone by the time I came back from a weekend journalism conference. Our relationship was over.

I had the locks changed, but I was still concerned about him. When I called to check on him, he apologized that he'd kept me from having the baby I'd always wanted. It was true, and it made me sad, both for him and for me.

Rich had conveyed his suicidal ideations as a form of emotional manipulation, and as a way to get attention. As I later learned, this had been a pattern in all three of his marriages. But on the Thursday that his body was found, I knew his demise was coming. I woke up with a heavy gray ache that I felt deep in my bones, and it lasted all day.

"I'm just waiting for the call," I told a friend after trying to nap that afternoon.

Ten minutes later, I heard from Rich's AA sponsor that there was a body in Mexico, but they still weren't sure it was Rich. I spent the next twenty-four hours struggling with my own ambivalence about the possibility that it might be someone else.

Although he was on a psychotropic roller coaster from prescription drugs, alcohol, and his own brain chemistry, Rich was still coherent enough to leave out his driver's license, presumably so I would be informed of his death. The maid also found a plastic bag of ground-up lightbulb shards, which he'd apparently been planning to eat if necessary.

I'd learned about some of his lies before he died, but many of them didn't become evident until after his death, when I found two locked briefcases full of documents, as well as letters, photos of women in tawdry hotel rooms, and other items that exposed the dark secrets he'd been hiding from me—including the police report about his shoplifting arrest.

I didn't see them at first, but the more I researched this case, the more parallels I saw between Rebecca and my late husband. Rebecca's family wasn't aware of how deep her relationship and self-esteem troubles went, or how much she ached to be loved by the right man, because she'd never talked to them about that. She never said she wanted to commit suicide, nor did she voice the deep sadness that she described in the notes on her phone or in the emails she sent to Michael Berger. She only showed them her happy face.

Rebecca told a lot of conflicting stories to various people, but none of them seemed malicious in nature. I still don't know whether Rebecca was truly abducted by Neil or whether she made up the story to avoid hurting Michael. Perhaps she couldn't face telling Michael that it was over, but he certainly believed that she was in danger at the time.

All I know is that my husband told me a lot of wild stories

too. His tears seemed just as real as Rebecca's did to Michael, and Rich managed to convince me too, for a time anyway, that he was telling the truth. Who knows? Maybe he believed his own lies.

Meanwhile, the suicide versus murder debate continued to rage in the Zahau case, escalating as it progressed to trial. I kept an open mind, because every time one alternative scenario seemed to make sense, I uncovered new evidence that pointed in another direction.

One scenario involved a New York prison inmate, whom I will call "Vincent Bruno," who claimed Max was killed by an assassin. Claiming to be an Italian Mafia associate, Bruno sent letters to Jonah and his friend Howard, warning them of additional "hits" on Jonah's family by Bruno's cellmate, another alleged Mafia associate. Bruno specifically cited Jonah's parents by name as other possible victims, and asked to meet with Jonah.

Bill Garcia got ahold of Jonah's letter while working on Dina's case, because it was delivered to her house. Garcia also met with Bruno in prison four times in 2016, spoke with him by phone, and also corresponded with him.

Prison officials subsequently told Garcia that Bruno may have known some low-level Mafia associates, but he wasn't one himself. Bruno had also been caught running catfishing scams by writing to private citizens and asking them to come to his parole hearings. That said, Garcia thought it was curious that Bruno had enough specific information to make claims about Jonah's business and his family without some kind of connection or source. For one, how would Bruno know a dermatologist named Howard Luber was Jonah's best friend?

I learned a lot of new information by sitting through the trial and found the testimony quite compelling. But as I watched through the lens of my own experience, I still had many unanswered questions.

What comes out in a trial is not a single truth. Each side tries to win its case by presenting witnesses who offer conflicting interpretations of the same evidence, which in this case was collected by sheriff's investigators. I came away convinced that the whole truth had not come out—from either side. I knew I would have to burrow into new areas, and come at this from every angle I could find.

The outside-hit theory, for example, was still floating out there. Dan Webb had even mentioned it in his closing argument, saying that if someone *had* murdered Rebecca, it wasn't Adam.

If she or Max had been killed by a hit man, I figured Jonah wouldn't want to discuss that out of fear for his family's safety, which meant it would likely never be proven. Had he mentioned that fear to Gore, and did that have anything to do with keeping this case closed? I wanted to talk to both of them, but I knew Jonah hadn't talked to any writer or news media but *20/20*, and only briefly at that.

So I set out to pick up where investigators stopped looking, and to delve into places they had not thought to go. What other dynamics were going on behind the scenes at the Spreckels Mansion, in Jonah's business life—and beyond—that could have generated a motive for murder, even if it was only a staged one?

Chapter 39

Despite what Adam, Jonah, and Howard told detectives in July 2011 about Jonah's loving relationship with Rebecca, it had become clear since the trial that relations between the couple and life at the mansion had not been so great after all. Both sides had since admitted that the relationship was actually falling apart.

But was Rebecca thinking of leaving Jonah and returning to her ex-husband for yet another fresh start and geographical cure, even though that had failed so many times before? Or had she resigned herself to stick it out this time?

Public records and news stories about Jonah's business showed that the stakes were high for him in the months before Rebecca's death, and even more so afterward, as the investigation adversely affected his company's bottom line. Jonah may have brought some of these tensions home with him, which would have added even more conflict.

Rebecca mentioned that she wished they'd kept the Doberman, that things might have been different for Max if they had, but she never explained what she meant. Was someone else at the mansion before one or both of these two fateful incidents, which occurred less than forty-eight hours apart?

Going further back in time, Jonah's complex web of business

dealings involved government investigations, class-action lawsuits, threats of a hostile takeover, and employee terminations
for a variety of reasons. Could any of these have produced a "hit
man," someone who might have wanted to hurt him or his loved
ones?

In 2008, Medicis executive Richard Havens and three employees under him pleaded guilty to conspiracy to violate the
Food and Drug Act for promoting an off-label use—diaper
rash—of the antifungal ointment Loprox, when FDA restric-
tions prohibited its use by children under ten. Jonah said Havens
took responsibility for the actions, pleaded guilty to a misdemeanor, and resigned.

As CEO, Jonah also entered into an agreement with the federal government stating he "accepted ultimate responsibility for
the conduct that gave rise" to the investigation.

"They came knocking on our door, we weren't even aware of
this occurring," he told me.

Medicis also agreed to pay the federal government $9.8 mil-
lion to settle all claims related to the case, without admitting liability. According to the federal DOJ, the case was triggered by
whistle-blower complaints from four former sales reps, who
ended up receiving about $1 million from the federal govern-
ment for reporting the use of Medicaid reimbursements for Loprox prescriptions.

Around the same time, a group of investors filed a series of
federal securities-fraud class-action lawsuits against Medicis,
alleging that the company committed fraudulent accounting practices by overstating profits from the sales and returns of expired
cosmetic products for more than four years.

After being audited and subsequently ordered to recalculate
its earnings, Medicis disclosed new values for the profits, which
triggered a dramatic one-day stock drop of $2.34 per share, or
13 percent, on trading of more than 3 million shares, and "wiped

out approximately $125 million of shareholder equity," according to the lawsuit.

Jonah and two top executives were named in a lawsuit that consolidated the claims, filed in 2009. Medicis denied all the allegations, saying that a simultaneous announcement about its product Solodyn was "of greater significance," and that none of the defendants showed any individual financial gain or had any motive to commit fraud.

In 2011, the parties negotiated a settlement for $18 million. Ernst & Young settled that lawsuit, and saw several of its employees disciplined, because the firm "bore all the responsibility legally and financially," Jonah contended.

"No one in our firm was in any way implicated or involved," he said.

Although Medicis admitted no wrongdoing, it was responsible for paying $11 million of the settlement, which Jonah said was covered by their insurance carrier. Ernst & Young paid only $7 million.

In the months preceding Rebecca's death, Medicis was being targeted for what Jonah described as "an unsolicited takeover" by several other companies. Fueled by rumors of mergers and acquisitions reported in the *Wall Street Journal*, the threat was bad enough that Jonah tried to take Medicis private with the help of some large private equity firms.

After Rebecca's death, publicity emanating from the sheriff's investigation caused a drop in stock prices that exacerbated Jonah's concerns about the reputation and future of his company. Speculation was running rampant that Rebecca had been murdered and that he was somehow involved, possibly as payback for something business related.

As Jonah tried to head off the takeover attempt by Valeant Pharmaceuticals, another large company, and several private equity firms, he said Valeant "took advantage" of the situation with Max and Rebecca and forced him and his company into crisis management mode.

"They even tried to reach me while I was at the Rady Children's Hospital," he said.

As a result, he said, he pleaded with sheriff's officials to consider his plight and to publicly state that he wasn't a suspect. Later, he tried to find a way to legitimize and gain public acceptance of the sheriff's conclusions.

But, he said, "I never wanted the investigation to go away. I wanted it to be completed in an appropriate and orderly fashion."

Although he declined to sell his company in July 2011, Valeant continued to purchase shares, while Jonah and his company continued to reel from this challenging series of events. The public's interest in Rebecca's death was simply unrelenting.

When Valeant resurfaced in fall 2012 with "a very aggressive cash offer for the company," he said, Medicis ultimately accepted. The sale was final that December.

Valeant paid $3.4 billion for Medicis, but shareholders received only $2.6 billion because of some debt on the books. SEC records show that Jonah personally walked away with $41 million, after he and seven of his directors lost or gave up their positions amid a termination of 95 percent of Medicis employees.

"I'd still be at Medicis if we hadn't been taken over, I don't want to say unwillingly, but it wasn't a welcome transaction," Jonah said recently. "I declined to participate in any way with the company that acquired us . . . even at a significant financial cost."

Keith Greer wanted the jurors to hear more about all of this so they could make up their own minds about whether Jonah had any undue influence over the sheriff's investigation.

"Although he admitted he told the sheriff about the stock crashing, and affecting people's pensions, he denied putting pressure on the sheriff," Greer said in pretrial court papers. "A jury should be able to hear the testimony and decide if this is believable or if it's contradictory and supports plaintiff's claims that Jonah Shacknai pressured the sheriff to wrap up the investigation quickly."

But the defense apparently won this fight, because none of this came out in court.

In a class-action lawsuit filed a year after the Valeant purchase, Jonah and his male leadership team from Medicis were retroactively accused of creating a hostile work environment and discriminating against female employees from 2008 through 2012.

In the era of #MeToo, when we, as a society, are encouraged to believe female accusers, these allegations—which Jonah deemed "outrageous," "absurd," and "spurious"—nonetheless raise questions about the scope of emotional challenges Rebecca may have been dealing with at home.

The lawsuit, filed by seven female former employees, ultimately encompassed claims from 225 women. Ninety-nine involved allegations of sexual harassment, and the rest concerned lower pay, smaller bonuses, and overall suppression of promotion and advancement for women.

In summary, the claimants alleged: Female sales applicants were told that Medicis was a "boys club," where women had to prove themselves. Once hired, they had to deal with objectification, groping, crude jokes, sexual propositions, and even sexually charged games of Charades at sales meetings. Forced to stay out late drinking with clients and male managers, female employees were made to "feel they were expected to be sexually available to their superiors," or lose out on favorable treatment and promotions. Pregnant workers were also discouraged from taking time off.

In July 2016, Valeant agreed to a $7.2 million settlement, which angered Jonah, because the former "Medicis manage-

ment never had an opportunity to respond. We would have denied all the allegations."

Jonah maintained that the original plaintiffs were all fired for
performance issues, and that many subsequent claimants acted
out of anger at Valeant for massive firings after it purchased
Medicis. Several women even apologized to him for filing false
claims, he said, for which they were paid about $20,000 each.

"The feeling was so bad, people came to the trough," he said.

In his defense, he said, expectations for the Medicis sales
force were "gender blind. They were all driven by numbers."
Medicis was recognized as one of the world's most ethical companies in 2011 and 2012 by the Scottsdale-based Ethisphere Institute. And eight of the thirty employees at his new company,
DermaForce Partners, which develops, manufactures, and sells
skin-care treatment products to dermatologists and plastic sur-
geons under the name of skinbetter science, are women who
used to work for him at Medicis.

Journalist Sean Elder, who mentioned the lawsuit during
Death at the Mansion: Rebecca Zahau, a documentary series on
the Oxygen network, called Jonah "a force" in the pharmaceutical industry, and agreed he never would have agreed to settle.

"He fights things to the last straw," he said.

However, Elder also described Jonah as "controlling" in
many aspects of his life, including his efforts to keep himself
out of the news and how his brand is portrayed.

"What frustrated him the most is that he cannot make this
[Zahau] story go away," Elder said.

Chapter 40

The public's interest in this case hasn't flagged, because many people still believe the sheriff's investigation didn't go far enough to resolve a multitude of unanswered questions and to fill in integral pieces of this story. The question is, why? Was it poor evidence collection and testing, confirmation bias, or a failure to ask the right questions of the right people?

While researching this book, I was given plenty of crazy "leads," heard a lot of conspiracy theories, and went down many a rabbit hole. Given the intrigue, many observers and outside experts have been inspired to offer their own interpretations of the evidence and alternative scenarios to the official finding of suicide. It just doesn't make sense to most people how or why Rebecca would come up with such an elaborate plan to kill herself.

Although Sheriff Gore dismissed attorney Anne Bremner's comments about the extreme rarity of women hanging themselves naked, claiming there was all sorts of literature about naked suicides, that is not, in fact, the case.

Only one medical journal came up in a Google search for "naked suicide," and it stated, ironically, that "the psychiatric and forensic literature is mostly silent on the topic." The author of the article, "Naked Suicide," is Robert I. Simon, a former clinical professor of psychiatry and director of the Psychiatry and Law Program at Georgetown University School of Medicine, who said he wrote it to encourage discussion of "this little understood phenomenon."

When Simon published the article in the *Journal of the American Academy of Psychiatry and the Law* in 2008, he wrote that comprehensive studies of naked suicides simply didn't exist. He could find little or no information in textbooks or journal articles, and only a "spate of news articles" about people who had "jumped to their deaths while naked." Other than the jumpers, he said, most "naked suicides occur indoors."

Of the lawsuits involving suicides that he reviewed, no more than 8 percent of the victims were naked. He also found that about 95 percent of all suicides were linked to mental illness.

Conventional wisdom has it that a woman found hanging naked is most likely a homicide or a staged suicide, he wrote. *It is thought that "feminine modesty" carries over into a suicidal death.*

He noted that women may accidentally hang themselves naked while engaging in erotic asphyxia—aimed at heightening an orgasm by cutting off oxygen to the brain—but this is typically done indoors with a partner, using a belt or soft restraint. Given the bindings, bloody knife, and painted message on the door at the Spreckels Mansion, no one believes that Rebecca's death was anything but intentional.

Simon offered several possible motives for naked suicide, which he said may be done impulsively while already unclothed: a desire for "rebirth and cleansing," a reference to Christ's resurrection; "anger and vengeance," with intent to "traumatize a survivor"; and in depressed people, "an expression of vulnerability, utter despair, desolation and worthlessness." In the case of one male psychiatric patient, his plan to commit suicide naked was a way to "atone" for his perceived sins, as "a sacrificial lamb, shorn of clothes."

* * *

But what makes this case so unusual and complex is that Rebecca's death was not just a simple case of "naked suicide."

The salient fact here, forensic and suicide experts say, is that case histories are virtually absent of women who have employed this particular *combination* of methods to commit suicide. Rebecca was not only naked, she was hanging outside, gagged, with her ankles tied and her hands bound behind her back. And the peculiar message on the door was written in the third person.

Wherever one stands on this case, what is perhaps most baffling is why anyone would stage a homicide *or* a suicide in this particular way, because it naturally drew tremendous media attention. To send a message, perhaps? If so, to whom and by whom?

Deciphering the cryptic note on the door could help demystify this case, but no one can agree on what it means. Some have described its tone as taunting or angry, others as lyrical or poetic.

But consider this: The message has a notable lack of punctuation, which could be a clue to identifying its author, like a handwritten signature. The message is in the form of a question, yet it ends without a question mark, and omits a possible comma in the middle. This could reflect an irrational state of mind, a perceived need to hurry, or a habit of writing texts or emails without punctuation. It could also signal that the author is not a native-English speaker, or that it is someone pretending to be one. It's even possible that the author wanted to create chaos, confusion, and open-ended intrigue as part of the staging.

Those who believe Rebecca was murdered say it sounds like a message from her killer—that no one could save her, because she was already dead.

Conversely, if she wrote the note before committing suicide, some say that she meant she had "saved" Max by giving him CPR, and now was asking, rhetorically, if anyone could save her from going to hell, as Christian beliefs dictate. Jonah suggested the "you" in the message could refer to God or even to him.

Adam signs his signature using block letters, which is not a common practice. Rebecca's sister said she scoured through Rebecca's handwritten materials and found nothing in block print.

Asked if the message sounded like her writing, Jonah said, "It didn't sound like her, it didn't sound not like her." He has resigned himself to the fact that he will probably never know what the message means, "particularly if you ascribe it to a psychotic act, and what precedes it to psychotic behavior, that makes it all the more unintelligible."

Nina Romano said she had "no clue" what it meant, but "if we could understand that message, then maybe all of us could understand what the hell happened. I want [the Zahaus] to know, I want them to have closure for what happened for their sister and their daughter, because I understand their pain and I understand why they can't let it go. I feel *awful* for them, my sister feels *awful* for them. She would never, ever want another mother to feel what she's feeling, because my sister, she will never be the same."

Another matter of debate is whether Rebecca's neck injuries were more consistent with homicidal manual strangulation or hanging by suicide. This can be put into a broader context by comparing her injuries with those in two other high-profile cases: the hanging deaths of Jeffrey Epstein in a New York City jail cell and Saddam Hussein's half brother, Barzan Ibrahim, who was executed in Iraq.

Controversy ensued when Ibrahim's execution resulted in his decapitation—with his head landing five feet away from his body and his severed neck spewing blood, after his body was dropped less than eight feet through a trapdoor.

Rebecca's body supposedly dropped more than a foot farther—nine feet and two inches—yet she had no cervical spine damage and her head was still attached. She suffered only a fracture to the cricoid and thyroid cartilages and a break to one arm of her hyoid bone.

Epstein, a financier facing charges that he and other wealthy men had sex with underage girls, was found hanging in his cell with ligature marks on his neck, and internal damage to the neck that was similar to Rebecca's. The guards who were supposed to be watching him fell asleep, then fraudulently altered their report to protect themselves. Cameras in the area were suspiciously not functioning.

Dr. Michael Baden, a renowned forensic pathologist with five decades of experience, was hired by Epstein's brother to observe the autopsy. He also went on TV to dispute the suicide findings by the New York City Medical Examiner's Office, where he once worked.

Baden said Epstein had two fractures of the left and right sides of the thyroid cartilage, as well as a broken hyoid bone, which "points to homicide rather than suicide."

"Those three fractures are extremely unusual in suicidal hangings and could occur much more commonly in homicidal strangulation," said Baden, who has weighed in on murder cases involving O.J. Simpson, Phil Spector, and Aaron Hernandez.

In fact, he added, he'd never seen three such fractures in a suicide in his fifty-year career. Neither had Dr. Cyril Wecht, who was also consulted on the Epstein case, saying it was "extremely rare."

"You don't get those three fractures in a suicidal hanging with someone leaning forward," Wecht said in the Netflix documentary series on the case.

These opinions on the Epstein case gibe not only with Wecht's findings for Rebecca, but also with conclusions drawn by four doctors who coauthored the article "Suicide by Ligature Strangulation: Three Case Reports," published in *The American Journal of Forensic Medicine and Pathology* in 2009:

Fractures of the hyoid bone or the laryngeal cartilages are rarely found in suicide cases and are restricted to only one broken upper thyroid horn in most instances.

The article cited a separate German review of 116 suicide ligature strangulation cases, in which *the number of laryngohyoid fractures generally was low and the involvement of the hyoid bone, as well as major injuries (e.g., a fracture of the cricoid cartilage) was extremely uncommon.*

When I interviewed Anne Bremner, the Zahaus' first attorney, about this case in 2019, she had a number of theories about who killed Rebecca. Although she thought Adam made the most sense, she didn't think he did it alone.

"Why was the lividity in Rebecca's back? She didn't die from hanging, she died from being on her back and being strangled. That's hugely compelling. That's where the blood settled when she died . . . She was already dead when she was moved. The subgaleal bruises on her head could have come from [being hit with] the heavy weight under the bed. It's in the pictures.

"It's like the Jeffrey Epstein case," she said. "There probably was some help in there, we just don't know what it is."

The state of the chandelier that Max apparently grabbed, and which fell to the floor next to him, also indicated murder to her: The cord was "severed right in the middle, like someone cut it. I thought that was really weird," she said.

As I combed through the sheriff's investigative reports one last time, I found a few surprising, relevant details that were never publicly released. Some were facts from the crime lab analysis that presumably weren't publicized because they would have either detracted from the suicide findings, or didn't specifically support Keith Greer's premise that Adam killed Rebecca.

For example, the blue T-shirt that was wrapped around Rebecca's neck and shoved into her mouth had "a mixture of DNA from at least three individuals," one of whom was Rebecca. Assuming that the second person was the tech who collected the shirt, at least one other contributor was never identified "due to the complex nature of the mixture." Adam, Nina, and Ariel were excluded, so who else's DNA is on that shirt? According to investigators, the shirt was a Massimo brand, size XS, which is typically a size for women. However, the authorities never identified whose shirt it was.

Similarly, the rope removed from Rebecca's wrists also indicated "a mixture of DNA from at least two individuals." Rebecca was deemed only a "possible contributor," but there were also "two foreign DNA types." Again, Adam, Nina, and Ariel were excluded.

One of the guest room doorknobs indicated a low-level DNA mixture from at least two individuals, but the lab could reach no conclusion on who they were.

Detective Tsuida noted that Rebecca's clothes—a white undershirt, a black long-sleeved T-shirt, and a pair of blue jeans—were laid out on the bed in the master bedroom, where the bedding was pulled down. This led Tsuida to conclude that Rebecca "was probably asleep prior to checking her voice mail" at 12:50 A.M.

But if her period was heavy enough to be dripping on the carpet, then why wouldn't she wear a tampon to bed or to walk around the house and garage to gather the knives and rope? Were the spots and smears of blood on Rebecca's left toes and foot really caused by scratches from the prickly succulent below the balcony?

Curiously, investigators didn't focus on the prints that were found on certain items, such as the eight-inch knife's blade, but that didn't belong to the excluded people. Combined with the lack of fingerprints or DNA from anyone but Rebecca at the death scene, and the absence of Adam's DNA on items he admitted to touching, some people say this indicates an incomplete investigation with questionable collection techniques. If investigators didn't swab certain areas that they know Adam touched, isn't it possible they also missed other places that he or someone else touched?

Some outside investigators say yes. "The investigation was sloppy," Doug Loehner, who recently retired from his job as a police officer in Missouri, told FOX 5 San Diego.

Based on his examination of the evidence, Paul Holes, a retired forensic criminologist and cold case investigator, said the SDSD's methodology for collecting and testing DNA seemed flawed.

"I'm fairly convinced something is amiss there," he said on the Oxygen network's series.

Holes noted, for example, that only one swab was used to collect DNA from items with large surface areas like the door with the painted message, where multiple swabs should have been used. A single swab can only hold so much material before it becomes saturated, causing secondary profiles to be wiped out or go undetected. This, he said, may be why investigators found none of Adam's DNA, even on items he admitted to handling.

Also, contrary to Linda Wright's testimony that she saw no recognizable texture marks left by someone wearing gloves, Holes said he found what he believes is the imprint of a leather glove in the black paint on Rebecca's right ring fingernail. Greer said that imprint could move this case firmly back into the criminal realm.

Holes also noted that investigators found no blood drops in the guest room or on the balcony, where they surely would have fallen if Rebecca, who was on her period, had hopped toward and over the railing. Similarly, he couldn't see how she could get over the railing by putting her weight on just her right big toe, as the impressions on the balcony indicate to him.

Furthermore, Holes noted that the figure-eight knot used to tighten the rope around Rebecca's wrists was on top of the bindings, rather than below them, where her fingers would need access to tighten or manipulate it. He saw the same problem with the knot on the sheriff's reenactment video.

The Oxygen series was one of at least seven TV documentaries and news shows on this case, several of which featured interviews with me.

First to air was a *20/20* episode, which ran during the trial. Then came a two-parter, *Marcia Clark Investigates The First 48*, which was broadcast soon after the trial.

"Do you believe Rebecca committed suicide?" Clark, who prosecuted the O.J. Simpson criminal case, asked Dina Shacknai.

"No, I don't," Dina said.

Mary Loehner-Zahau told Clark that she couldn't prove it, but she was sure that Adam and Jonah Shacknai held Rebecca responsible for Max's fall.

"It was not a suicide," Mary said. "I still believe in the goodness of the system. And the truth always comes out."

The Oxygen series producers took the recording of Adam's 911 call, which has a lot of strange background noise, to forensic audio engineer Brad Murphree to search for digital anomalies. Murphree said he found one: a second person's voice, to whom Adam was talking at the house.

Murphree said he could hear Adam saying, "Hold her still" to the second person. But on TV, the words weren't definitive, even when vocally enhanced.

That series also featured another polygraph examiner, who said Adam failed his test. Pointing to waves on the voice chart,

John Grogan said Adam conclusively showed deception on two of the most important questions.

"If it was half this size, it would be a fail," he said. "This is an explosion. Terrible. Textbook fail."

As I watched the trial and all the documentaries, I kept coming back to memories of my husband's behavior before he killed himself. While he'd made suicidal threats for twenty years to his family and all three of his wives, Rebecca never once mentioned wanting to kill herself. And unlike my husband, who had addiction and mental-health issues, Rebecca had no such diagnosis.

The night she died, she told her sister that she would talk to her the next day, then took a shower. Why would she shower if she was about to hang herself? And why would she delete Jonah's voice mail before doing so?

Still, based on her erratic and emotional behavior, her cell phone notes, and the fact that her fingerprints and DNA are the only ones found on key items of evidence, I couldn't eliminate suicide as a possibility. The more I learned about her, the lies she told, her codependency on Neil, and her troubled, disintegrating relationship with Jonah, the more it seemed possible.

If, as Tsuida suggested, Rebecca felt hurt or angry because she felt Jonah blamed her for Max's injuries, it's conceivable that she staged her death to embarrass him. Conversely, she could also have done so, thinking it would save him and her family from embarrassment.

Some have theorized that she painted a cryptic message that only Jonah would understand. "I've heard that theory," Jonah said, though he had no idea what the hidden meaning might be.

But what I learned from my husband's last, desperate act is that you can't apply reason or rationality to an irrational act like suicide, because the person committing that act is not of sound mind.

One nagging mystery is where Rebecca would have obtained the idea or knowledge to tie herself up that way, given the lack of searches for such methods in her internet browser history.

Jonah said he didn't know about her past experience with these particular knots or how many times she may have practiced tying them. However, he noted, she had small hands and "exceptionally fine motor skills, which is why she was so effective and well regarded in [Lasik] surgery."

He added that "the only time I ever saw her tie a knot other than a shoelace was as [our] boat was coming into the slip," and that Adam certainly didn't know his way around Jonah's garage and also "didn't pack a rope with him when he came to Coronado. He's not the most organized guy in the world, to begin with."

Greer's claim that Adam sexually assaulted Rebecca with the steak knife handle is a stretch for some folks. Jonah, for example, said he believes that Greer completely made it up "without any factual or evidentiary basis" to rile up the jury.

"At some point, you just say who is it that committed the perfect crime, left no hint of their involvement, so much so that some guy who attempts a rescue actually gets framed by a plaintiff, despite having been completely exonerated by the police, who were looking for a bad guy. It just doesn't hang together," Jonah said. "This jury found Adam responsible by the same token, with the same lack of evidence. It's beyond a nightmare. It's surreal. It's Kafkaesque."

But others, including several experts featured on the Oxygen series, said the death scene shows recognizable signs of a sex crime. Combined with nudity, rope tying, and gagging, they said, the sexual assault scenario makes sense.

"Everything that you see here is very humiliating," said Dr. Rebecca Hsu, a forensic pathologist. With sex crimes, "you want to punish [the victims]."

Criminal psychologist Eric Hickey has seen a lot of suicides during his career, but never one like this: "Someone did this to her," he said. Someone who knew her.

Loni Coombs, a former prosecutor, said she believes that Rebecca was murdered, and that the criminal case should be reopened. "If she was sexually assaulted, she wasn't committing suicide," she said.

To Laura Pettler, who specializes in staged crime scenes, the message on the door reflects a great deal of anger and a tone not seen in Rebecca's other writings.

"This is an abrasive, harsh form of speaking," she said. "Crime scenes are a reflection of the victim and the offender if it's a crime . . . This is angry, this is black, this is dark. How is this a reflection of her?"

In addition, Pettler said, the items found in the guest room tell her that this was an "opportunistic" crime. "This wasn't planned. It has a spontaneous feel."

An attorney with ties to this case said he believes someone hired two men to kill Rebecca. To him, the lacerations all over her back looked more like puncture wounds from a screwdriver than scratches from the vegetation below.

"These marks show personal anger," he said. "They want to humiliate her. This girl had perfect skin."

The injury on her finger also didn't look like a rope burn to him. "It is more like a gouge. There's a piece of meat missing," he said, noting that this was the same hand where she usually wore the ring that Jonah gave her, but it was missing too.

He said the knots used to bind Rebecca's wrists weren't nautical in particular, and he was told by a bondage expert that they're frequently used in that world because they're easy to tighten and loosen at will. That said, a bondage expert featured on one of the TV shows voiced the opposite opinion.

*   *   *

Although some have speculated that Dina was involved in Rebecca's death because she blamed Rebecca for Max's injuries, she and her sister Nina insisted from the start that Dina had nothing to do with Rebecca's death.

"She wishes Rebecca was here so she could get answers," Nina said early on. "It was almost like when Rebecca committed suicide, she took every piece of information she had with her, and my sister is a very information-driven person."

Nina couldn't understand why anyone would think that she, Dina, or Jonah, all of whom like their privacy, would subject themselves to rabid media attention by killing Rebecca this way.

"That is crazy talk," she said. "It makes no sense whatsoever. Their son is in the hospital fighting for his life, and they're going to bring this on themselves? You have to know [Jonah] to know that is the craziest thing. He would never in a million years want that kind of publicity." And yet, "all of a sudden you see people blogging, we're all conspiring, it's bizarre. I just don't understand how people think."

There is also a supernatural twist to this case.

Private investigator Bill Garcia gained possession of the bed to which Rebecca had been tied, in a way he sees as no coincidence.

As he was standing in line at a Mexican restaurant in San Diego, a man recognized him from being on TV. Garcia often gets hired, and also volunteers, to help search for missing children.

The man had acquired the bed while doing some remodeling work at the mansion after it was sold. He gave the bed to a female employee, but she didn't want it after learning its history, so Garcia said he would take it off her hands.

Wearing gloves, he wrapped the bed in plastic and stored it in his garage, where he invited a medium and healer friend to do an energy reading on it.

As soon as Jackie Bensinger walked into Garcia's garage, she felt the bed's energy, almost as if it were electrified. She felt an even stronger charge when she touched its legs, sensing the placement of the rope that had been tied there.

Almost immediately, she said, she tuned into Rebecca, who communicated what had happened to her. "I felt her lying on the bed. I saw her look up" with surprise at the man she knew, who was hurting her as they wrestled.

"Why are you doing this to me?" Rebecca asked.

Bensinger said she actually felt the presence of two men in the room with Rebecca.

"After that, I got the sensation that I was being choked," she said, and began to cough so much that Garcia became concerned.

"Are you okay?" he asked.

Psychics often cough when connecting with someone who has passed over, she explained, but in Rebecca's case, it was more than that. "I feel that she did die from being choked."

Bensinger had to take several breaks during the reading, in between bouts of coughing and shaking all over. "It took me a bit to recover," she said.

"It definitely wasn't a suicide," Bensinger said. "[Rebecca] told me that several different times, and the energy from the bed was a confirmation of that."

She said Max also came to her, very supportive of Rebecca and with an energy that was even more forceful than his caretaker's. "Children are very strong once they have passed over," she said.

Bensinger said Max showed her how "he was taken down, that he was murdered. Although he said somebody was behind him and basically threw him over" the railing, she felt it was two men: one who was short and balding, with a little black hair, and one who was taller.

She later conveyed this information to Dina Shacknai, saying she sensed that the men had some kind of business connection to Jonah and came to the house seeking revenge.

Bensinger also got a negative vibe from the mansion when she stood outside it. Because the house had been sitting on the market for years, she offered her services to help clear the mansion of the bad juju, but the real estate agent declined. That energy, she said, actually predates the Shacknai family's time there.

"I definitely feel like there's all kinds of energy, from the very beginning. Spreckels—he was probably very mean to his wife," she said. "Not good energy, and people being hurt. Sometimes when people are in a place like that, it can kind of push people who live there to the edge. That energy is going to make things worse."

Garcia subsequently gave the bed to Keith Greer.

Chapter 41

As Adam's defense team was putting together its appeal, they asked Bill Garcia to interview jurors about any misconduct or inappropriate contact with media, the judge, or attorneys. It's unclear if they knew he'd already worked this case on Dina's behalf.

Garcia was told that one female juror said she would talk at some point. The defense had tried unsuccessfully to reach her, but had yet to try using a PI.

Garcia was willing to take the job, but was told he needed to speak with Adam first. During their thirty-five-minute phone conversation, Garcia heard Adam react with increasing anger and anxiety as he tested Adam with provocative comments and questions.

"I did read the ME's report and, personally, I think her life was taken," Garcia said.

"Oh, you do," Adam said.

"I do not believe she committed suicide," Garcia said. "I think you were put in a position that, well, screwed you over."

"Who, how, or why would somebody take her life, and why that method?" Adam asked. "Why would somebody go and be painting s—t all over the house?"

Garcia said he'd watched Adam's attorney's "strong" performance in the courtroom for a couple of days, and he'd also listened to the 911 call.

"What's your take?" Adam asked, complaining that he couldn't believe he'd been accused of staging that call.

"My take was that I believe that you were sincerely scared and it was something that was hard to comprehend, but you went through it, and it's actually pretty amazing that you were pretty much able to document that whole discovery," Garcia said. "I don't believe you, Adam Shacknai, were responsible for Rebecca's death."

"Thanks for nothing, but thanks nonetheless. I don't take it as a compliment, but whatever," Adam replied. "But who else? Who would do that? Not leave any fingerprints, no signs of wiping away. How do you explain that?"

"That is a difficult one," Garcia said. "So, you believe she took her own life?"

"I probably would have," Adam said. "When you mess up, something goes wrong with someone else's kid. They were going to break up anyway. They were running on fumes."

Garcia asked Adam why he thought Rebecca killed herself. "She was temporarily, at least, under a hell of a lot of pressure. This we know," Adam said. "Having someone's kid die under your supervision, to be living in my brother's world like that, it's pressure anyway. She was really not completely accepted as it was by his friends, by his ex-wives. A rich guy and everything else, and everything that went on, and then all of a sudden under your supervision, his kid is dead. It must have been pretty tough."

During his eight years as a paramedic, Garcia said he saw multiple suicides, including some hangings, but never anything like this one. As he explained the four reasons why he thought Rebecca had been murdered, Adam wasn't impressed.

"You're a rational person, yet you still say that somebody else killed her," Adam said. "So that's what I'm up against. So, either you're an idiot or you're smart. Which is it?"

Garcia said he'd take the job and work hard for the appellate team, but Adam didn't seem interested.

"I don't respect your intellect," Adam said, comparing Garcia to "one of the animals from the jury, like a mule or something."

Needless to say, Garcia didn't get the job.

Instead, the defense team found another private investigator to question jurors about what transpired during deliberations.

According to a seventy-nine-year-old male juror, who ultimately voted with the nine-to-three majority, the men and women were pretty evenly split in their first few votes.

The women were in agreement, finding Adam responsible for Rebecca's death, at least in part because they thought he "looked like he did it."

The man said he initially voted that Adam wasn't responsible, but the women were passionate and persuasive. The forewoman strongly believed that Rebecca had been murdered. A second woman asserted that Adam was culpable, because she'd "been around a lot of this stuff" as a probation officer. A third female juror stood up and motioned as if she were writing the message on the door, but said she couldn't at that height.

The man said his mind wasn't changed by any mention of Asian porn or bruising on Rebecca's scalp. It was a point raised by the forewoman about the women's panties in the guest house trash can that pushed him over the line, because he saw no reason for them to be there.

In the months after the verdict, however, he had problems sleeping, as he kept turning it over in his mind. If Adam had killed Rebecca, then why weren't his footprints found on the balcony?

The man felt guilty, because he believed he was the ninth and final vote that found Adam responsible for Rebecca's death.

"I feel like I convicted an innocent man," he said.

In the end, however, none of the jurors interviewed by the defense would sign an affidavit under penalty of perjury, a precursor for their statements to be admitted as part of the motion to overturn the verdict.

"They didn't get a single juror to write a statement," Keith Greer noted. "Not one."

Chapter 42

Sheriff Gore won the primary election in June 2018, but the findings of his department's review of the Zahau case weren't released until December, five months past the estimated completion date.

After asking the SDSD months in advance to attend the next news conference, I was promised entrance this time. But once again, I was blocked at the last minute for lack of a press pass.

Keith Greer already knew what the sheriff was going to say, because his client had been briefed on the review team's findings, but he wasn't allowed in either. The Zahaus had hoped that the verdict and subsequent review would trigger the reopening of the criminal investigation into Rebecca's death, he said, but the SDSD had simply reconfirmed its original findings.

Speaking to the media before they headed into the news conference, Greer vigorously denounced the effort as superficial at best.

"We hoped it was incompetence, but it's corruption, it's got to be," he said. "The [Shacknai] family has a lot of money."

Greer threatened to pursue his allegations of impropriety with higher authorities, perhaps with a civil rights lawsuit, noting that the timing of the sheriff's announcement corresponded suspiciously with the filing of a new-trial motion by Adam Shack-nai's attorneys that same week.

Afterward, Greer invited me to watch the live-streamed news conference in his car, where a TV producer sat behind us, recording, as Greer interjected comments like, "This is outra-geous," or "How can he say that with a straight face? That's a bald-faced lie."

Sheriff Gore told reporters that he'd asked for a "thorough" and "objective review of the first investigation with fresh eyes, however, the new team found no evidence that would lead us to believe that Rebecca Zahau died at the hands of another . . . [or] that would dispute or be inconsistent" with the medical exam-iner's original suicide finding.

Responding to Greer's fresh allegations of corruption and collusion, Gore said his personal interaction with Jonah was only to further the investigation.

"I never took any money from Jonah Shacknai in my election or reelection campaigns," he said. "That's just not the way we operate. To be quite honest, I take personal offense to that, im-pugning the reputation of this fine department, one of the best in the country."

During the review, he said, he asked the FBI's Behavioral Analysis Unit to conduct a psychological autopsy of Rebecca. The intent was to examine her state of mind through personal writings to determine whether it was likely that she committed suicide, and if not, to debunk that conclusion.

But when Gore reached out to the Zahau family for such writ-ings, "nothing was forthcoming," he said, which was partly why the review took so long. In contrast, he said, he "personally called Jonah Shacknai" to ask for any letters or writings in his possession, and within a week, Jonah turned over what he had.

This was years after Rebecca's death, and Jonah had already returned all of her personal belongings, including some journals, to her family, so Jonah said that all he had left were some cards and letters that she'd given him.

"It wasn't enough for them to come up with a real good analysis, which is unfortunate," Gore said. "I know in a lot of cases they do very good work, but we didn't have enough material to look at."

The sheriff acknowledged that skeptics have often confronted him about this case at public appearances, and he predicted that would probably continue.

"I know there's a lot of uneasiness about this [case]," he said. "What we're trying to do is take the facts, and the physical evidence, the forensic evidence, where it leads us, and try to debunk . . . some of the conspiracy theories that have come up in the last seven years."

Gore left it to sheriff's homicide Lieutenant Rich Williams to address questions and theories that came out of the trial. Williams, however, pointed out up front that this was "not an investigation. We're doing a review of the existing investigation," which made the scope quite limited.

He said the review took five months longer than anticipated, in part, because the team had to wait for Greer to hand over trial transcripts. But even then, they didn't learn any new evidence, only new interpretations of existing evidence.

Because two outside experts had said that Adam failed his polygraph test, Williams was asked if the team had reviewed the exam. Williams said no but gave no explanation.

Williams noted that questions arose at trial about whether certain items had been tested for DNA. He said several gloves, found in different parts of the mansion, were tested back in 2011, but the amount of DNA was "insufficient" to form a conclusion. All they could tell was that a right-handed garden glove "contained a mixture from at least two different individuals."

The chef's knife, found in the bedroom, was also previously

tested for DNA and prints. The prints matched Rebecca's and the DNA included "a mixture from at least two individuals, however the sample provided an insufficient amount of information for conclusions or comparisons," he said.

Williams didn't explain why these items weren't retested, using the more advanced technology available in 2018, or why the team saw no reason to reinterview any witnesses, and Adam Shacknai in particular.

He said the one evidence item that *was* tested for DNA during the review period in 2018—a point the judge raised during a hearing, and jurors asked about during deliberations—was the pair of panties found in the guest house. But the profile didn't match Rebecca or Adam, because they belonged to Jonah's daughter, Cindy. She'd been partying with some friends there, and had thrown away the underwear several days before Rebecca's death.

Asked about Greer's claim that prints and DNA were wiped away, Williams said he could only theorize why investigators didn't find DNA on certain areas, such as the doorknobs. In his experience, doors are frequently left open, so people don't touch the knobs much.

"I can only tell you what we did find, and what we did find were Rebecca's prints, and essentially only Rebecca's prints, at the scene," he said.

He said eleven DNA swabs were taken from areas on the rope that investigators believed were likely to have been manipulated while the knots were being tied. Of those, nine matched Rebecca's DNA, one showed a mixture of DNA from at least two people, with Rebecca as a possible contributor, and the last contained no human DNA. Adam and Nina were excluded from the human samples.

Asked how investigators could conclude no sexual assault had occurred if the steak knife had vaginal blood on it, Williams replied that tests conducted during the autopsy "revealed no evidence of a sexual assault." Even if it was menstrual blood on the knife, he said, it could have "made its way to the knife through another means rather than the insertion of that."

As for the theory that Rebecca had tried to free herself from the bindings with the chef's knife blade, he said, "There were no cuts or fraying to the rope to indicate that Rebecca was trying to escape . . . and the bindings were loose enough to be removed intact."

He also said the description at trial of the fingerprint positioning on the blade didn't match the actual prints, an apparent reference to a minor error Lisa DiMeo made on the stand when she misidentified one of the fingerprints.

Concerning the testimony that Rebecca was too short to have painted the message on the door, Williams said the letters were within a span of four feet to four feet eleven inches from the floor. Acknowledging that the door would be elevated when mounted on the frame, he showed a photo of a woman, who was an inch and a half shorter than Rebecca, standing next to the door, with her arm comfortably in position to paint it. The unspoken message was that it would be no problem for Rebecca to have painted the letters.

Finally, Chief Medical Examiner Glenn Wagner addressed the disparity between Dr. Lucas's autopsy report and the analysis by the Zahaus' expert, Dr. Cyril Wecht, about the subgaleal hemorrhages on Rebecca's scalp.

While Wecht contended they were serious enough to have caused a loss of consciousness from blunt-force trauma, Wagner called the injuries "superficial," and "not capable" of causing unconsciousness.

He also lumped the hemorrhages in with the scratches on her forehead, back, and around the ear, which Lucas attributed to the vegetation under the balcony.

"In the scalp, there are no skull fractures, no subdural subarachnoid hemorrhages, no injury to the brain," Wagner said. Given the "broken plant material" on the ground near Rebecca's body, "the evidence, based on the abrasions, contusions throughout the body, indicates to me that Rebecca went face-first over the railing and impacted, slid down the wall, breaking the foliage, as well as leaving marks on the wall before the full length of that rope was reached, and did, in fact, hang herself."

After watching the sheriff's presentation, Greer repeated his corruption allegation and charged that the review was a sham to support the department's original "improper and biased decision."

Even worse, he said, the review team included no women, which caused them to overlook and misinterpret evidence pointing to sexual assault and murder.

"Why not do a psychological profile on Adam?" he asked.

For many people, the SDSD's confirmation of its original findings reinforced the opinion that the "review" was merely a campaign ploy "to appease the public and just to postpone further scrutiny until after the election," as Greer put it.

Chapter 43

Because I wasn't allowed into the news conference, sheriff's sergeant Paul Michalke a member of the review team, agreed to sit down with me privately.

In a three-hour meeting several days later, I did something I've never done in my thirty-plus years as a journalist and author: I shared some of my investigative leads and findings with law enforcement.

Explaining my own personal and legal safety concerns, I suggested that the SDSD explore some of my leads, because I didn't have subpoena power to compel anyone to talk to me or to produce documents.

Michalke started by telling me how and why he thought Rebecca had committed suicide: She was likely in the shower when she got Jonah's call, "lost it" when she listened to his voice mail, then deleted it. He believed that she'd done this as a "creature of habit," based on the lack of other saved messages on her phone. Still wearing a towel, she then staged the suicide scene to look like a murder to avoid embarrassing her devout Christian family.

Echoing his colleagues at trial, Michalke said it was "the totality" of the evidence that convinced him it was a suicide. But in particular, it was the heel and toe impressions on the balcony that fit Rebecca's feet, the portion of disturbed dust on the railing where her body went over, and the absence of anyone else's DNA and fingerprints.

Why not retest those items with "insufficient" DNA? He said the team decided not to do that on the gloves and other evidence after a discussion with the sheriff's crime lab.

"It's their belief that even under the new technology they'd still be unable to identify" specific contributors, although the amount of DNA was "still enough to exclude" Adam and the others as "contributors," he said. But he thought the gardening gloves, found in the living room, had probably been used to pick up the pieces of broken chandelier.

They did, however, do DNA testing on a couple of items for the first time. In addition to the women's panties, he said, they tested a tissue with two blood spots sitting near a razor in the master bathroom. The blood came back to "an unknown male," and Adam was excluded. Jonah's DNA, blood, and prints weren't collected in this case, although he later said that he would have cooperated if asked.

What did Michalke make of the overturned chair in the guest room? "There was no other indication of any physical altercation" in the very small room, he said, so it may have fallen over as Rebecca stood up from it.

Why not at least change the cause of death from suicide to "undetermined," given the jury verdict, and the push by numerous outside experts, including former prosecutor Marcia Clark, to reopen the criminal case?

"I can't answer that," he said.

Although he acknowledged that "the medical examiner came to their determination based on our investigation," and their own autopsy findings, he insisted that it wasn't circular reasoning.

We also discussed other topics, such as the New York prison inmate's claims about the alleged hits out on Max and on Jonah's parents, and the card reader and cameras that weren't working at the Ronald McDonald House, but he had no real comment.

When we were done talking, I asked for a response for this book. The sergeant said he would take "all this new information" that we'd discussed, of which he said law enforcement wasn't previously aware, and get back to me.

Although I was cautiously optimistic, I didn't really believe that the SDSD would be willing to let go of its suicide findings and rationale. It had become clear as we talked that afternoon that the department had placed itself into a box from which it couldn't escape without losing face.

After closing the criminal case into Rebecca's death long ago, Michalke explained that the department couldn't obtain search warrants or compel anyone to provide documents or evidence of which the SDSD wasn't previously aware, even if they might reveal the motive for one—or even two—murders.

"We now have a case that's closed, and how do we go about asking for documents?" Michalke asked.

The obvious answer, many would say, is to reopen the case.

When I followed up a week later, I was correct. Michalke said he didn't want to get drawn into Adam's appeal, and saw any potential "violations" I'd described during the meeting as within federal, not local, jurisdiction, even if they might lead to uncovering motives for murder.

"I'm not going to nose around in something I've been told we're done with," Michalke said. "The captain is sticking with the sheriff's position—the investigation is remaining closed. It will not be reopened."

"So, I'm on my own?" I asked.

"Pretty much."

Chapter 44

On January 25, 2019, Judge Bacal issued a tentative ruling denying two motions that Adam's lawyers had filed. The first requested a new trial to overturn the verdict; the second asked to overturn the judgment that was based on the verdict.

Although new-trial motions are quite routine, Bacal's comments were anything but. She caused quite a stir by highlighting flaws in the sheriff's department investigation and challenging its suicide findings. She also appeared to support, at least in theory, the Zahaus' continued quest for answers.

The court feels remiss if it does not state that the sheriff's investigation leaves almost as many questions unanswered as it answered, her ruling stated. *The lack of Adam's DNA and fingerprints does not necessarily mean he was not at the scene . . . Common sense says Rebecca did not paint the amateurishly painted message on the door. And if she did not, someone else did . . . This was only one of numerous pieces of circumstantial evidence that puts the sheriff's conclusion into question. As a result, it is not unreasonable to still ask, who killed Rebecca Zahau?*

But before Bacal could announce her final ruling on the motions, Adam's insurance company agreed to settle the case for $600,000—over his strenuous objections.

I was out of town on February 6, the day of the hearing, which meant I had to follow news developments on my phone. That was problematic, however, because different news outlets published contradictory "facts" of the ruling, including the erroneous claim that the verdict had been "erased." It was days before one major newspaper accepted its mistake and issued a correction.

In fact, the verdict still stood; it was only the $5 million judgment that had been thrown out. The case was dismissed with prejudice, which rendered Adam's motions moot and left him no avenue to file the appeal he'd planned.

Adam said he was told by his insurance company, in essence, "We would've never gone to trial if we didn't believe in you, but this is so fricking bizarre that we see no end in sight in legal costs. Appeals being what they are."

Although the attorneys kept the amount confidential, Adam independently announced that it was $600,000, furious that he'd lost his ability to be vindicated in court.

Immediately after the judge's ruling, Adam gave a rambling twenty-minute statement, peppered with expletives, to TV cameras at the courthouse.

Asked if he killed Rebecca Zahau, he replied, "Hell, f—ing no. I wouldn't f—ing waste my time killing Rebecca Zahau." He called Greer a "scumbag," and a "sleazeball," and described the entire case against him as a "hoax" built by Greer using theories he picked up from internet trolls.

Shrugging off the hyperbole, Greer countered that the family wasn't giving up. Armed with the jury verdict and the judge's criticism of the sheriff's investigation, he said his clients planned to petition the ME's office to change the cause of death from "suicide" to "homicide." They would use the settlement money to investigate leads they couldn't afford to explore previously, to try to meet the higher criminal standard of proof.

If their petition was rejected, he said, they would file a writ of mandamus in court to force the matter before a judge.

Before trial, he said, the Zahau family had been offered—and turned down—$1 million to settle the case.

"This was never about money," he said. "This was about justice."

In the coming days and weeks, Adam continued to profess his innocence in media interviews, attacked the judge's integrity and professionalism, and claimed that his defense team had found "some jury misconduct."

He characterized Greer as a profiteer—winning the jury verdict, collecting this settlement, and now going after the ME's office, as if he were "working the next table" at a casino.

He also accused the judge of a host of "ticky-tacky things," saying she seemed to have some kind of "vendetta" against law enforcement, and had used "a mystery novel to analyze the case," doing her own "failed experiments" to copy the knots.

"I thought she was almost sort of like—a nudge and a wink—'I'm going to help the Zahaus now, and try to get them some money, and I'm going to help you later on appeal by writing this stuff down,' because it's pretty much ludicrous and unprofessional," he said.

The settlement also triggered a spontaneous call to me on a Friday afternoon. It was 3:19 P.M. on February 22, 2019, to be exact.

"This is Adam Shacknai," he said.

Shocked, I was temporarily at a loss for words. "Oh, I'm so glad you called," I said.

That was true, although I wasn't really prepared to talk to him right then. Although I'd been planning to call him down the line, I didn't have a book deal yet, and I was deep into another project.

I have a research-and-writing process, and it goes in that order. Normally, I approach primary characters for an interview with a list of specific questions in hand—but that's after doing a ton of research so I can spot a lie when I hear it.

Because killers are often con men and liars (I'm referring to those who are convicted in criminal court), I usually chronicle these conversations in separate chapters at the end of my books, rather than weave the information into the narrative. That way, readers can see exactly what was said and determine the person's credibility for themselves.

But this case was quite different from others I'd written about. Yes, Adam had been found responsible for Rebecca's death, but only in civil court. Also, because he had very accomplished attorneys, and a brother with a ton of money, I didn't want to say the wrong thing now and lose my chance to talk to him or Jonah later.

It had been two weeks since the hearing, so I asked what he was still doing in town. I figured he'd be back in Memphis by now.

He made some kind of nonresponsive literary reference, presumably because I'm an author. But he didn't answer my question until the third time I asked, and even then he was flippant.

"Courtroom tourism," he said.

"How did you get my number?" I asked.

"Mary gave it to me," he said.

He seemed to be apprehensive about talking to me, or trusting anyone whose allegiances he didn't know, as he fished around to see if I was close to Keith Greer.

Then the negotiations began about if, where, and when to meet, and inside or outside, as he cracked jokes.

"It's cold," he said, agreeing that we should meet somewhere warm. "I can't be cagey outside."

He can actually be funny and charming, I thought, *much different from the angry man on the TV and radio, who cusses and*

makes defamatory statements about Greer and the Zahau fam-
ily, comparing the judge to an internet troll "who wore a black
robe during the whole trial."

Adam said he was frustrated with the way things had gone,
that his attorneys had done "absolutely nothing," when they
"should have been on the ground," investigating and checking
people out, following up tips.

One of the attorneys sent an investigator to talk to a girl who
had "insinuated herself in the case—she said I hadn't done anything wrong," he said, the same thing people told him back in
Memphis. But I couldn't follow where he was going with this,
because he spoke in non sequiturs, incomplete thoughts, and
colloquialisms.

"So, are you here investigating?" I asked.

"Seeing what comes my way," he replied.

From what I could tell, he was determined to gather whatever
intel he could—from me—and try to clear his name by hook or
by crook.

"Did you ever look into those people on the internet?" he
asked.

"Like who?"

Like the people who had posted on Websleuths about him,
he said, which made him feel sick after reading them. I told
him I'd read some of them, and that some had personally attacked me too.

He'd also been reading the "trolls" who posted on the *Patch*
news site for Coronado and on a couple of blogs, one of which
featured animated videos that raised questions the authorities
had either glossed over or refused to answer in a meaningful way.

"Do you know if [the blogger] and these other people are
friends with, or have anything to do with, Greer?" he asked,
clearly looking for a conspiracy. "Or the judge?"

No, I said, I didn't know anything about that, but Greer didn't tell me all that much. "If you hear anything, I'm happy to listen to anything you have to tell me."

But I also informed him of my ground rules for our interview the next day: I wasn't going to give him my opinion or share information I'd uncovered in my research, and our talk had to be on the record.

"Can I tape our conversation tomorrow?" I asked.

"No," he said firmly.

"Why not?" I asked. I'd heard him on TV and radio, what was so different about letting me tape our interview?

"TV is one thing, but a book is for posterity," he replied, using derogatory terms to describe the superficiality of TV reporters and their questions.

When you look into TV reporters' eyes, he said, you don't see anything but them trying to get "the shot" or the quote.

Okay, I thought, *so he's scared of me and my book. That's not a bad thing.*

He said he was tired of being criticized for revealing the "confidential" amount of the settlement, which he didn't even want or know much about.

"I didn't sign a goddamn thing," he said, so he wasn't violating any confidentiality.

Then he asked if I knew anyone who was a lowlier scum and deserved less respect than Greer.

"Yes," I said cautiously.

"Are you friends with Keith Greer?"

"I'm not friends with anyone, I'm a journalist. I had a hard time getting anything from him," I said, referring to documents I'd asked for during the trial.

"What do you think of Ann Rule?" he asked.

"That's a trap," I said, and he had to agree. He told me he didn't much like the book chapter she'd written about him and this case, which was no big surprise, because he was obviously her leading suspect.

Many of his questions started out with "what do you think of," so I reminded him of my rule against sharing opinions.

Okay, then, he said. Where was I on reporters who only look for and write what's most sensational?

"I'm not looking to be sensational, I just want to tell the truth," I said.

"How you can let people pull off the biggest hoax?" he asked. "I guess they deserve credit."

I wasn't letting anyone do anything, and I wanted to hang up before I upset him, although I felt like that was almost inevitable, judging from his media interviews. We agreed to meet in La Jolla, which was halfway between us.

I hung up, contacted investigator Bill Garcia and my agent, both of whom warned me to be careful. My agent said he was concerned that Adam didn't want me to record our conversation, and Garcia said he was worried for my personal safety.

They asked if I could call law enforcement to be there, wear a wire, or surreptitiously record the conversation. In California, Garcia said, it's not against the law to record a conversation with someone you think could be guilty of murder.

I said that if Adam looked in my purse and saw my cell phone recorder was on, then he'd never talk to me again for the book. I also didn't want to become an arm of the law enforcement investigation to that degree—especially after my recent attempt to share information with them had gone nowhere.

My agent asked if my partner could accompany me as a second pair of ears, or at least to make sure I was okay. My partner wasn't thrilled that I was meeting with the man a jury had found responsible for Rebecca's death, but he was reluctantly willing to covertly sit in a café to watch over me.

Still, I didn't believe that Adam would hurt me, and I also reminded Garcia that he didn't think Adam killed Rebecca.

"No, I don't think he did it," he said, "but I do think he was a participant, and that makes him at the very least an accessory to murder."

Good point. "But he isn't going to do anything to me in Peet's Coffee," I said.

"Make sure to look around and make sure no one else is in there watching you," he said. "He may try to threaten you, or suggest that if you write a book accusing him that he'll sue you."

That night, as my partner and I were returning from a sushi dinner and a walk, Adam texted me at eight twenty-five, asking if I might want to change our meeting to Sunday. Not up for dragging this out all weekend, I said no, but I could wait until the following Tuesday.

I didn't want him to think he could jerk me around, as if he was the only thing happening in my life at the moment. It felt manipulative, and I didn't want him feeling that he had the power in this situation.

Half an hour later, my phone rang in my purse. It was Adam calling. To put it bluntly, I was tired and not in a professional head space to talk to him.

Thinking we were going to clarify the meeting time and be done with it, I didn't have a notepad or pen ready. I was walking from the parking lot to my partner's place, and probably shouldn't have answered the phone, but then again, I also didn't want to keep texting with him and create a written message history.

He told me that he was on the treadmill before meeting someone for dinner, and didn't want to get up too early. So we agreed to move the meeting an hour later to 1:00 P.M.

"I want to have a clear head," he said.

"Better not stay up late drinking, then," I said, trying to keep it light, as he'd been doing with me since he first called.

"I don't drink," he said.

I was surprised to hear that. "Oh," I said. "Well, then, don't take any Ambien tonight. That stuff will mess you up."

Looking back, I realized that was not the smartest thing to

say, given that he had taken Ambien the night before Rebecca was found dead. But honestly, I was thinking of my own past experience with the drug, how just half a dose had left me in a half-sleep state with weird dreams, then groggy and exhausted in the morning. I only used it a few times before learning that it can cause far more serious side effects and memory loss in some people.

Given the circumstances, it was a dumb offhand remark, but I really meant it as an innocent, if perhaps a bit tongue-in-cheek, comment. I obviously hadn't thought it through, and had even noted during our conversation that I wanted to stop talking and keep things professional until the next day. He didn't seem to take offense, so we hung up.

Frankly, I wasn't even sure why Adam's attorneys hadn't used the Ambien defense as an excuse for all the weird things he'd said to police and to Rebecca's sister the morning he called 911. I made a mental note to ask him about it, then tried to put the conversation out of my head. But when I checked my phone before going to bed around midnight, I saw that I had struck a nerve.

If the Ambien remark is a harbinger of things to come, I'll take a raincheck, he texted at 9:13 P.M., adding that I should try not to let innocent people get sued over someone's parlor games in the future.

Clearly, he'd been looking for an out, and I had given it to him. I sent him an apology, saying I hadn't meant any offense. When I didn't hear back, I figured he must be asleep—or had taken an Ambien.

The next morning, I was heading to do some work at a coffee shop when Adam texted me again, saying we could still meet if I wanted. But he said he could "take it or leave it," and had other things to do, like possibly leave town.

I told him it would be best to meet Monday or Tuesday, so

we could leave it open until then. *What is he doing here any-way, I wondered, and why can't he commit to being here two days from now?*

On Tuesday, Adam agreed to meet me at a café in Mission Valley, where he took an Uber from his hotel downtown. My partner was at work, so I went alone. It was a public place, after all.

We talked for three and a half hours in an eye-opening exchange that I hoped would encourage more transparency and cooperation in the future by him, his girlfriend Mary, and Jonah.

First, as I'd said to the folks who described Adam as "cocky" or "arrogant," he seemed more socially awkward than anything else. He was pretty angry about all of this, but based on his brashness and the continuous unfiltered, inappropriate comments, I wondered if he might be on the autism spectrum. Or was it more of a defense mechanism to cover his fear and anger over being falsely accused?

Adam was quite protective of Jonah and his privacy. But based on what he was saying, they didn't seem all that close. Or, as Dina pointed out, perhaps Adam was just cautious about boundaries and didn't ask his brother probing questions.

For example, Adam danced around my question about whether he'd attended Jonah's most recent wedding, to his third wife.

"Small ceremony" was his response, adding that now he was worried I was going to say that he and Jonah had a falling-out. That signaled to me that he wasn't there or hadn't been invited.

All of that goes to my other premise, which is that Jonah likely didn't disclose to Adam certain details about his life, including what was going on in his relationship with Rebecca, at the time of her death.

Adam acknowledged that was true, saying some things had come out since then. Such as? He declined to elaborate.

Asked again what he was doing in town, he said that after the settlement, he went home to Memphis, then returned to San Diego.

"I'm doing what I should've done all along—be on the ground to some extent. Just see what I run into, just for my edification," he said.

"Are you looking to see if maybe it was someone else [who killed Rebecca]?" I asked.

"No."

Why not? I asked.

"The police would know. I just know what I felt. That seems to be borne out. That was a first impression. If the evidence dictated otherwise, that'd be great." But, he said, "the ropes appeared to be self-tied," at least that's what the detectives determined. "I don't disagree with that."

What he did disagree with was his attorneys' strategy of arguing that the knots were so simple to tie. "To me, you had to answer for those damn things. Don't seem that simple to me, when I couldn't do it," he said. "That's a logic thing, so I pursued that on my own."

His conclusion? "I'd say they were more bondage knots than nautical knots," he said, explaining that he thought they were like Shibari, a Japanese type of "erotic bondage," which he described as a mix of art and sexual ritual.

After finding a Shibari video online, he said, the first thing they talked about was how to self-tie your hands behind your back.

"Was Rebecca a kinky person?" I asked.

"I do not know," he replied. "It wouldn't surprise me at all. This whole Goody Two-shoes stuff. There were other sides to her."

He said he didn't care that she "went guy to guy," and he also didn't mean that to sound judgmental, or to imply that it was okay for a man, but not a woman, to do, but "she got around."

"If this were a criminal case, I'd get to all the bottom of that stuff . . . and I may find out anyway," he said.

Based on Adam's insistent Shibari claims, and the theory that some people have suggested, that Rebecca and Jonah may have participated in consensual sexual acts involving rope tying or choking, I asked Jonah about it directly. Did they ever play with ropes or bondage in private, or watch any movies with that sort of content?

Not surprisingly, he said no. "I don't think either one of us ever brought up the subject."

As for the abduction incident involving Michael Berger, Adam said, he believed "she kidnapped herself. She probably didn't want to break up with him and took it too far."

While we were talking about the financial issues involved in his defense, he said that his insurance company was suing him, but didn't want to explain why.

He expressed regret that he'd gone with the team of corporate business lawyers rather than a criminal defense attorney who knew his way around a murder trial, even a young, hungry one. He also wished they'd spent some of the massive legal fees to hire some private detectives.

"The budget spent on these attorneys, with a tenth [of it], we could've blown this wide open," he said. "I thought I was working with the best attorneys," but as it was, "it was very expensive and [had] no impact."

Adam also wasn't happy with the way they handled his case in the media, telling him to keep quiet during the trial, regardless of what was said about him, without ensuring that they had better "optics."

But first and foremost, he wanted to be clear that he'd thought from the very beginning that Rebecca committed suicide, because she must have been very sad.

"I believe that Rebecca and Jonah were in the process of breaking up," he said.

To him, Jonah's description during his testimony that he and Rebecca were "evaluating" things between them that summer was really code for "get the f— out," because Jonah was usually the one to end his relationships.

We didn't talk about the case in depth. He offered up some of his musical tastes, and I let him say what he wanted, but I did manage to work in some substantive questions on topics such as the Ambien he took that night.

He said he was taking Ambien at that time because it helped him, but his attorneys wanted to keep that out of the trial in light of bad publicity that the drug caused some people to hallucinate.

"By the time the depositions were over, they tried to keep everything out," he said, adding that he'd also wanted to let his girlfriend testify, but they wouldn't allow that either. Referring to Greer's inference that Mary had prescribed him various drugs, Adam clarified that it was migraine medication, not Ambien.

He said he and Mary had a normal relationship, even though they didn't live together, and that he wasn't the sexual pervert Greer made him out to be. He and Mary had met in Memphis at a "cheap fund-raiser" to benefit people dying of HIV.

"She's got a really nice house," he said. "I'm satisfied with where I live. She's got a magical property," with lots of trees and greenery.

She was also a fantastic cook. "She's got a real touch. She measures up well. She's real smart too," he said. "I need an advocate. I deserve an advocate."

He said he had no history of violence against women, and no criminal history at all. "I just don't do s—t like that."

Switching gears, I asked him about the 911 call. "What did you mean by I got a girl in the guest house?" I asked.

"I didn't mean anything by it," he said.

He said he'd stayed in that guest bedroom in the main house

before, but when I asked if he misspoke on the call and meant the guest *room*, he said no.

"It was a 911 call," he said, a cryptic, nonresponsive answer like others he'd given in the past.

Based on his attorney's closing argument, I figured that Adam meant he was trying to do the right thing by calling 911, and he was in the middle of an emergency, trying to get help, so he was frazzled, and it didn't matter what words he used. He also acknowledged that his attempts to be sarcastic or funny often didn't make sense to other people.

But words matter. People can't always figure out what others are thinking, or understand their shorthand language. Most of us take each other and our words at face value.

As the interview progressed, Adam seemed to grow more comfortable with me, because his cussing escalated, and his words grew more callous about Rebecca and her family.

"Do you see a chance that someone else did this?" I asked again, hoping that he might let something slip about an accomplice or other people at the scene, as others had speculated.

"As long as it ain't me, I don't give a f—," he said. "I wouldn't waste my time [killing her]. I could talk s—t, but it wouldn't be honest based on who she was before this."

Who was that? I asked.

"What Sigmund Freud called meshuga to beat the band," he said, explaining that the Yiddish term "meshuga" means crazy.

"I'm trying to be sarcastic," he explained. "She was goddamn sad, that's what I said to myself. Call it emotional intelligence. Sorry if I was right."

But overall, he said, he was mostly just angry at the Zahaus. "They're going to sit there and make up a lawsuit against me. F— them . . . They'd better pray there's not a God, because they're f—ed."

My overall impression of him didn't change from the man I'd

seen and heard on TV and radio: He was an odd bird who was easily triggered.

About a week later, I saw him at a jazz club that we'd talked about, where he consumed what looked like a glass of cola. I went over and said hello, and we left it at that.

After speaking with someone who knew the crew Adam had worked with on the tugboat, I learned that he was moved from boat to boat after *Dateline* aired its show on the case.

This person gave me a better handle on a tugboat captain's life, split between his home and the Mississippi River, and also the size of his income. Turned out Adam wasn't poor, because he likely earned at least $500 per day on the river.

He was one of six crewmembers who worked a rotating shift—with three running the boat, while the other three slept or watched TV. One crewmember thought Adam was trying to cover for something, like being gay, because he went "overboard" with comments that he wanted to have sex with women they saw on TV and how "hot" his girlfriend was. His coworkers were surprised to learn that she was in her seventies.

At first, Adam didn't mention that he was going to be on trial, but they all knew. He later proclaimed his innocence to them, and tried to get them to speak to the media on his behalf. But he got no takers.

Chapter 45

In the months after the trial, Keith Greer said he'd give me a copy of whatever legal document he filed next, which he described as a formal complaint or petition against the ME's office and the SDSD.

After several unfulfilled requests, I approached Doug Loehner directly. He told me he would release it to me with Greer's approval, which never came.

Greer later told me that Doug and his wife Mary "went rogue" on him and filed it themselves. What was it exactly? An administrative grievance, he said, which was worded so strongly that he didn't feel comfortable releasing it to anyone, but essentially documented what he'd been saying at news conferences, including the corruption claims.

After I told Greer and Loehner about my book deal, they both congratulated me. But subsequent calls, voice mails, and texts to Greer went unanswered.

As I started calling people who had been involved in the case, such as attorney Marty Rudoy, I was told that everything had to go through Greer, who still wouldn't respond to my queries. Several other people I'd previously interviewed also wouldn't call me back.

Why wouldn't they want the truth to come out? I wondered. I knew that Greer had been working on his own book for months, but I still thought it was unfortunate that he didn't want to cooperate.

Doug, with whom I'd been chatting by phone and texting after sending him a couple of my books to read, told me that Mary was thinking about writing a book herself, so she didn't want to talk either.

Meanwhile, Greer appeared on all the TV shows, trying to move the case forward, as he continued to modify and add to his story of what happened to Rebecca.

In August 2019, he and Mary held a news conference, to which I was not invited, to announce a $100,000 reward for any information leading to the arrest and conviction of Adam Shacknai. They said the money would be paid out of the $600,000 settlement paid by Adam's insurance company, and urged anyone who heard screams coming from the mansion the night Rebecca died to call or email them.

Sheriff Gore also "respectfully declined" my request for an interview. Invited to appear on KUSI to talk about my new book deal that October, I made a plea to Gore on the air, respectfully requesting that he reconsider.

In the end, I saw this clampdown as an attempt to control the narrative. But that only spurred me to work harder to try to find the real truth.

As I went back over the investigative reports one more time, I was still finding details I'd overlooked, or that now made more sense in the context of what I'd since learned, and helped me connect more dots.

In reviewing the internet browser history for the two computers taken from the mansion, I noticed a ninety-minute session on Rebecca's laptop from November 13, 2010, which evidenced her struggle with the Shacknai family dynamics.

The internet searches, which fit with Rebecca's discussions with Snowem six weeks later, came in this order:

How to deal with stress

How do I deal with a difficult stepdaughter

How to let go of painful memories

How to have a healthy relationship

Discipline issues with children

During the week prior to Max's fall, when Rebecca and Jonah were debating whether to keep the Doberman, her laptop showed numerous searches for puppies for sale, specifically Weimaraners and German shepherds.

On Monday, July 11, 2011 at 4:35 P.M., about six and a half hours after Max's fall, her laptop was used to access the Calvary Chapel Maricopa website, which lists the phone and email contact info for the local pastor in Maricopa County, Arizona, where Rebecca and Jonah lived the rest of the year. So, as much as she conveyed doubts and a lack of faith to Jonah, it appears that she still wanted spiritual guidance or relief that day.

Fifteen minutes later, someone made a change to an online Southwest Airlines reservation. This was likely when Rebecca decided to send Ariel home to Missouri, and changed her return ticket to fly out the next day.

A few hours before the ticket change, someone had used the same laptop to access music videos by Justin Bieber and Selena Gomez, and teen TV series such as the sitcom *iCarly*. This may have occurred after Rebecca and Ariel returned from urgent care, or they could have taken the computer with them.

Then, twelve hours later, in the early-morning hours of Tuesday, July 12, another browsing session began. It started off innocently enough at 1:34 A.M., logging visits to YouTube sites similar to those from earlier in the day, including the teen shows

Wizards of Waverly Place and *iCarly*, as well as a search for "Friends Rachel and Joey Kiss." But then the user took a sharp turn. Starting at 1:50 A.M., the search veered into a long series of porn sites, using keyword phrases such as "boy f—s girl." The session, which took the user to some Asian porn sites, continued for two hours, as the content grew increasingly bondage- and violence-related. The final searches were for "evil kitty," "family guy hard sex scenes," and a music video, "sexy back justin timberlake," at 3:42 A.M.

A local news story from 2011 stated that investigators found "bondage porn" and "Asian porno" on a computer in the house. This led some people to erroneously conflate these details with Adam's volunteered admission to police that he'd masturbated while looking at porn on his iPhone shortly before calling 911.

But investigators never seized Adam's phone, so we don't know what type of porn he was viewing that morning. The only Asian porn that investigators found came during this early-morning browsing session on Rebecca's laptop a good twelve hours before Adam came to town. Conversely, Ariel flew back to Missouri at least fifteen hours before Rebecca's body was found.

For me, what was most troubling was the viewing of bondanime.com, an animated bondage site, on Rebecca's laptop at 3:22 A.M. The content was highly disturbing, not just because it showed women being tied up and tortured, but also because it seemed to telegraph some of what Keith Greer believes happened to Rebecca about twenty-four hours later.

The only *known* people in the house at the time this site was accessed were Rebecca and her thirteen-year-old sister, Ariel, and I saw no evidence in the sheriff's investigative records that this site was accessed again, either before or after this session.

This was not one of the Asian porn sites. It featured a series of frames, showing a topless young woman wearing a cheerleader skirt, tied to the metal frame of a bed similar to the one in the guest bedroom where Rebecca's hanging rope was anchored. An older man, wearing nothing but a long-sleeved dress shirt, stood next to her, sexually aroused.

Another frame showed a rear view of the girl's genital area as she was sexually assaulted with a wooden stake. The girl was crying and her face was racked with pain in every frontal view of her. (Using the Wayback Machine website, which allows archived web pages to be viewed by date, I could tell that these particular "cartoon" anime frames have not changed since July 2011.)

"I'm certain something had to inspire Greer's imagination," Jonah said, referring to the claim that Adam sexually assaulted Rebecca with a knife handle. "His theories were extraordinary and certainly not responsible."

Greer insisted that the website didn't inspire his theory about the sexual assault. He said it came together when his expert, Lisa DiMeo, noticed that the knife handle had blood on all four sides. She correlated that with the blood smear on the inside of Rebecca's thigh, because it looked like a transfer mark from pulling the knife out of her vagina.

When Dina's attorneys tried to ask Ariel during her deposition about her computer use at the mansion, Greer said it wasn't relevant to the case, arguing that Ariel was already traumatized by her sister's death.

In pretrial court papers, he wrote, *Plaintiffs respectfully submit that which web sites a teenager accesses on a computer is clearly a "private" matter, of potential embarrassment, and thus the teenager should not be forced to reveal such information unless there is clearly direct relevance to the litigation, and if Defendant should ever meet the burden of establishing such relevance, it should only be disclosed under an appropriate protective order in this high media profile case.*

The question is, who was looking at these sites? Was it Ariel or Rebecca, viewing it together or alone, or was someone else in the house? Ariel has since admitted that it was her, which Doug Loehner reluctantly confirmed on a podcast in late 2020—and to me as well.

Greer did allow the attorneys to ask Ariel about Rebecca's state of mind, however.

"Had your sister ever talked to you about being very, very sad or depressed or anything that she didn't like about her life?"

"No," Ariel replied.

"Did you ever see your sister other than after Max's fall in this incident, did you ever see your sister cry?"

"No."

When I interviewed Anne Bremner in 2019, she gave me a tidbit that I'd never heard before, which I went back into the investigative file to explore further: A DVD of the Korean movie *The Housemaid* had been entered into evidence, and Bremner—as well as others who read the file—thought investigators had found the DVD at the mansion. A remake of a 1960 thriller, the movie was released in 2010 and was an official selection at the Cannes Film Festival that same year.

Bremner called its presence "eerie." After ordering the movie from Netflix and watching it, I had to agree. If this had been Rebecca's DVD, it would be quite telling, because the parallels between the movie plot and the events at the mansion were too close to be coincidental.

The main character, Eun-yi, is a young, pretty, and poor nanny-housemaid who comes to work for a wealthy Korean family in an opulent home. At least two stories high, the house has a chandelier hanging over an open area below, very much like the Spreckels Mansion. The little girl whom Eun-yi is hired to watch looks about five, close to Max Shacknai's age.

Partway through the movie, I was taken aback when Eun-yi, who is on a ladder dusting the chandelier, is purposely injured by her boss's wicked mother-in-law. As the older woman kicks out the ladder and tries to kill the baby Eun-yi is carrying after having sex with her boss, Eun-yi grabs the chandelier to avoid falling to the ground floor. However, she loses her hold and comes crashing down. The long drop puts her in the hospital, but doesn't kill the fetus.

Moving on to Plan B, the boss's wife, pregnant with twins, schemes with her mother to coerce Eun-yi into accepting $100,000 to abort the fetus, and disappear. But Eun-yi refuses. She wants to keep the baby.

So, the wife and her mother poison an herbal drink and feed it to Eun-yi as a healing potion. That puts Eun-yi back into the hospital, where her dead fetus must be surgically removed.

In the last scene, Eun-yi decides to get revenge for the forced abortion and the cruel, callous treatment by this nasty, narcissistic family. As the entire family watches, Eun-yi ties a noose around her neck, then simultaneously hangs herself from the chandelier and lights herself on fire.

"Oh, my God," I said out loud as I sat up on the couch.

Coupled with the foreshadowing nature of the bondage porn on Rebecca's laptop, this movie plot made it difficult to explain away the uncanny similarities.

But something still seemed amiss here. The single-page investigative report said Detective Tsuida entered the DVD into evidence on September 29, 2011, nearly a month after the SDSD had closed the case and announced its findings. Was this a human error in documenting when the evidence was taken from the house, or had someone gone back and found the DVD later?

Chapter 46

Sheriff Gore changed his mind while on vacation and agreed to do an interview with me on December 5, 2019. Only he didn't meet with me alone as he did for my last book. This time, he was flanked by his chief legal advisor, Robert Faigin, and the lieutenant in charge of media relations, Justin White.

What I really wanted to hear was what Gore, as our county's only elected law enforcement officer, thought had happened to Rebecca and why. I also wanted to ask him personally about the allegations that he'd had an improper relationship with Jonah, leading to special treatment, undue influence, and rushing the investigation to a close.

During our ninety-minute interview, Gore was friendlier and seemed more nervous than I expected, perhaps because his competency had been challenged in the media lately.

Just a week earlier, *The San Diego Union-Tribune* had run an editorial with the headline A DECADE IN, SAN DIEGO COUNTY SHERIFF BILL GORE'S LEGACY CRUMBLES. The editorial didn't specifically mention the Zahau case; it simply stated that Gore was either "inattentive or in denial," and that he needed "control of both his deputies and his jails" to do "his job effectively. Or he needs a new job."

As I asked Gore about the collusion and corruption allegations, I reminded him of Jonah's admission to Detective Tsuida
that his company lawyer had reached out to the DA's and sheriff's offices, asking them to issue a statement that he wasn't a
suspect in Rebecca's death.

"Do you remember that?" I asked.

"I don't ever recall talking to a lawyer for his company,"
Gore said. "He never made that request of me." He added that
he didn't know whom Jonah's attorney may have talked to at the
SDSD, because the request never got back to him.

"I'm not saying they didn't, but if I'm a corporate lawyer,
that's probably not a completely illogical request to make, looking at the business concerns," he said.

He also noted that Jonah was cleared of any involvement in
Rebecca's death early on in the investigation. "It was pretty
clear that we had his location. I think we had him on videotape.
I think he was at Rady. His whereabouts were accounted for."

When I brought up the investigative report I'd given to
Sergeant Michalke about the nonfunctioning hallway cameras
and card reader at the Ronald McDonald House, Gore had no response. In fact, he indicated that none of the information I'd
presented during my lengthy meeting with Michalke had
reached his desk.

So I moved on, asking him to walk me through the times he'd
met and spoken with Jonah personally by phone. He was fuzzy
on the details, but said he recalled four phone conversations.

"I've met with Jonah in the office here and I've met him off-
site . . . He might have come in for interviews . . . I just don't recall because it wasn't relevant. I wasn't being accused of being
a corrupt person at the time."

The latest call was more recent, he said, in response to the
FBI's request for Rebecca's writings for the psychological autopsy. While Jonah produced a few items within a week, he said,

Greer never submitted a single document. Gore theorized that Greer didn't want to take the chance that the FBI would say Rebecca was troubled.

"That's false," Greer countered recently, explaining that he'd handed over samples of Rebecca's writings, including the notes on her phone, as well as testimony and exhibits related to his handwriting expert, who testified at trial, as requested for the review. "We gave him the entire trial, all the transcripts, and all the evidence."

Throughout the entire case, Greer said, Gore spoke directly to Jonah, and yet never to the Zahau family. Greer said he had only one phone call with Gore, and that came after the trial and before the election.

"[Gore] asked if we had any new evidence," Greer said.

I asked Gore if Jonah had ever made a personal plea to him, along the lines of "Can you try to end this soon? Because it's really weighing on me, or it's financially a problem for me."

Gore said no, but Jonah "lost his son, darling Max, and his girlfriend, and because of this big cloud that's been over this investigation. What kind of gets lost is that he's the ultimate victim in this. I mean, clearly there's a lot of victims in this. The family that lost their sister to suicide, and Max's mother, Dina." And yet the inference from Greer's allegations was that Gore had accepted some kind of financial incentive or had relented to political pressure because Jonah was such a high-profile wealthy guy.

"For the record," Gore reiterated, "I take great offense at Mr. Greer's accusation that I'm corrupt, that this department is corrupt, because Jonah Shacknai has a lot of money. That's preposterous, and it's insulting. And I know they've checked my campaign records."

Greer clarified recently that he wasn't alleging there was any "direct bribery," as in, "Here's a bag of money."

"I think these things are much more complicated and much

more indirect and we may never know exactly what or how," Greer said. "You've got a rich brother backing the alleged murderer and you've got a sheriff's investigation that was clearly corrupted. Now do we have the line between the dots? No. Will we ever? Probably not. Just two facts in this case that are highly suspicious."

Asked why the SDSD didn't release more specific information about the investigation sooner, Gore said he was trying not to further upset the Zahau family.

"It's traumatic enough for a family," he said. "I don't want to revictimize a family that has gone through a tragedy like that."

But he also never thought the public would challenge his department's findings to this extent.

"You keep hoping—because in our opinion, the evidence was so overwhelming, you can only come to a logical conclusion—that the family would accept that. That the public would accept it."

Responding "I don't know" to many of my other questions, Gore said he didn't get "down in the weeds" on this case, as his detectives did. He seemed to think this would satisfy questions of his accountability, but I'll leave that to my readers to decide.

That said, he did engage with me in a number of what-if scenarios as he laid out his interpretation of the evidence, showing that he had thought them through.

Asked for the strongest piece of evidence that convinced him this was a suicide, Gore said he was actually one of the last members of his department to reach that conclusion.

"I wasn't ready to say it was one way or the other until I saw the last bit of evidence, which was the toxicology reports," he said. When he learned that Rebecca had not taken any drugs or been drugged by someone else, that was the final determining factor that she'd done this to herself, "without signs of a fight or a struggle."

"Maybe they were totally unconscious and all these things

were done to them, and somehow they took that body and levitated it out and threw the body over the balcony. That's not going to happen with somebody that has not been drugged or unconscious at the time," he said.

As for the claims that the four hemorrhages on her head could have rendered her unconscious, he deferred to the medical examiner's opinion to the contrary.

"So many times you sit back and you try to come up with a logical explanation for a completely illogical act of committing suicide," he said.

Contrary to the Zahau family's claims, Gore said he had "great sympathy" for them. "I don't think you'll ever find a statement where this department had bad-mouthed them in any way. I understand their concern. No one wants to believe that their loved one committed suicide."

But Rebecca was "very unhappy," he said, which came out in witness interviews, and the notes on her phone discussing where her "off and on" relationship with Jonah was going. Then came Max's tragic fall, followed by Jonah's voice mail to her.

"We'll never know exactly what happened up there. Were they playing? Were they running around? Did she feel—I mean, obviously, she's going to feel guilty because she was responsible for watching them. Was there more to it than that? Were they chasing around back and forth on that upstairs balcony and he tripped? We'll never know."

Gore said their expert thought that Max didn't go over the top railing on the second floor, but rather over the railing that ran down the staircase, which Gore claimed was only knee-high for an adult. In photos, however, that railing doesn't appear to be any lower than the one on the second floor above.

His summation of the civil trial, which resulted in the verdict against Adam, was that the judge made some bad rulings, allowing the jury to see "some things they should have never seen and some prejudicial stuff," such as the nude mannequin.

Also, Rebecca's sister and mother were "very sympathetic" in the courtroom, he said, while Adam was "kind of a long-shoreman tugboat captain kind of guy," who was not so sympathetic.

But Gore laughed off Greer's murder scenario, calling it "completely illogical," even though it had persuaded the jury.

"If you want to go and make it look like a suicide, then you put a gun to her head and put the gun in her hand and walk out. The end. But no, you go through these extraordinary means to make it look so complicated, people go, 'Well, that's not how you commit suicide. It must be a murder,'" he said, chuckling. "Adam comes up with this scheme in a day from the time he gets into town, to come up with this big conspiracy, and sexually assault her with the knife while he's there."

Nonetheless, the jury bought it. Why? "I think that Adam's lawyer got outlawyered," he said.

Because Gore couldn't answer my specific questions about the investigation, I asked to interview Detectives Tsuida and Palmer, the latter of whom had since retired. Tsuida declined and Palmer couldn't be reached for comment.

My public record request for the "administrative grievance" filed by the Zahaus had been denied, so I asked the sheriff's in-house counsel about it. Faigin said he didn't even know what Greer meant by an "administrative grievance," noting that the only document the Zahaus had submitted recently was a letter complaining about the sheriff's investigation.

It wasn't for lack of trying, but I didn't get substantive answers from Gore about why the review team didn't reinterview anyone, and why they didn't try to retest the gloves that had "insufficient" amounts of DNA.

"I'm sure they coordinated that with the lab, and the decision was made there was no reason to reexamine the DNA evidence," Gore said.

"But why—"

"I wasn't involved, it wasn't my decision, I couldn't tell you."

When Gore had no real comment on the several new findings that came out in the Oxygen series, Faigin piped up that this was "not new evidence, it's interpretation of evidence that was collected by the sheriff's department."

"So, none of this matters?" I asked. "Doesn't seem like it's worth reopening the case for?"

"I didn't review all of the Oxygen channel [documentary]," Gore said. "I just didn't."

By the end of the interview, it was clear that Gore was firmly invested in the suicide scenario. From what I could tell, the only way that would change is if new witnesses came forward with evidence that the SDSD accepted as "new," or if someone confessed to killing Rebecca Zahau.

What else could be done at this point? Under the California constitution, if the attorney general found that the SDSD had committed malfeasance, a different law enforcement agency, such as a sheriff's office in a different county, the FBI, or even the state DOJ, could take another look at the criminal case. Or, if a new sheriff were to be elected, he or she could decide to reopen the case.

About two weeks later, Adam's girlfriend, Mary Bedwell, emailed me out of the blue.

I wanted to ask you . . . to periodically and thoughtfully consider justice from the perspective of a completely innocent individual who is accused and essentially convicted of murder—as if you had walked past the Spreckels Mansion, discovered Rebecca hanging and must now spend the rest of your life trying to prove you didn't kill her, she wrote.

I wrote back and asked to interview her, saying she could tell me about the Adam she knew. Even though she was biased as his girlfriend, I still believed that the more I could learn about him from someone other than Greer, Adam's lawyers, and from his own awkward statements, the better I could illustrate what he was—and wasn't—capable of. She thanked me, because no one else had asked for her input.

When we talked in January 2020, she was quite open, funny, and, from what I could tell, genuinely honest. Asked about the claims that Adam was a sexual deviant, she said, "I have to laugh. Adam is a sexual deviant? No."

She said she was surprised to hear about him watching porn, but they laughed about it together. "He probably had too much time on his hands," she said. "He won't lie in bed, or go back to sleep, he's got to get up and get moving."

"But as far as masturbation goes, if every man who woke up and masturbated, then went next door and killed someone, then the world would be a pretty scary place to live in," she said, recalling former surgeon general Joycelyn Elders's support for the practice. "In fact, I think it's supposed to do the opposite."

When she heard people like Greer challenging why Adam went to such lengths to cut Rebecca down, when other people would have waited to let the police handle it, Mary thought of Adam's reaction when her cat, Sinbad, disappeared.

Mary figured Sinbad might or might not come back, but not Adam. "He wouldn't give up. He went door-to-door, badgering people, to look in their sheds—maybe he got locked in. And after a week, he encountered a man who worked in the power plant. He said, 'Your cat got electrocuted. We still have the body.'" Only then would Adam give up the search for that cat.

Mary said she believes Adam is harmless. "There's nothing in his character that would make anybody think he could do something like that, any more than you could or I could. He was a convenient person to accuse for a lot of reasons," she said. "I've known him for [more than] twenty-five years. It's just not him."

Mary had her own theories for why Rebecca would kill herself in this way.

"Rebecca wanted Jonah to think that somebody had tried to kill Max and failed, and came back and killed her," she said. "She wanted him to think that she died a hero. I think Rebecca wanted Jonah to think that strangers or enemies or somebody had killed Max."

She said she also thought Rebecca feared for her family because she felt "she'd disgraced them" with what she'd allowed to happen to Max while under her care. If that was the case, the message on the door was more of a billboard than a suicide note.

"It's enigmatic, that's for sure. My theory is, if she was trying to make her suicide look like a murder, then that message makes sense. We tried to kill him, and we failed, and now we've come back and tried to kill you."

In light of the accusations against Gore, and because so many private citizens—even strangers approaching me at Home Depot—had pleaded with me to find out why "someone was paid off" and why the SDSD didn't conduct the Zahau investigation properly, I looked for an outside voice.

As one of three assistant SAICs under Gore at the FBI office in San Diego from July 1999 to February 2003, John Kingston had only praise for his former supervisor.

"He was the most, or next most, reasonable, rational, great bosses I ever worked for," said Kingston, who now works security in the private sector.

Chapter 47

About a month after my interview with Gore, sheriff's Lieutenant Justin White emailed me some brief, general answers to my long list of specific questions. I got no response to my subsequent requests for more detailed answers.

I'd asked, for example, what importance did the SDSD give to the statements by all of Rebecca's friends, ex-lovers, and family members, who said she never would have committed suicide? And what did they think of Adam's instantaneous determination that Rebecca had committed suicide when investigators thought the scene was suspicious and bizarre enough to immediately call in the homicide team?

As with any case, all evidence is reviewed and considered, White wrote.

White confirmed that detectives never seized Adam's cell phone, which several outside investigators have said was a major misstep in the overall investigation. He also said detectives never considered Neil Nalepa, Dina Shacknai, or Nina Romano as suspects.

We don't start out a case with suspects then work backwards in order to make the evidence fit a theory, White wrote. *We follow the evidence and let it lead us to a suspect/no suspect.*

White also didn't directly answer whether investigators had

determined whose T-shirt was shoved into Rebecca's mouth, saying only that the DNA on it matched Rebecca's and excluded Adam, Ariel, and Nina.

Asked why no one was reinterviewed or newly interviewed during the 2018 review, he wrote, *A witness's recollection of an event is more accurate closer to the event so nobody that was interviewed initially was reinterviewed.*

White did clarify one important point, however, and that was Detective Tsuida had *not* actually found that Korean DVD in the house. This information came as a big surprise to several people involved in the case who had read the investigative file, including me, because the report seemed to indicate otherwise.

The Housemaid *DVD was purchased by the Homicide Unit and entered into evidence on 9/29/2011,* he wrote. *It was purchased because of suggestions that the circumstances in the movie were similar to those in the Zahau case.*

Therefore, what could have been an important, decisive clue now seemed to be another red herring, because there was no actual evidence that Rebecca had ever seen the movie. Or was it?

When I asked Jonah about the DVD, he told me it was possible that he and Rebecca had watched foreign movies with subtitles, but she didn't watch many movies period, because "it was hard for her to sit still for two hours or two and a half hours." He said he certainly would have remembered this particular movie, because "it would have made an impression," even before all of this happened.

But based on the "screw you" scenario that Tsuida had painted for Jonah, it appears that she submitted this movie into evidence because it supported an alternative motive for suicide—that Rebecca turned her death into a horrific spectacle as an act of revenge, not guilt.

Epilogue

After Jonah Shacknai sold the Spreckels Mansion in late 2011, its new owner did a remodel and planted half a dozen mature palm trees in the front yard, with the intent of flipping the tainted property.

In 2013, the home was purchased for $9 million by 1043 Ocean Blvd., LLC, the principal of which was Robert D. Harris, an entrepreneur from Utah who ran a private aircraft company and also founded the carpet-cleaning company Chem-Dry.

Despite more renovations by Harris, and the addition of a low stucco wall, ornate metal gates across the driveway and front walkway, and some lush landscaping that enhanced the mansion's privacy and security, no one was willing to buy what some Coronado locals still call "the murder house."

In 2019, the mansion was on and off the market with an asking price of from $16.9 to $17.5 million. After COVID-19 hit in early 2020, the house finally sold for $11 million. It was listed as a monthly rental until the new owner began making interior and exterior modifications, such as removing the palm trees and some of the new landscaping, to restore a more historic look.

Right after my cordial interview with Adam's girlfriend, Mary, who said she enjoyed talking with me, he started to send me emails. His surprisingly angry, accusatory tone sent up red flags as he insulted me personally and professionally, described me as "evil," "a mental midget," and a "Nazi," among other slights I don't care to mention.

Because he'd been respectful and polite to me before, I had no idea where this sudden vitriol was coming from. His language was so extreme I wondered if the emails might have been sent by a fake Adam or the hacker who had recently hijacked my email account. But after I left concerned messages with Mary, Adam wrote to assure me that he was indeed the author.

Upon the advice of my publisher's attorney, I never responded to any of his messages, but I did forward them to the SDSD and the SDPD, and asked the latter agency to file a report. The SDPD officer told me that this type of harassment was indeed a crime, but he, too, advised me not to respond so as not to escalate the situation.

Here is a brief excerpt:

> If I did not think you were evil to the degree of a Josef [*sic*] Goebbels cosmic hatred I could supply you with information that could be of interest to readers who have not been stained with the agenda you have had against God knows who or what (I have some guesses), since BEFORE day one. I would never pretend that you would relinquish a chance to seek revenge against your perceived enemies or forfeit an opportunity to exorcize your demons over a little peon like myself or a trifling issue like justice.

My editor thought the emails would stop if I didn't engage or respond, but Adam's bitter rants continued unabated, with the same inflammatory and defamatory content, sometimes landing in the middle of the night. By their sheer number, what started as harassment and attempted intimidation soon felt like he was stalking me.

Sheriff's sergeant Michalke advised me that I could apply for a restraining order, but I might not get one because Adam hadn't threatened to inflict physical harm, and since he lived in Memphis, and worked on a tugboat across the country, he might not be viewed as an imminent danger. When I reminded him that a jury had found Adam responsible for Rebecca's death, he said, "But that was in civil court."

One set of emails contained screenshots from an unidentified social media thread, asking loaded questions about the Zahau case. Posted using a Facebook plug-in for "Tara Chung," the queries included points the defense had raised in court. They also made baseless claims against the judge, and fired personal, defamatory accusations at the Websleuths owner, Keith Greer, and two respected local TV reporters I know personally.

I found "Tara" on Facebook, where she'd posted only two substantive items since creating her page in 2015, and both were about the Zahau case. Her profile photo featured a young Asian woman posing with her cat. She supposedly lived in San Diego, had attended a Christian law school, and "liked" a martial arts school, yoga, a famous jazz duo, the *Memphis Flyer*, an arts-and-entertainment publication, and a Memphis-based legal justice center. She didn't appear to have any friends, or at least none who were visible, and she seemed to be following only one person: me.

Because her posts used similar hyperbolic language and tone as Adam's emails to me, and her bio reflected Adam's hometown and tastes, mixed with Rebecca's, it looked like Tara was Adam's social media creation.

By email #25, he was grasping at straws to find new ways to insult me, so he went back to belittling Dan Webb and his team of corporate lawyers, and pointing to his loss at trial to disprove my "utterly mundane" claim of how good they were. As an admirer of the Reagan administration, he said, he never would have let Webb represent him if he had known about Webb's role in prosecuting Admiral Poindexter.

All told, he sent me forty emails over three months, sometimes four a day, and offensive to the end. Whatever his intent, the messages did not help his cause. Rather, they only made me reconsider what I'd previously thought about his involvement in Rebecca's death.

Was this the behavior of an innocent man?

Jonah kept a low profile in 2020, but his LinkedIn bio showed that he had been involved in a new pharmaceutical company as the founder and executive chairman of DermaForce Partners, LLC, and was also board chairman of the skin care side of Illustris Pharmaceuticals, Inc.

About six weeks before my deadline, my repeated attempts to reach the elusive multimillionaire finally paid off. He emailed me, we chatted by phone, and he said he would be willing to meet with me. Within days, however, COVID had made that too risky, so we did eight lengthy Skype interviews instead.

Jonah still hadn't spoken to anyone other than briefly to *20/20*, but he answered all of my questions, offered me new information, and told me his side of this whole story. He also responded to the nagging allegations that he was somehow involved in this case and that he had some sort of undue influence over the sheriff's investigation.

"I never knew or had any relationship with Sheriff Gore," he said, adding that he didn't even know the sheriff's name until after Rebecca's death. During the investigation, "I spoke to him on one occasion. He called me to express condolences and to thank me for cooperating with law enforcement. That was a non-substantive call."

Jonah said he never had any "involvement in or around or after the investigation with any law enforcement official other than as a cooperative fact witness." Just like the Zahaus, he wasn't briefed by Detective Tsuida and Dr. Lucas until shortly before the first news conference, and he wasn't allowed to ask questions.

"That was the first time I learned of their conclusions," he said.

Given everything he's been through, he requested that I keep his personal life private, revealing only that he married his current wife in 2014, they have two children together, and they live in southern California.

As for Adam's emails to me, he said, "We're all accountable only for our own behavior. I've never written anything like that to anyone, and I don't excuse it. I'm just empathetic only to the extent that he's been through an extraordinary trauma and he got a very raw deal in all of this, but it doesn't excuse his behavior. I'm sorry you were on the receiving end of this."

That said, the emails didn't change his mind about Adam's involvement, or his firm belief now that Rebecca took her own life.

"If I'd been a guy who worked as an insurance salesman, if Rebecca hadn't been naked, and if Adam's comportment wasn't unusual or odd, nobody would be talking about this. So, I think you've got to look at the dynamics of this whole case. It makes for great theater, which is why it's of interest to the public, but it doesn't change the underlying facts."

After long ignoring my texts and calls, Keith Greer agreed to answer some questions right before my deadline, saying he'd been previously restricted from doing so for reasons he couldn't disclose.

When I told him about Adam's emails, he made this chilling prediction about the case.

"It's going to end in a weird way," he said.

"How?" I asked.

"I don't know," he said. "Big, big money, nasty happenings. Time will tell. I just have this feeling it's going to end in a bad way."

Greer and his clients waited until July 13, 2020, the ninth anniversary of Rebecca's death, to announce that they were ready to take further legal action. At a news conference, Greer released a petition for a writ of mandate, which he filed in court three days later, demanding that Sheriff Gore and the SDSD release investigative records that had been denied to Doug Loehner and Pari Zahau over the past several months. These records included detective notes, workbooks, phone messages, and emails, as well as correspondence and records of phone calls between Gore and his legal team. The petition doesn't ask for money other than reimbursement of legal fees.

"We think that we will find correspondence between the investigating officers . . . which question whether this is homicide or suicide," Greer said.

The SDSD had previously denied these record requests—including one that asked for correspondence reflecting why detectives chose not to obtain Adam Shacknai's cell phone records as they did Jonah's, Rebecca's, and Nina's—stating that such records were "exempt from disclosure" under the California Public Records Act.

Records of a law enforcement investigation, or any investigatory or security files compiled by a law enforcement agency . . . are not public records, the SDSD stated, noting that Gore's legal communications were also exempt under attorney-client privilege and work product protections.

The writ petition points out, however, that the SDSD has previously released a "substantial number of documents" and other evidence that would otherwise be considered exempt, even posting them on a website.

The petition states, *It is improper for the Sheriff to use the exemption privilege as a sword rather than a shield,* selectively waiving it to release only the materials that support the agency's suicide findings.

"The sheriff is playing this game of only releasing that which helps his position, and then snuffing and hiding all of the evidence and all of the analysis of his officers which contradict that finding," Greer said. "That's wrong."

As part of the legal action, Greer commissioned a new report with forensic animations and scene reconstructions by Scott Roder of the Evidence Room, which bolster the homicide and sexual assault scenarios Greer presented at trial.

There is evidence of another person's involvement in almost every facet of the crime scene, Roder's report states. *One has to work very hard to fit the sheriff's conclusion into evidence.*

Greer also released a six-page letter, addressed to Dr. Lucas at the ME's office in Los Angeles. The letter set out the main points argued at trial and excerpts of the judge's tentative ruling before the settlement, asking that Lucas, as the pathologist on Rebecca's case, amend her death certificate to cite the manner of death as homicide or—"at a minimum"—undetermined.

Mary Zahau-Loehner, who renewed her offer of a $100,000 reward for new information on the case, accused the SDSD of conducting a racially and socioeconomically biased investigation.

"I would like the public to really know what happened behind the scenes, and Sheriff Gore is full of lies," she said. "This was a biased investigation motivated by power and wealth. This is nothing but racial and socioeconomic discrimination. If Rebecca was a white, wealthy woman, we would not be standing here . . . Justice has not been served for my sister yet."

Responding to these new developments, Dave Myers, Gore's opponent in the last election, tweeted: I've said for many years, why would the Sheriff take a phone call from the millionaire boyfriend and discuss his company stock price dropping because the investigation continued? A day later, he added: We can't trust Sheriff Gore to bring justice to #Zahau.

A statement issued by the SDSD described its investigation as "objective and thorough," but said the agency doesn't comment on pending litigation.

In media reports, Adam Shacknai characterized the Zahaus as "brain damaged jackals," and their latest move as "a shakedown of yet another party where Greer smells free money."

He also said, "I really wish for them to admit what happened."

But the Zahaus seemed just as determined as ever to continue this fight. "Rebecca is not going to be forgotten, and this family is not going to rest until the murderer is in jail," Greer said.

As of mid-November 2020, the writ petition had been assigned to a judicial officer, with a case management conference scheduled for March 19, 2021.

But the Zahaus still hadn't sent the letter to Dr. Lucas. Doug Loehner said they had since learned that any request to change the death certificate would have to be handled by the ME's office in San Diego, to which they hoped to submit a similar letter soon.

"This has to end," Doug said.

Author's Note and Acknowledgments

I still can't say for sure what happened to Rebecca. There were parallels between my husband's and Rebecca's lives, but there were also differences. As complicated and controversial as this story was to write, it chose me, and I've been compelled to stick with it. In so doing, I applied the same unbiased, investigative, and exploratory approach to this multifaceted case that I always do, following the evidence no matter where it took me. Knowing that I have a unique perspective on this topic, however, I kept an open mind, hoping to elevate the level of understanding about what really happened and let readers reach their own conclusions right along with me.

Adam Shacknai's inflammatory emails made me rethink things, and after speaking with Jonah, I had to rethink them once again.

Lest anyone think I'm "exorcising my demons" by writing this book, as Adam alleged, my professional interest in suicides and bizarre deaths came long before my husband died in 1999, starting with my studies in abnormal psychology at the University of California, Berkeley, where I earned my bachelor's degree.

Years later, the *Union-Tribune* nominated me for a Pulitzer Prize for my 1998 investigative feature story about a nineteen-year-old who came to a painful end after setting himself on fire outside a Walmart. I also won an award for a story about a lonely divorced man who failed to kill himself in multiple ways, but finally succeeded in starving himself to death. He was found mummified in bed eighteen months later, hidden behind the foil-covered windows of his condo.

If you're interested in learning more about my personal story and my husband's suicide, it's chronicled in a short memoir, *Secrets, Lies, and Shoelaces,* which took me nineteen years to finish—after watching the Zahau trial.

I believe that the community at large still actively engages in conspiracy theories about this case partly because many evidentiary details weren't released until the Zahaus' lawsuit went to trial, and even then, only a portion of them came out. I've tried to remedy that here, by exploring all the evidence and theories—in context. The result is a more detailed, balanced, and current account of what happened to Max and Rebecca than you'll find anywhere else.

Based on my previous reporting, I can tell you that a victim's family often doesn't see a suicide coming or know their loved one as well as they think. By the same token, no one has heard of a suicide quite like this, and many people, including a good number of outside experts, still can't see how a woman could or would have done this to herself.

I've already written several narrative nonfiction crime books involving staged murder *and* suicide scenes, created to mislead investigators, and it's clear to me that Rebecca's death was staged to look like something it wasn't. But we may never know, definitively, whether the perpetrator was Rebecca or her alleged killer(s).

Despite the sheriff's firmly-held accident and suicide scenarios for Max and Rebecca, her family and Max's mother still believe their loved ones were murdered. The bottom line is, if Rebecca didn't commit suicide, then her killer is still out there.

As someone who has become an unwitting suicide expert, both personally and professionally, my continuing investigation placed me squarely into this story. But in the end, I had no agenda, no verdict, and no financial settlement to protect.

I reached out to all the key players involved in this story, as I always do. Some didn't want to cooperate, saying they're working on their own books, or felt they've already said enough.

Others didn't respond or couldn't be reached. That said, I was still able to represent their views here from court testimony or interviews with law enforcement and the media.

After observing the entire civil trial, I set out to write a book to incorporate as many never-released details as possible. In addition to culling through public records, I thankfully have good sources who supplied me with inside information, including the sheriff's investigative files and photos, discovery materials from the various lawsuits, witness interview transcripts and audio files, trial depositions, and outside expert analysis. I also conducted countless interviews myself.

I've given several people pseudonyms to protect their privacy. Also, some quotes have been edited down for storytelling purposes, such as the removal of repetitive verbal tics, stumbling, or extra words that interrupt the natural flow of conversation. But nothing has been changed or added to alter the context or meaning, and no details have been embellished, exaggerated, or created. Any errors are unintentional.

On a more personal note, as I sat in the courtroom during the trial, I also served as a pool photographer when professionals like Nelvin C. Cepeda couldn't be there. Nel, an old friend and former colleague from the *Union-Tribune*, took many of the shots in the photo insert.

When Nel and I flew to a military base in Pennsylvania for a week to do a series of stories on Kosovar refugees in 1999, it was my first assignment back from bereavement leave after my husband's suicide. Nel was a great partner to work with at that fragile point in my life, and that series also won a journalism award. So, it felt like synchronicity when we sat side by side in this trial nearly twenty years later.

Many days, also right beside me was *Union-Tribune* reporter Pauline Repard, with whom I wrote the first news article on the Kristin Rossum case in 2001, the topic of my first book, *Poisoned Love*. Pauline and I go back to 1993, when we both worked for the editor who was married to private investigator Bill Garcia, the one who brought my husband's ashes back from Mexico in 1999. Small world.

I'm grateful to Bill, Nel, and all the other people who helped me produce this book, and I want to thank them for their contributions: Anne Bremner, Jonah Shacknai, Michael Berger, Alma Cesena, John Gibbins, John McCutchen, Pauline Repard, Michelle Madigan Herman, David Gotfredson, Keith Greer, Sheriff Bill Gore, Sergeant Paul Michalke, Lieutenant Justin White, Denys Williams, Mary Ann Castellano, Steve Walker, Paul Pfingst, Doug Loehner, Mike Workman, Mary Bedwell, Dwight Smith, Jackie Bensinger, Kris Grant, J.W. August, Paul Ciolino, Tara Schneider, Maurice Godwin, Tricia Arrington Griffith, Howard Breuer, and Ben Metcalf.

A big thanks also goes to my beta readers—my mother, Carole Scott, and my fellow author Georgeanne Irvine. To my partner, Géza Keller; my editor, Michaela Hamilton; and my agent, Peter Rubie, I express my deep gratitude for their longtime and consistent support of and belief in my work.

Connect with U s

Visit us online at
KensingtonBooks.com
to read more from your favorite authors, see books
by series, view reading group guides, and more.

Join us on social media

for sneak peeks, chances to win books and prize packs,
and to share your thoughts with other readers.

facebook.com/kensingtonpublishing
twitter.com/kensingtonbooks

Tell us what you think!

To share your thoughts, submit a review,
or sign up for our eNewsletters, please visit:
KensingtonBooks.com/TellUs.